EDUCATION
for the
EXCEPTIONAL CHILD

EDUCATION

for the

by

LONGMANS, GREEN AND CO.

EXCEPTIONAL
CHILD

L. X. Magnifico

UNIVERSITY OF TENNESSEE

NEW YORK · LONDON · TORONTO · 1958

LONGMANS, GREEN AND CO., INC.
55 FIFTH AVENUE, NEW YORK 3

LONGMANS, GREEN AND CO., LTD.
6 & 7 CLIFFORD STREET, LONDON W 1

LONGMANS, GREEN AND CO.
20 CRANFIELD ROAD, TORONTO 16

EDUCATION FOR THE EXCEPTIONAL CHILD

FIRST EDITION

LIBRARY OF CONGRESS CATALOG CARD NUMBER: 58–10761

Printed in the United States of America

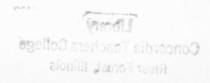

PREFACE

THIS TEXT presents a survey of the field of the education for exceptional children. It is intended for advanced students, experienced teachers and administrators who wish to enter the area of special education, and all others who desire a knowledge of the over-all field, particularly, but not exclusively, guidance counselors and educational consultants. It presupposes that the student has an orientation in professional education and is familiar with elementary educational psychology. The topics that are synthesized briefly in this volume serve as introductions to courses that are entities unto themselves.

The text is not intended to do more than offer a compact survey of special education in a manner that is neither tedious nor unduly repetitious. At the same time it attempts to keep the reader abreast of the current sociological and economic trends, both pertinent to the entire field of education in the American democracy.

The text has been written from the point of view of one who

has had grass-roots experience both as a teacher and as a guidance counselor of exceptional children, particularly of those diagnosed as mentally retarded, slow learners, gifted, and socially handicapped. One of the author's many activities in education was a summer camp for exceptional children, which he directed for three years. And so it follows that the author is sensitive to the problems peculiar to teaching children who are different or handicapped in some way. Hoping not to seem presumptuous, the writer feels inclined to offer several suggestions for the instructor and student. First, the instructor and student are admonished not to consider this book as a source within itself, and, for this reason, the basic concepts underlying this work have been presented in a deliberately controversial style to stimulate and provoke further study and research. Second, illustrations and halftones have been omitted, since the author believes that there are no substitutes for live demonstration classes and visits to public and private schools, institutions, hospitals, and the like. In the smaller college communities, audio-visual aids can certainly serve as better instrumentalities than halftones.

L. X. M.

Knoxville, Tennessee
May, 1958

ACKNOWLEDGMENTS

THE AUTHOR acknowledges particularly the excellent counsel of Dr. Walter B. Barbe, professor of education, University of Chattanooga, Chattanooga, Tennessee, for his rich information and comments on the chapters concerned with the education of the gifted. Then, too, he is grateful to his colleague, Professor Lorin C. Staats, Jr., for his valuable comments and criticisms pertaining to educational theories, philosophies, and practices in the areas of speech and hearing. Also, he is indebted to Dean N. E. Fitzgerald, of the University of Tennessee, for his inspiration, encouragement, and many courtesies which he extended the author during the preparation and writing of this volume. And finally the author conveys his thanks to Mrs. Lucy Petree, of Knoxville, Tennessee, for her tireless efforts and good humor while working with the many crises that inevitably arise in typing a manuscript.

CONTENTS

ix

EDUCATION
for the
EXCEPTIONAL CHILD

CHAPTER ONE

The Over-all Problem

IN 1938, the Educational Policies Commission of the National Education Association reported an investigation designed to determine precisely what the purposes of education in a democracy —specifically, our democracy—were. After many months of assiduous effort, the commission concluded that the education of an individual in this country should be based upon the following objectives:

1. Self-realization
2. Achievement of satisfactory human relationships
3. Economic efficiency
4. Civic responsibility (**24**, p. 4)

Education for Everyone

Actually, almost from its very inception, the government of the United States had been concerned with nurturing the type of education that would best promote the happiness of all the people under its protection. Article Three of the Ordinance of 1787 states that—

Religion, morality, and knowledge being necessary to good government and the happiness of mankind, schools and the means of education shall be forever encouraged.

But, in spite of the encouragement given to education by the national government and by several state governments during the late eighteenth and throughout most of the nineteenth centuries, and, in spite of the influence of such individual leaders as Horace Mann, Henry Barnard, James Carter, DeWitt Clinton, and others, the concept of an education for everyone in the United States was slow in coming to full fruition.

The chief concern of the American people during the period preceding the Industrial Revolution was the obtaining of food, clothing, shelter, and things of immediate utility. They had little or no time to devote to things of the mind. In a country of virgin lands and forests, most of them were busily engaged in clearing lands for farming and building homes, in planning and constructing towns, cities, and roads, as well as the factories and the warehouses for processing and storing the raw materials and finished products they were turning out.

With the exception of a few metropolitan areas in the East, nearly all of the families in this country, living on farms and in isolated rural communities, were in effect entities unto themselves, since the very nature of their existence required considerable self-sufficiency. Education, though generally recognized to be "a good thing," was also considered as essentially a luxury. Although there was free public education of one kind or another throughout the country, it was not until 1852 that the first state compulsory attendance law was passed,[1] and it was not until as recently as 1918 that every state had such a law.[2] Even then, during the earlier years of the Republic, few young people pursued their studies beyond the elementary grades—even in areas where secondary education was readily available—since most of them could not be spared from the family work force, either on the farm or in the "sweat-shop" factories to be found in the villages and towns.

[1] In Massachusetts.
[2] Mississippi was the last state to pass a compulsory attendance law.

Early Attitudes toward Educating Exceptional Children

There was no question in those early days of educating the handicapped. Children who were sick, afflicted, or mentally defective to such a degree that they could not be employed usefully in any way were either confined secretly to their homes or sent to institutions where they vegetated until they died. The majority of the people, even those with some education, did not really recognize mental deficiency as distinct from insanity. In the first half of the nineteenth century, according to Albert Deutsch—

. . . sick poor, old poor, able-bodied poor, infant poor, insane and feeble-minded—all were grouped together under the stigmatizing label "pauper" and all were treated in very much the same manner. (8, p. 116)

From the colonial period up until very close to the present, most American schools were organized and administered along the lines of the political philosophy that dominated all our country's thinking almost to the point of obsession, namely, that all men are *born* equal. School curricula were consciously designed "to offer children equal opportunity," but "equal opportunity" simply meant that all children were expected to be capable of performing the same tasks and acquiring the same skills.

Yet all men are *not* born equal when it comes to capacity, and, by offering the same education to all, the school system was merely compounding the original inequalities of birth. Even during the early days of the American school system, teachers and parents could not avoid noticing that not all children responded in the same way to the "equal opportunities" so handsomely offered them. Even so, slow-learning children would often be excoriated and punished for not performing well. If one acted on the premise that all were born equal, then all should be able to learn the same skills and acquire the same knowledge at the same speed. If they did not, it was their own fault. Therefore, either the children learned the prescribed curricula or they would be advised to drop out of school. And so it was that the slow-learning children, the children with low intelligence, the dull children, and the educationally retarded children did drop out of school in droves—usually at the end of the seventh grade.

Although J. F. Rosenkranz lived and worked in Germany, he reflected the general attitude prevailing throughout Western civilization in the nineteenth century regarding children's abilities, when he classified them into three different groups: "1—incapacity, as the want of all gifts; 2—mediocrity; 3—talent and genius." [3] (**25**, p. 107). As far as he and his fellow educators were concerned, the child who fell into the first classification was not educable; therefore, there seemed to be little sense in wasting time or thought, not to speak of money, on him.

And so the customary method of "dealing" with handicapped children—especially the mental defectives—by institutionalizing them or "letting them rot" remained quite consistent down through the Industrial Revolution, and in many areas it predominated through the 1930's. As a matter of fact, in a few isolated spots in the country, such a pattern prevails to this very day.

THE GROWING PROBLEMS OF EDUCATION
IN THE TWENTIETH CENTURY

The masses of the people can hardly be blamed, however, for holding such an attitude when, up until the early years of this century, as Walter S. Monroe has pointed out, psychologists "gave relatively little attention to individual differences" in children's learning capacity. (**23**, p. 46) Educators of that time seemed

---

[3] Although he wrote in 1848, a translation of his book did not appear in this country until 1896.

equally unconcerned. Although there were, of course, exceptions, as, for example, Preston W. Search, who spoke up in 1895, during his tenure as superintendent of schools in Los Angeles, for "individualism in mass education" (**27**, p. 399), for the most part they tended to agree with E. E. White, who wrote in his *Art of Teaching* (1901) that "children are endowed with common powers and . . . face common interests and needs, those of the common civilization into which they are born." (**33**, p. 133) His implication was that children of approximate age should simply be lumped together in heterogeneous classes, and most of them would manage to get through somehow. The bright ones would manifest themselves readily and the dull ones would fall by the wayside—and rightly so, as they were not deemed worth the trouble of salvage. And it must be admitted that there are many educators today who, although they might not be willing to admit it openly, agree substantially that elaborate methods of teaching and training the mentally retarded and the mentally deficient are in large part a waste of resources that might more profitably be applied to the children of higher intelligence.

It was in the early 1930's that the problem of educating *all* of the people of the United States became accentuated, for reasons that rested on a material rather than a spiritual or ethical basis. The urbanization of our society, coupled with the mechanization of industry, had made it increasingly possible for fewer and fewer individuals to produce for larger and larger numbers of people. Now that child labor was no longer needed, laws protecting children from hazardous work were rigidly enforced, and so it became important to find a niche for those youngsters who were gradually becoming excluded from the labor force but who did not seem to fit into the academic organization.

Furthermore, mechanized industry required not only engineers and technicians with extremely specialized educations, but also labor that was highly skilled and needed a good deal of training.

In addition, new discoveries in medicine and improved public health programs were bringing about an increased longevity for the total population. Not only were people enjoying longer life spans than ever before, but a longer period of productivity within that life span as well. Hence, older workers were able to stay on the job longer. In fact, today it is expected that most of those gainfully employed will remain on the job until the retirement age—which, at present, is sixty-five.

The Depression Augments Education's Dilemma

The problem of what to do with the healthy young people between fourteen and twenty-one years of age who could not be absorbed into the labor force was increased by the advent of the depression and the consequent shortage of jobs for adults. What was to be done with the children? "Keep them in school longer" was a cry heard from industrialists, businessmen, labor leaders, political leaders, and some educators. Certainly that was the simplest solution for everyone concerned. As a result, compulsory attendance ages were raised by law in a number of states, largely so that youngsters would not compete with their fathers and older siblings for jobs.

Although they were now adding a different kind of student to their enrollment, the majority of schools during the 1930's persisted in remaining still largely academic in nature. Certain attempts were made from time to time to cope with the varying capacities of children. Roy O. Billett listed twenty-nine that were used in various high schools during that era (1, p. 1), but, in the main, the elementary schools continued to prepare children for high schools and the high schools prepared youngsters for colleges and universities. In 1934, Ellwood P. Cubberley did suggest suitable alterations in the school curricula to cope with the needs of exceptional children. The category, "Central Schools for Peculiar Boys and Girls," would seem to have been his delicate way of classifying the feebleminded and possibly, as some of the courses suggested seem to indicate, the exceptionally bright as well—though this point is not clarified. (**5**, p. 568)

It was during the depression that the various modern philosophies of education gained impetus, becoming involved in sharp conflicts with the traditional philosophies. The opposing theories of how to deal with the problem of educating the diverse masses of children and young people attending elementary and high schools and the junior colleges were never fully reconciled. By the late thirties, the problem of educating the masses and, at the same time, dealing with the depression was becoming a critical one.

The problem did not come to a head then only because the Second World War broke out. Not only did the country need an expanded labor force to deal with military production, but the existing force was diminished by the drafting of young men into the armed services. Young people of both sexes were able to find a ready niche in the world as long as they had minimal capabilities.

Those young men with mental handicaps that were not too severe were inducted into the army, where many proved to make perfectly acceptable soldiers. Thomas R. Weaver discovered that, of eight thousand mental deficients inducted by the army, more than half made a successful adjustment. (**32**, p. 246) At the same time, of course, enough men were rejected for service because of their mental inadequacy to demonstrate just how serious the problem was in this country.

Other mental retardates, both men and women, as well as individuals with minor physical handicaps, also were able to find jobs, although most of them had been previously considered unemployable or marginally employable. And young people were urged to take jobs now that there was no longer the economic and social necessity of keeping as many as possible of them in school. Aside from that, the exigencies of a wartime civilization tended to minimize the importance of education, particularly to those young people who had little scholastic aptitude or academic inclination.

Present Problems of Education

Now, thirteen years after the cessation of hostilities, we are faced more intensely than ever with problems in the area of specialized education. Today more children than ever are in schools. In 1953–54, 34,025,000 children were enrolled in the elementary and secondary schools, as compared to 16,854,832 in 1899–1900— a rise of over 100 per cent. (15, p. 101) Not only do we have the perennial problem of how to educate all sane children, from the borderline mental defective to the genius, to achieve the objectives spelled out in the opening paragraphs of this chapter, but we also must know how to meet the crisis of the coming labor shortage ahead.

That there is bound to be a labor shortage, most authorities seem to agree. Writing in *Harper's Magazine,* Peter Drucker has prognosticated the following:

There will be a population increase of one-fifth in the next ten years.

But total population of working age will increase only by one-tenth.

Population actually available for work will increase only by six per cent.

And total hours worked by the whole economy in the course of one year *may not increase at all.*

And in the next twenty years, total population will increase by at least two-fifths.

Population of working age, however, will increase by less than one-third.

Labor force will go up by one-fifth and total hours worked by ten per cent.

And even more intensive employment, on a larger scale, of older people who are willing and able to work—however desirable in itself—would not materially affect these considerations. (11, p. 30)

It would seem that, as automation increases in its scope, the need for labor should be decreased; however, according to John Diebold, this is very far from being so. "Even if we do no more than maintain the over-all rate of increase in our standard of living," he says, "the demand for labor will in all probability exceed the supply available, particularly if the work week is cut or the retirement age lowered" (9, p. 20)—two procedures which seem, barring another war, to be inevitable.

Beyond a doubt, automation offers considerable promise for the increased employment of the physically handicapped. Dr. C. Richard Walmer has commented, in discussing the future of automation in relation to the worker's welfare:

Certainly there will be a lessening of physical stress, so that physical standards for many jobs need not be so rigid. If a job requires that a man sit at a control panel and work with his hands, it will not matter that he is crippled. He may even be much happier doing such work than someone who has the physical ability to move about freely and who may become restless and dissatisfied if forced to restrict his movement. The worker, in short, must be considered in relation to the machine and to the working environment, and, in the light of this, handicaps are often quite unimportant. (31, p. 118)

On the other hand, automation seems to offer less encouragement to the mentally retarded. By relieving human beings of the "dirty, unpleasant jobs and the backbreaking labor," and by taking them away from "the repetitive, monotonous, highly specialized tasks such as those found on the assembly line, where keeping pace with the machine can build up tensions and frustrations," automation will be cutting down on the number of jobs those thus handicapped can hold. As Walmer says:

. . . Workers will in many cases be shifted to better, more skilled jobs to handle the servicing, repair, and construction of the necessary equipment, but not all will have the ability to handle such jobs. (31, p. 118)

Although at the present moment mechanization appears to be proceeding toward a point where machines will be able to think so competently for themselves that the lowest human intelligence will be able to operate them, that time is also approaching when the machines will virtually be able to operate themselves. When that day arrives, not only the mentally deficient may find themselves without a place in society, but the human beings of average intelligence may also find themselves displaced persons.

Furthermore, the criteria of the future may well rate individuals who are considered to be of average intelligence by present-day standards as mentally defective. Therefore, society's only hope is to start now to prepare places for those whose mental capabilities are bound to fall below the ever-rising norm, for, as Drucker has pointed out:

> The really serious social problem is not employment but the need to upgrade whole segments of the population in very short time. Automation requires trained and educated people in unprecedented numbers. . . . (12, p. 45)

With the proper education and training, the mental retardate of today, as well as that of tomorrow, probably will be able to cope with many of the new jobs. Without them, he will have lost his niche in our social structure, while, at the same time, jobs go begging. And, since the average individual of today may well be the mental defective of tomorrow, it behooves every thinking individual to give some consideration to the training of the mentally handicapped, because it may be his own children and grandchildren for whom the bell will toll.

The Future of Present-Day Education

One thing is certain: Because of the increases in individual life spans, community urbanization, mechanization of industry, and the rigidity of labor laws, our schools can no longer continue to operate according to a pattern and a strategy geared to the late nineteenth-century mode of living. As George S. Counts has written:

. . . Even though we thought it desirable, the young could not be reared and inducted into our complex and far-flung industrial civilization as they were reared and inducted into the relative simplicity and confined society of the agrarian age.

. . .

. . . industrial civilization has greatly enriched and complicated the educational undertaking, but it has also increased immeasurably the institutional resources through which the responsibility of rearing the young and the old can be discharged. . . . (3, p. 299)

THE NEEDS OF YOUTH

Today the schools are called upon not only to teach skills as well as academic subjects, but also to provide a program that will enable youth to slough off excess energy in a wholesome manner. The needs and drives of young people, particularly those of high school age, are complex. According to Marguerite Malm and Olis G. Jamison, "it is the function of the high schools to meet whatever needs of the adolescent are not expressly or incidentally being met elsewhere in sufficience," and they go on to list his needs generally as:

1. The needs that he has in common with all people of his culture:
   To feel secure.
   To have a sense of worth.
   To have companionship and affection.
   To have variety.
   To maintain physical well-being.
2. The special adjustment needs of adolescence:
   Adjusting to his physical changes.
   Adjusting heterosexually.
   Emancipation from childhood dependence and restrictions.
3. The need for adult help on personal problems of adjustment.
4. The needs set by coming adulthood:
   Learning the ways of democracy.
   Developing adult directives of behavior.

Developing the ability to work and making a vocational choice.

Preparation for marital choice and marriage.

Acquiring the other knowledges, abilities, and attitudes which are of genuine necessity in adulthood. (**21**, pp. 457–58)

John Dollard has touched upon the difficulties arising from the adolescent's need to adjust his own primitive emotions to conform with his changing status:

It is possible that under ideal circumstances the new behavior patterns might be learned without producing a measurable amount of frustration. . . . In American society, however, these newly acquired abilities are prevented from functioning. Although the individual is physiologically an adult, he is sociologically a child. . . . He is expected to conform to the adult restrictions and mores, and yet he is allowed very few of the advantages and privileges which should accrue at maturity. . . . (**10**, p. 94)

According to Herbert and Lois Stolz, at this point in a young person's life, a spurt in growth begins, starting at any age from ten to fifteen, with the average at fourteen. (**29**, p. 15) Adolescents become more preoccupied with their physical problems because their bodies assume so much importance at this time. (**28**, p. 16) However, their emotional problems—which are, of course, a direct outgrowth of these bodily changes—are of even greater importance, at least as far as the school is concerned. Adolescence is an age of transition between savagery and civilization, and it is as much the task of the school to curb the primitive impulses of the savage as to instruct the young person in the arts and sciences of civilization; otherwise those impulses might find antisocial outlets.

Sheldon and Eleanor Glueck have discovered that delinquency is more prevalent among "energetic, adventure-thirsty" mesomorphic boys:

The excess of mesomorphy among delinquents as a class ought to suggest that special allowance must be made in all major channels of self-expression for the greater energy output of certain boys, if their drives are not to take antisocial expression. . . . There is obviously a need for greater variety in curriculum patterns, in leisure-time provisions, and in vocational opportunities and a more specific fitting of types of boys into areas of activity. (**14**, pp. 194–95)

There will always be some students for whom the academic subjects and skills are of paramount importance, just as there will always be some for whom school is never much more than a place where such meager abilities as they have can be channeled into optimum usefulness. Gearing the teaching program to a hypothetical average would mean that education's first objective—self-realization—could not be met adequately, if at all. The effect of such programing in the past has inevitably been only to frustrate both the gifted child and the child of inadequate mental capacity. As far back as 1895, the United States commissioner of education admitted that "in some cases the graded school system is so managed that it is made to do harm to all pupils except those of average ability." (**16**, p. 40)

Differences among Children

There is no such thing as an absolute norm applying to all individuals. From earliest times it has been recognized that virtually everyone will vary in some respects from what has been arbitrarily considered standard for the sake of convenience. And, of course, such standards have varied from century to century, as well as from place to place. It was Binet who pointed out that a man who was accepted as normal in a rural district of France might find himself considered mentally deficient in Paris. (**2**, p. 188)

Even on a purely physical level, there are enormous variations among members of the same group. As Wallin showed:

In one group of ten-year old boys, the highest ten-percentile group was 1.2 times taller, 3.4 times heavier and stronger, possessed 2.6

times more lung capacity, and was capable of performing 7.1 times more muscular work than the lowest ten-percentile group. (30, pp. 32–33)

Most often the variations are relatively minor or occur only in certain areas which are not of the first importance and are compensated for by other traits or aptitudes in other areas. However, sometimes the differences are so pronounced or in so important an area that they cover virtually all aspects of the individual's total personality.

Treating all children as if they were alike in capability and intelligence is as if all children were considered to be of the same height, whether they are tall, short, or average in actual fact. Even though differences in mental ability are perhaps more serious than any other kind when it comes to effecting social adjustments, they are as *natural* among members of the human race as differences in height. Therefore, the concept that all children should be taught in the same class, regardless of major individual differences, so that they can learn to "get along well with each other" is as absurd as to require that all of them wear the same size clothes.

As a matter of fact, such a system is degrading to the American ideal. Democratic education should not be a Procrustean bed that endeavors to lop the gifted and stretch the handicapped until they conform to the conventional gray norm or break down. Instead, its purpose should be to develop a child's capacity to the point where he can think and discriminate rationally to the fullest limits of the cortex with which the Creator endowed him. According to Counts, mass-production methods of education belong to a totalitarian society, and, even though we give equal educational opportunities to all, "we must never forget that the supreme value of a democracy is the unique quality of the individual human being. The great role of the culture in the development of excellence in the individual must not be allowed to obscure the fact of individual differences." (3, pp. 312–13)

All of us, no matter what our abilities or our handicaps, have the same basic needs, and important among them is the "need for achievement." Yet, Karl C. Garrison and J. Stanley Gray have stated too often it is not allowed expression in our schools:

. . . The child's feeling of security and personal worth is not enhanced by the teacher insisting that he achieve a certain level of competency in his school activities, especially when such a level is beyond his ability. (**13,** p. 202)

According to Christine P. Ingram, special education actually is the only way of achieving equality for the mentally retarded:

. . . Objectives for the mentally retarded may be said to differ from those for all children only to the extent that they are narrowed down to prepare the individual to fulfill special adjustments in a limited occupation and social sphere. (**17,** p. 61)

The street sweeper occupies a place in our society as useful and as productive as the nuclear physicist, and each one, if he is well-adjusted, respects the other's work.

There are no truly "bright" individuals, nor are there truly "dull" individuals; there are only *different* individuals. There appear to be the brilliant, the superior, and the gifted in particular fields and areas. The gifted in one specialty may be the dullest in another specialty. Only those who are mentally defective by structure can be placed in a category where they must be cared for or supervised all through life. And yet many of the latter who have received appropriate special education are making worthwhile contributions to society.

The Value of Special Training for Exceptional Children

William M. Cruickshank has offered the following definition to explain the admittedly loose term "exceptional child":

Who is the exceptional child? He is first and foremost a *child.* Secondly, he is a child who deviates from the normal in some degree or other. Too frequently the community forgets that these children are children. Too frequently the handicap is the facet of the child's life by which he becomes known to his teachers, to his friends, and even to his parents. . . . The degree to which the child with a handicap is accepted by his peers, his family, and his community as a *child* and the degree to which he can accept himself as a *child* will determine the extent to which he becomes an exceptional child. (4, pp. 9–10)

As a matter of fact, when he wrote the above, Cruickshank was *questioning* the value of the special class program, at least in some of its current manifestations, for he went on to say:

. . . *general educators must recognize that education for the exceptional child is a part of total education.* . . . As children, these young people are as essential a part of the total school plan as is any child in the community. . . . Placing the exceptional child outside the regular educational program has meant removing him from the immediate acquaintance of general educators. The emphasis has been to separate and keep apart. . . . (4, p. 10)

However, a personality cannot develop in a vacuum. Neither the dullard nor the genius can develop a personality or learn to get along well, each with the other, in an atmosphere and environment geared to a hypothetical average. The school has an obligation to provide training for gifted and superior children in academic subjects, but it also has an obligation to provide education for all the other different children who have different abilities. Special education classes and special schools should be viewed as avenues leading toward the exploitation of our very valuable human resources. Educators, therefore, should not be derelict in informing the school patrons that such classes are a necessary and very valuable component of a truly democratic school system.

The training of the gifted separately does not in itself produce intellectual snobbery, nor does the training of the educable mentally retarded or the socially maladjusted produce warped personalities and feelings of inferiority. Such developments are far more likely to occur when classes are heterogeneous, so that the child of low IQ and the child of high IQ find themselves in direct competition—each one blaming the other for his frustration or boredom and each as likely to stray off into mischief and possible delinquency. According to a bulletin put out by the U. S. Department of Health, Education, and Welfare:

Under the system of school progress by grade, retarded children are frequently subjected to tasks which they cannot possibly understand or perform; and frequently they are permitted to go from grade to grade without achieving anything of satisfaction to themselves or to their teachers. To escape the sense of inadequacy and blameworthiness they may become truants or engage in mischief. Studies of undesirable behavior among pupils show that there is a tendency for disciplinary problems to be concentrated among retarded children who are not given the special educational help that they need. (6, p. 7)

As for feelings of inferiority, the mentally retarded child is far less likely to find rejection from his peers than from his mental superiors and far more likely to find rewards in a curriculum adjusted especially to his capacities. Harold A. Delp has pointed out that, although "the goals for the retarded, in general, are the same as for all children . . . some aspects, nevertheless (though) desirable for all . . . become necessities for the best interests of the mentally handicapped." (7, p. 248)

Henry C. Lindgren has termed "the emphasis and insistence on conformity and submission," which is characteristic of the emotional atmosphere of all too many schools today a decidedly "disintegrative influence." (19, p. 390) It arouses maladjustments among those children who, because of their inherent differences, never can conform to the standards of the classes of average students, being above, below, or possibly beyond their scope. And these maladjustments, in their turn, give rise to prejudice and hostility.

Experience has shown that a teacher is much more likely to encounter difficulties in discipline and poor morale if she attempts to teach a class at the average pace, with two or three pupils deviating to both extremes, than if she conducted a special class for either the advanced or the retarded.

In itself, however, the special class is not enough. It must not be organized merely as a dumping ground for the exceptional child, a place to dispose of him so that the community need feel neither guilt nor apprehension as regards his future. However, as Cruickshank has pointed out, dumping grounds are what all too many of these special classes prove to be:

While the recognition of the exceptional child has gradually developed in the United States, there has been an appalling lack of a well formulated educational philosophy for provision for these children. National, state, and local programs often have developed without recognition by administrators and teachers of any inherently sound point of view. Too frequently classes have developed simply out of the interest of a parent or of a group of parents, out of pressure by some community service agency, as the result of the humanitarian interest of a single principal or teacher, or possibly as the result of direction by a higher educational authority. Many, many classes for exceptional children have developed in this spirit. . . . As a result, a vast network of special classes, different and apart from general education, has developed throughout the entire United States. These developments have, it seems to me, been the result of faulty thinking on the part of general educators and the specialists alike. This in turn has been due to the lack of a carefully developed philosophy or point of view on the part of the general education which encompasses these children. (4, p. 9)

Naturally, there would be no serious problem for education if the schools were open only to the superior and gifted who were physically and mentally in good health, and if all other children who achieved biologic maturity could be wholesomely occupied in a family situation outside of school. But we must face reality, and, in a democracy, every living human being who is not confined to some institution and who is considered sane by law must be given an opportunity to exploit whatever talent or talents he possesses. Otherwise, as the Gluecks have warned, he may exploit his talents in an antisocial manner:

> Forcing certain types of children into the traditional mold results in increasing tension, frustration, revolt, and delinquency. Much greater flexibility in school curricula is called for; a rich variety of satisfying school experiences must be devised which will enlist the interests of different types of children. (**14**, p. 200)

Ten years ago, Lawrence Link wrote that only about 10 per cent of the exceptional children in the United States "have been furnished the special facilities and programs required for their education." (**19**, p. 131) And, in 1954, Romaine P. Mackie issued the following statement under government auspices:

> In the United States only about 15 per cent of the estimated number of exceptional children of school age [4] are reported to be in special schools or classes. Undoubtedly, others are being served, but, even so, there is a great gap between the services rendered and the number of children requiring special help. (**20**, p. 7)

Although some progress is constantly being made in this area, there is no reason to suppose that special educational services leaped by 50 per cent during those seven years. Most of the difference, therefore, may be ascribed to the fact that both percentages are estimates and added very little to improved educational services for these children. The most conservative estimate of the number of exceptonal children who have not been provided with the special facilities they need could not be put at less than 80 per cent of the total number of such children in this country. What is happening to them? Educationally, they are still in the nineteenth century, still—especially if they are handicapped mentally—being forced into leaving school because they cannot cope with its problems.

Studies have shown, as Grieder and Romine point out, that the larger part of those individuals who tend to drop out before they

---

[4] Which would amount to from four to five million.

complete the elementary grades tend to be those of low intelligence. (15, p. 106) It is to be assumed that such dropouts would tend to occur most frequently in areas where special educational facilities are not provided. Thus these young people are being deprived of their rightful due as citizens and human beings.

The state governments have come to recognize their educational responsibilities to the handicapped, at least. In 1950, a council of governors was moved to issue an official declaration, which included the following statement concerning the feeble-minded:

. . . There is needed broad state planning for the care of the mentally deficient. In such planning, the most careful attempt should be made to integrate and make use of normal community resources to preclude the unnecessary use of special institutions and (even where these need to be used) to permit a rapid return to the community of as useful as possible a citizen. (22, p. 207)

Even where progress has been made, it has been dilatory and uneven. As Louis Rosenzweig has commented:

Public education has moved slowly in the direction of educating all the children of all the people. The present century has witnessed the inclusion of handicapped children in programs of public education. Thus we find that provisions have been made for almost all levels of the physically handicapped. . . . Since 1900 state and local legislation has made some provision for the mentally retarded, although almost without exception such public education has been limited to those children with I.Q.'s above 50. (26, p. 181)

Furthermore, as will be discussed in the chapters that follow, children with IQ's over 130 find themselves in almost the same predicament as those with IQ's under 50—or whatever arbitrary intelligence limit is set—for little or no attention is being given to their very real needs. It seems, therefore, that a substantial majority of those of our children who deviate from the norm in some direction are not being given the true equality of educational opportunity that should be theirs under a democratic government.

References

1. BILLETT, ROY O. *Provision for Individual Differences, Marking, and Promotion.* (National Survey of Secondary Education, Monograph No. 13. Office of Education, Bulletin No. 17.) Washington, D. C.: Government Printing Office, 1932.
2. BINET, ALFRED, and T. SIMON. "La mesure du développement de l'intélligence chez les jeunes enfants," *Bulletin de la Société Libre pour l'Etude Psychologique de l'Enfant,* II (1911), 187–248.
3. COUNTS, GEORGE S. *Education and American Civilization.* New York: Bureau of Publications, Teachers College, Columbia University, 1952.
4. CRUICKSHANK, W. M. *The Exceptional Child in Contemporary Education.* Syracuse: Syracuse University Press, 1952.
5. CUBBERLY, ELLWOOD P. *Public Education in the United States.* Boston: Houghton Mifflin Co., 1934.
6. *Curriculum Adjustments for the Mentally Retarded.* (U. S. Department of Health, Education, and Welfare. Bulletin 1950, No. 2 [2nd ed.]) Washington, D. C.: Government Printing Office, 1953.
7. DELP, HAROLD A. "Goals for the Mentally Retarded," *Training School Bulletin,* LIII (January, 1957), 248–56.
8. DEUTSCH, ALBERT. *The Mentally Ill in America.* (2nd ed.) New York: Columbia University Press, 1949.
9. DIEBOLD, JOHN. "Applied Automation: A Practical Approach," in *Keeping Pace with Automation.* New York: American Management Association, 1946. Pp. 20–28.
10. DOLLARD, JOHN, and OTHERS. *Frustration and Agression.* New Haven: Yale University Press, 1939.
11. DRUCKER, PETER. "The Coming Labor Shortage," *Harper's Magazine,* CCX (March, 1955), 27–32.
12. ———. "The Promise of Automation," *Harper's Magazine,* CCX (April, 1955), 41–47.
13. GARRISON, KARL C., and J. STANLEY GRAY. *Educational Psychology.* New York: Appleton-Century-Crofts, Inc., 1955.

14. GLUECK, SHELDON, and ELEANOR GLUECK. *Delinquents in the Making.* New York: Harper and Brothers, 1952.
15. GRIEDER, CALVIN, and STEPHEN ROMINE. *American Public Education.* New York: Ronald Press Co., 1955.
16. HARRIS, WILLIAM T., in *Addresses and Proceedings.* Washington, D. C.: National Education Association, 1895.
17. INGRAM, CHRISTINE P. *Education of the Slow-Learning Child.* New York: Ronald Press Co., 1953.
18. LINDGREN, HENRY C. *Mental Health in Education.* New York: Henry Holt and Co., 1954.
19. LINK, LAWRENCE J. "Toward a More Advanced Program of Education for Crippled Children," *Journal of Exceptional Children,* XLVII (1947), 131.
20. MACKIE, ROMAINE P. *Some Problems in the Education of Handicapped Children.* (U. S. Department of Health, Education and Welfare. Pamphlet No. 112). Washington, D. C.: Government Printing Office, 1954.
21. MALM, MARGUERITE, and OLIS G. JAMISON. *Adolescence.* New York: McGraw-Hill Book Co., 1952.
22. *Mental Health Problem of the Forty-Eight States, The.* Chicago: Council of State Governments, 1950.
23. MONROE, WALTER S. *Teacher-Learning Theory and Teacher Education, 1890–1950,* Urbana, Ill.: University of Illinois Press, 1952.
24. *Purposes of Education in American Democracy, The.* Washington, D. C.: Educational Policies Commission, National Education Association, 1938.
25. ROSENKRANZ, J. K. F. *The Philosophy of Education.* New York: D. Appleton and Co., 1886.
26. ROSENZWEIG, LOUIS. "Report of a School Program for Trainable Mentally Retarded Children," *American Journal of Mental Deficiency,* LIX (October, 1954), 181–205.
27. SEARCH, PRESTON W. "Individualis in Mass Education," in *Addresses and Proceedings.* Washington, D. C.: National Education Association, 1895. Pp. 398–406.
28. STOLZ, HERBERT ROWELL, and LOIS MEEKS STOLZ. "Adolescent Problems Relating to Somatic Variations," *Forty-third Yearbook,* National Society for the Study of Education. Chicago: University of Chicago Press, 1944. Part I.

29. ——— — ———. *Somatic Development of Adolescent Boys.*
New York: Macmillan Co., 1951.

30. WALLIN, J. E. WALLACE. *The Education of Handicapped Children.* New York: Houghton-Mifflin Co., 1924.

31. WALMER, C. RICHARD. "Worker Welfare in the Era of Automation," in *Keeping Pace with Automation* (**10**). Pp. 118–30.

32. WEAVER, THOMAS R. "The Incidence of Maladjustment among Mental Deficients in a Military Environment," *American Journal of Mental Deficiency,* LI (October, 1946), 238–46.

33. WHITE, EMERSON E. *The Art of Teaching.* New York: American Book Co., 1901.

CHAPTER TWO

The Problem of
Handicapped Children

IT IS difficult to classify with complete accuracy those children who stand in need of special education, because the term "handicapped" can be extended to include an enormous number and variety of disabilities. Merle E. Frampton and Elena D. Gall compiled a list of the common, uncommon, and rare disabilities which would require special educational facilities for those afflicted with them:

. . . The Blind, the Partially Sighted, the Deaf, the Hard of Hearing, the Speech Defective, the Mentally Retarded, the Feeble-minded, the Cerebral Palsied, those with Muscular Dystrophy, Multiple Sclerosis, individuals with Special Health Problems, the Tuberculous, the Cardiopathic . . . the Emotionally Disturbed and others with acute psychopathic conditions, the Neurologically Impaired, the Socially Maladjusted, the Orthopedically Handicapped, those with Lowered Vitality, the Delicate, the Epileptic, the Multiple-Handicapped, the Aged, the Chronically Ill, those with Endocrine Disturbances, the Narcotic, the Alcoholic, the Hemophiliac, the Juvenile Delinquent, those with Dental Defects, Leprosy, Brain Injuries, Spina Bifida and allergies, Paraplegia, Diabetes, Poliomyelitis, Asthmatic conditions, Chorea, Tics, Lateral dominance, Osteomyelitis, Legg-Perthis disease, Encephalitis, and many other medical, psychopathic, and emotional defects. (2, p. 32)

However, as far as the question of educating them is concerned, handicapped individuals can be divided into four broad classifications: (1) the physically handicapped, (2) the mentally handicapped, (3) the socially handicapped, and (4) those which combine all three. Frampton, in collaboration with Hugh G. Rowell, further subdivided the physically handicapped into three groups:

(a) those whose handicap involves one or more special senses, including the blind, the partially sighted, the deaf, the hard of hearing, and the deaf and blind;

(b) those whose handicap results in motor disability or limitation, including orthopedic cases (infantile paralysis, spastic conditions, osteomyelitis, bone tuberculosis, and congenital defects and deformities); cardiacs; those suffering from respiratory diseases in certain stages; malnutrition cases;

(c) those with various types of defective speech of whatever origin. (3, I, 1)

They have also broken down the category of mental handicap into three principal subdivisions:

(a) persons who in natural intellectual capacity fall in the lower ranges of human intelligence;

(b) persons who have suffered accident or disease resulting in the impairment of mental functions;

(c) persons suffering from emotional instability, psychopathic states, and insanity. (3, I, 1)

THE HISTORY OF EDUCATING THE HANDICAPPED

The Physically Handicapped

Attention was given to the problem of educating physically handicapped children long before it was thought possible to educate the mentally handicapped, since their defects, first of all, were more apparent to earlier and less sophisticated civilizations, and, second, seemed less irreconcilable with mental attainment than defects that were, in themselves, mental. It was not until the Age of Enlightenment in the eighteenth century, however, that education of the handicapped began to take great strides and, in effect, assume its modern form.

Through history it has been the blind who have received more attention and sympathetic consideration than any other handicapped group. Many individuals handicapped by visual disability were nonetheless able to achieve eminence in their respective fields, and not only did their prestige tend to raise the status of those similarly afflicted, but also they themselves made considerable efforts to help those with the same handicap.

It was not until 1784 that Valentin Haüy founded the famous school in Paris that marked the beginning of formal education for the blind, specifically adjusted to the capabilities of those so afflicted. This school not only revolutionized French methods of instructing the blind but also exerted a tremendous influence upon the education of the blind in all of Europe, notably Great Britain.

In 1790, the first English school for the blind was established at Liverpool. This was followed by many others throughout the British Isles, all of which had, as Frampton and Rowell pointed out, a drawback:

> The English idea of blind school education shows no distinction between charity and education, the asylum idea remaining uppermost. The only exception was the Bristol school whose aim was "to teach [the blind] a means of getting a living by work. . . ." (3, I, 28–29)

The first school for the blind in Austria, the Vienna Institute for the Instruction of the Blind, was founded by Johann Wilhelm Klein in 1804. This institution was actually a school rather than an asylum, and Klein himself "contributed a truly educational point of view to the methodology of teaching the blind. He introduced a new psychological approach, and brought about a realization of economic conditions for the blind." (3, I, 29)

The psychological approach was new in practice rather than theory, for, Berthold Lowenfeld wrote:

> Psychological problems of blindness received early attention in the eighteenth century with the question of how a successfully operated congenitally blind person would react to his first optical impressions. The philosophers Locke, Berkeley, and later Diderot theorized considerably about sensory problems of the blind. (11, p. 215)

This interest continued during the nineteenth century:

> During the early period of scientific psychology, William James, as well as Wilhelm Wundt and others discussed in their standard works problems of the blind, particularly their spatial perception. The first systematic study dealing with psychological problems of blindness as such also dates back to the experimental laboratory of Wundt where Theodor Heller conducted investigations which he reported in his *Studien zur Blinden-Psychologie* (1885). (11, p. 215)

It was with the development of the point alphabet that education for the blind really came into its own. Although such an alphabet had been suggested as early as the seventeenth century, it was not until 1825 that the Frenchman Charles Barbier actually developed an efficiently functioning one. This system was improved by Louis Braille, after whom the point alphabet we use today was named and who was himself blind. In 1920, the Braille alphabet was universally accepted.

Closely paralleling the history of the education of the blind has been the consideration of the deaf. Actually, while there were no schools established for the deaf before the first decade of the eighteenth century, history records efforts to educate the deaf as early as the seventh century. But it was not until the sixteenth century that practical education of the deaf began, in Spain. The Benedictine monk, Pedro Ponce de Leon, "was the first recorded teacher of the deaf." (3, I, 55) He was followed by Juan Pablo Bonet and Ramires de Carrión in the seventeenth century. All three achieved notable results in teaching the apparently mute to speak, as well as to read and to write.

During the seventeenth century, England took over the leadership in the education of the acoustically handicapped. William Holder emphasized lip reading, but his contemporaries, John Wallis and George Dalgarno, did not accord it a particularly significant status. (3, I, 57–58) In the eighteenth century, France forged ahead in this aspect of education, after Jacob Rodrigues Pereire, having been forced to leave Madrid, made his home in Paris. Pereire, not recognizing that the problems of instructing the various types of handicapped often overlapped, was fearful of trying to teach retarded children in Spain. It was this timidity that caused him to be driven into exile.

As a result of the introduction of Pereire's methods, several schools for the deaf were started in France during the eighteenth century. The most famous was the one established by the Abbé de l'Epée in Paris in 1755. It was l'Epée who developed the manual alphabet—which was improved by his successor Sicard and is still in use to some extent today.

However, the oral method of teaching the deaf to read lips and to speak is much more prevalent, and this, in the form that we know it, was originated by Samuel Heinecke—who is also noted for having founded the first German school for the deaf. In England, the oral system of educating the deaf was the preferred method. During the eighteenth century, however, it was available only to those who could afford it because this type of instruction was virtually a monopoly of the Braidwood family who, by refusing to divulge their methods to Gallaudet, were responsible for the lingering hold the manual method had upon teaching the deaf in this country.

Unlike the sympathy demonstrated for the blind and the deaf, the speech defectives were not granted educational consideration until recent times. While unusual emotional fervor has been aroused on behalf of the blind and the deaf, the speech defective is quite often ridiculed. In any event, the speech defectives comprise the largest number of handicapped children in our public schools today. The education of speech defectives probably received less impetus than did the education of the blind and the deaf because speech defectives are difficult to isolate at a glance. Their trouble may stem from another handicap, and those thus afflicted, therefore, should be receiving special education for the total disability rather than just for the defective speech. Garrison and Gray have identified three principal types of speech disabilities:

(1) those resulting from faulty habits, such as lisping and baby talk;

(2) those resulting from emotional instability or maladjustment, which includes the stutterer;

(3) those having a definite physical basis, such as the cleft palate. (**5**, p. 44)

Obviously, only the third category should be considered under the heading of *physical* handicap, since the second and, in a sense, the first are more properly classified as social disabilities. However, in earlier times the prevalent belief was that all such defects had a physical origin and attempts—often disastrous—were made to treat them medically and even surgically.

It was not until the eighteenth century that it was suggested, by the philosopher Moses Mendelssohn—although he may have been one of the most celebrated, rather than the first to advance the idea—that stuttering really was psychological in origin. And Jean-Marc-Gaspard Itard, the otologist who was later to achieve celebrity as a result of his work with the mentally retarded, was the first to have treated stammering as "a pathological symptom." (**3**, I, 98) As for education, toward the end of the nineteenth century, a school for speech defectives was established in Germany, but not much remedial work was actually done in the area until well into this century.

Brief mention at this time should be made about the education of the crippled, a term which was used to refer only to those who were orthopedically handicapped. Actually, it was not until the eighteenth century that any interest was taken in the specific problems of those so afflicted, and it was not until the nineteenth century that any considerable degree of attention was paid to the actual care, let alone the education, of orthopedic cases. For the most part, they attended the regular schools, unless it was absolutely impossible for them to do so—in which case they were generally kept at home, and, if possible, educated there, or, more often, left ignorant.

Although the first public school class for crippled children was established in England in 1899, that country made no provision for institutional care of the crippled. It remained for Germany and Austria to carry on "most of their orthopedic programs of education through the medium of hospitalization." (3, I, 12)

A more elaborate and detailed treatment of the problem of the education of the physically handicapped is presented in Chapter Nine.

The Mentally Handicapped

Scholarly interest was first aroused in the possibility of educating the mentally deficient toward the end of the eighteenth century. It was in 1798 that the famous "wild boy" was discovered in the French forest near Aveyron. This boy—who appeared to be thirteen at most—was discovered living there like an animal: naked, speechless, walking on all fours. He was brought to the Academy of Science in Paris, where Dr. Philippe Pinel, France's leading authority on the mentally disordered, pronounced him to be an idiot; therefore, it was to be assumed, it would not be possible to teach him anything, since the feebleminded were incapable of learning.

However, Itard, then a young physician at the Institute for the Deaf in Paris, ventured to disagree with Pinel. His reasoning was actually based upon a false premise: it was not that he failed to subscribe to the generally accepted theory that it was impossible to impart instruction to the feebleminded, but that he believed the boy to be suffering from a cultural rather than a mental lack. If he were to be exposed to the influences of civilization, Itard maintained, his condition would be improved, possibly to the point where he would become a normal individual.

Accordingly, Itard attempted to teach the boy, utilizing the techniques he had devised as suitable for a savage of presumably normal intelligence who had simply been deprived of a civilized upbringing. However, the boy actually *was* feebleminded and so, little by little, Itard was forced to modify his original methods. Finally, in despair, he gave up the project as a failure and turned the boy over to the mercies of one of his students, Edouard Séguin.

The French Academy of Science did not agree that Itard had failed in his work with the "wild boy." Instead, some time later, they hailed him as the discoverer of the fact that it was, after all, possible to impart some degree of training, if not education, to the mentally deficient; for, although Itard could not ever give the boy a measure of intelligence that he did not inherently possess, he had succeeded in achieving such improvements in the child's condition as had hitherto been considered impossible. In effect, Itard had taken a human beast and taught him to speak and understand and even to read and write a little. What was even more important was that he had taught the boy to adjust to civilization.

During the nineteenth century, Itard's methods were expanded upon by Séguin, who became known as "the apostle of the idiot"

(3, I, 178), because of his devotion to the cause of mental retardation. He made that field his lifetime study, his ambition being to educate the feebleminded to their fullest bent by exploiting every capacity latent in them. In 1846, he published the first scientific classification of mentally retarded children.

Schools had been opened for the training of the feebleminded previously, but Séguin's, established at Paris in 1839, was the first to succeed. After that, numerous institutions for the feebleminded modeled after his were opened in England and Switzerland as well and flourished.

The Socially Handicapped

Very little historical background can be given concerning the education of the socially handicapped, because it has been only during this century that the existence of such a disability as a *social* handicap has been recognized. And, even so, it has not been universally acknowledged or conceded to be a serious disability, particularly when it comes to its less outwardly destructive aspects.

Generally speaking, social handicaps and emotional handicaps can be considered as virtually synonymous in this context, because it is the individual's emotional development that determines the degree of his adjustment to the society to which he belongs. Since the physically or mentally handicapped child is usually a victim of greater adverse environmental pressures than the average child is, he frequently suffers from emotional maladjustment and, hence, is doubly handicapped. As Garrison and Gray have pointed out:

. . . The greater amount of maladjustments found among the physically handicapped results primarily from the limitations which such a condition entails. . . . The child who because of cerebral palsy is unable to participate in many out-of-door games is thereby restricted in the full realization of certain needs. He is thus forced, through circumstances beyond his control, to narrow his goals of self-realization. . . . The child with defective vision or who is hard of hearing is seriously handicapped in his personal and social development as well as in his school performances. . . . (5, pp. 444–45)

Very often teachers unequipped to deal with the problem of exceptional children either because of training or personality will simply classify their handicapped pupils, particularly those with acoustic and the less serious visual defects, as stupid, rather than attempting to look deeper for the cause of their scholastic failure. Or the teachers and the parents might go to the other extreme and overprotect the handicapped child in a mistaken effort to help him.

Social handicap, therefore, is an aspect of both mental and physical handicap, as well as an area of disability in itself. As Frampton and Rowell have said, concerning the education of those handicapped in this way:

While its historical background is negligible, its significance in the educational pattern is paramount, inasmuch as it cuts through every area of human accomplishment and integrates every successful program of achievement. Therefore, the socially handicapped group must be considered as a basic unit in each and every area of the handicapped. (3, I, 3)

EDUCATION OF THE HANDICAPPED IN THE UNITED STATES

The Physically Handicapped

Schools for the blind were started in the United States early in the nineteenth century. In 1829, the Perkins Institute and Massachusetts School for the Blind was incorporated under the directorship of Dr. Samuel Gridley Howe, who is also known for his pioneer work in other areas of physical and mental disability, as well as for his innovation of the cottage system in educating the handicapped. Three years later, in 1832, the New York Institute for the Blind was founded as a result of the efforts of Samuel Wood.

The other states soon followed suit. Pennsylvania founded a school for the blind in 1833, Ohio in 1837, Wisconsin in 1849, Indiana in 1847, Illinois in 1848, Missouri in 1850, Georgia in 1851, Iowa in 1852, Maryland in 1853, South Carolina in 1855, and Texas in 1856. Twenty-nine states had schools for the blind by the end of 1875. (3, p. 34) The most recent statistics in this area, those for 1947, indicate that there were fifty-six public and private residential schools for the blind in this country, serving some 5,235 students in forty-three states and territories. (29, p. 13)

Public school classes for the blind were also organized in various states. But the government's 1952 to 1953 report on education showed that only 839 pupils in nineteen states were served by these classes, primarily because it has been found most practical to instruct the blind in residential schools. However, there are 8,024 partially sighted children being served by special classes in the public school systems of most of the states and territories. (28, p. 28)

Thomas Hopkins Gallaudet was the man who brought about the establishment of the first permanent free school for the deaf in the United States, at Hartford, Connecticut, in 1817. Some of the other states began sending their deaf children to be educated there at the public expense, and subsequently the various states began to establish such schools of their own, New York being the first, opening the New York Institute for the Deaf and Dumb in 1818.

Since Gallaudet used the manual method rather than the oral one, owing to his having worked with Sicard in France after a rebuff from the Braidwoods, the Hartford School continued to use and promulgate that system, even after the oral method became more popular, first in Europe and then in America. Dr. Howe and Horace Mann, after visiting the schools for the deaf in England—

. . . became convinced of the practicability of teaching them speech. The campaign which he and . . . Mann began was opposed by the Hartford School, but . . . Mann and Howe established the class for teaching deaf mutes by the oral method which led to the founding of the Clarke School at Northampton. (3, I, 3)

One of the best-known workers in the field of education for the deaf was Alexander Graham Bell, and it was as a result of his endeavors to produce a machine that would visibly represent speech movements that he gave the world the telephone.

Public school education for the deaf started with the opening of the Horace Mann School in Boston in 1869. As of 1952–53, there were 3,935 deaf pupils enrolled in the public school systems of thirty-four states and territories. (28, p. 20) The latest figures for the residential schools as reported in *American Annals of the Deaf* of January, 1956, show a total of seventy-two schools with an enrollment of 14,464.

Classes for speech correction in the United States did not start until the beginning of the twentieth century. In 1952–53, 306,747 children were enrolled in public school classes for speech defectives in every state and territory of the union. (28, p. 19)

The education of the crippled lagged far behind education of the blind and deaf. Dr. John Paul Brown opened a private hospital for the treatment of orthopedic cases as early as 1829, but it was not until 1861 that he opened a public ward for orthopedics in Boston. The Hospital for the Ruptured and Crippled was opened in New York, in 1863, largely as a result of the efforts of Dr. James Knight. In the decade from 1880 to 1890, a number of similar institutions were founded: the Home of the Merciful Savior in Philadelphia; and, in New York, the Visiting Guild for Crippled Children, the Children's Aid Society, and the Rhinelander School for Crippled Children. According to Mackie:

Until the beginning of the twentieth century almost no provision was made for the public education of physically handicapped children in the United States, except for the deaf and the blind, who were publicly served . . . in residential institutions. A number of private and public institutions and homes had been established during the nineteenth century, but the trend toward public day-school care for crippled children is a movement of this century. (3, p. 129)

The first public school class for crippled children was opened in the United States in 1899 as a project of the Chicago board of education. However:

Even as late as 1914, except for the four large cities of New York, Chicago, Cleveland, and Detroit, there were almost no public education programs for crippled children in this country. (14, p. 9)

The condition has, of course, improved since then, and the 1952–53 statistics show that there were 17,813 crippled children enrolled in the special schools and classes of the United States public school system at that time. (14, p. 111)

The Mentally Handicapped

After the revolution of 1848, Séguin emigrated from France to the United States, where he helped organize five institutions for the mentally retarded, four in the northeast—in South Boston; Philadelphia; Syracuse, New York; and Lakeview, Connecticut—and one in Columbus, Ohio. (31, p. 9) Although the American Asylum for the Deaf and Dumb in Hartford had, in 1818, opened its doors to a limited number of mental defectives, it was Dr. Harvey B. Wilbur who started the first school in this country specifically organized for the education of mental defectives—in Barre, Massachusetts, in 1848. That institution was a private one; however, later that same year Massachusetts opened the first state-supported school for mental defectives in the United States as a division of the Perkins Institute for the Blind. In 1891, the school was given a permanent location in Waverly, and subsequently named after one of its most celebrated superintendents, Walter E. Fernald.

New York opened a similar school in 1851 under the direction of the same Dr. Wilbur. In 1855, the school was moved from Albany to Syracuse, where it is now known as the Syracuse State School. That same year Pennsylvania established a school (now the Elwyn Training School) for the education of feebleminded youth, and, two years later, Ohio and Connecticut followed suit by opening schools which have today become respectively the Columbus State School and the Mansfield State Training School and Hospital.

By now, every state in the union except two has some kind of institution or institutions to deal with the education and, if necessary, housing of the mentally deficient. The systems in New Jersey and New York are the most elaborate and diversified of all, and, indeed, the rest of the country has not kept pace with the Northeast in this area of education, just as, in its turn, the country as a whole has not kept pace with the work of other countries, notably Great Britain.

In many states, these institutions represent an attempt to solve the problem of the mental deficient for the community rather than for the benefit of the deficient himself. Sarason has suggested that, in many cases, institutions were built for the care of the subnormal:

. . . not because they reflected a new idea or approach or reflected an attempt to cope with this many-sided problem, but because there were either no facilities in the community or because some well-intentioned or misguided individuals believed that all such children should be in institutions. (**27**, p. 33)

In 1952, the National Institute of Mental Health reported that at least 124,210 mental defectives, both adults and children, were in the care of either public or private institutions. (**22**, p. 69)

The public school systems did not seem to consider attempting to deal with the needs of mentally deficient children until considerably later. Although Germany had established a public school class to train mentally backward children as early as 1867, it was not until 1896 that the first public school classes for backward children were established in the United States—in Providence, Rhode Island. After that, special classes for the mental retardate gradually came into being in public schools throughout the country. Springfield, Massachusetts, opened one in 1897, Chicago in 1898, Boston in 1899, New York in 1900, and soon the other cities followed suit, with the Northeast, as usual, taking the lead in development. According to Katherine Lynch and Louis Scharf, the New York classes really represented the first genuinely "experimental classes" for the training of defective children. (12, p. 337)

The progress of the special classes for these children was probably held back by the viewpoint expressed by such educators as L. A. Hollingworth, who felt that feebleminded children differ from the average only in the extent rather than the type of abilities they possess.

. . . No mysterious or unique matter or method is necessarily required in the task of training them. They can learn the same things that other children learn up to the limits of their capacity. (7, p. 5)

This attitude was subsequently proved to be untenable, and the theory behind these special classes today is that they should not only be designed to keep the mentally retarded or deficient children from hopeless competition with average students, but also that they should be set up to develop the deficients' special abilities, and thus, wherever possible, keep them from becoming a burden upon the community.

According to Monroe, as the century progressed, there came to be—

. . . widespread recognition of the marked individual differences in typical grade groups and of the desirability, or even necessity, of effecting a better adaptation of the school to pupils differing in capacity to learn. . . . By 1925 there had been a variety of experimental attempts to deal with the problem.

"Ability grouping," which had become popular by this time, was in many cases essentially a scheme to provide for varying the rate of progress for groups of pupils. In such plans the adaptation of instructional procedure was typically left to the teacher and usually very little was done beyond varying the pace of the assignments. Another means of adaptation within the class organization was some form of "coaching" or additional instruction for the "laggards." . . . Some schools developed "hospital classes," and, of course, many teachers on their own initiative kept pupils after school or in other ways provided "coaching" for the "laggards." . . . (**21**, pp. 105–106)

Laws were passed by many states requiring that special training be given to all educable handicapped children. The majority of the states now allot grants to provide special classes for the mentally deficient and retarded. As an example of one state's provision for children with this handicap, in 1947 California made special education *mandatory* for all "educable mentally deficient minors" of school age, with the state agreeing to reimburse the schools for the excess over normal operating costs that such programs would entail.

Even in those states where no such provision has been made by the state government, many local governments have organized appropriate classes to care for their mentally deficient children. However, at a conference of the governors of the forty-eight states held in 1950, it was recognized by all that this problem should really be the concern of the state governments. Moreover, the governors went on to define categorically the responsibility the state owed to these children:

There are three major aspects to the care of the mentally deficient. In the first place, his potentialities must be accurately *assessed* by appropriately qualified personnel. Second, the *educational* phase of his life must be so adjusted as to enable the defective person to make the best use of whatever potentialities he may have. Finally . . . it is necessary to make appropriate arrangements to adjust his life-situation in such a way that his potentialities can be used to give him the maximum occupational advantage and to give the community the benefit of his productive services. (**19**, p. 206)

In 1952–53, there were 100,903 "educable mentally retarded" children enrolled in the public schools of all the states, except Nevada and Vermont, and 4,662 "severely mentally retarded" in forty-one states and the District of Columbia. (**28**, p. 22) The most elaborate and comprehensive public school system of training for retarded children exists in New York City, where Lynch and Scharf have described the 692 such classes as "the world's largest laboratory for the study and education of the mentally handicapped." (**12**, p. 337)

The Socially Handicapped

Special education for the socially handicapped is perhaps the area in which the least educational and rehabilitational work has been—and is being—done, even though it could be the most rewarding, since it is the only one in which the handicapped stand such an excellent chance of being brought to full normalcy. In the early years of this country's existence, delinquent children were, for the most part, treated like ordinary criminals. Late in the nineteenth century, classes for delinquents and incorrigibles were established in several of the larger United States cities, and currently there are a number of so-called disciplinary classes organized in the public school systems. In 1947, 15,301 delinquent children were reported enrolled in special classes and day schools in 92 cities in all the states, as well as Hawaii, Puerto Rico, and the District of Columbia. (**29**). Outstanding among the public school work in this area is the Montefiore School, established by the Chicago board of education in 1929, which is one of the few day schools for the socially maladjusted child.

However, most of these touch on only one aspect of the problem of social handicap, for they are, as a rule, planned primarily for those children who actively misbehave or are conspicuously antisocial. They do not deal—at least, not adequately—with those children who, although "good," insofar as they do not create any classroom or community disturbances, are disturbed within themselves . . . though they may show little or no sign of their maladjustment to the untrained or undiscerning eye.

The Total Problem

The realization that basically education of all the handicapped actually presented a single ramified problem for the schools came around the end of the nineteenth century. It was Dr. Alexander Graham Bell who stated at a meeting of the National Education Association in 1898 that—

. . . We have in the public-school system a large body of ordinary children in the same community. We have there children who cannot hear sufficiently well to profit by instruction in the public schools, and we have children who are undoubtedly backward in their mental development. Why should not these children form an annex to the public-school system, receiving special instruction from special teachers, who shall be able to give instruction to little children who are either deaf, blind, or mentally deficient without sending them away from their homes or from the ordinary companions with whom they are associated? (**2**, p. 10)

It was largely as a result of Dr. Bell's efforts that a "Department of Special Education" was established as part of the NEA, in 1901. In 1902, the name of that department was expanded to "Department of Special Education—Relating to Children Demanding Special Means of Instruction."

Hazel C. McIntire has provided an excellent picture of the progress one state, Ohio, has made in dealing with special education, first as a series of disparate projects and then as a unified program. Ohio began by building state residential schools for the deaf in 1829 and 1837.

In the period beginning about 1910, there began to appear in the larger cities of the state special classes and schools for physically handicapped children. In this movement it is noted that the local school districts not only set up special classes for deaf and blind children, but went a step further by setting up special classes for crippled children. Financial records for that period show that the State Department of Education granted "state aid" to these special classes from the funds available to the department. . . .

By 1919, public interest in the education of physically handicapped children in the public schools had crystallized to the point that there was strong demand for legislation that would recognize existing classes and provide a basis for the organization and financing of such classes throughout the state. The law enacted that year gave the state superintendent of public instruction authority to "grant permission to local boards of education" to set up special classes for deaf, blind, or crippled children. . . . This basic legislation recognized the provision of schooling for educable handicapped children as a function of the state and the local school district, not the responsibility of related agencies, such as health and welfare. (13, p. 183)

In 1945, the Ohio state law was broadened "to include provisions for special classes for slow-learning children, child study, and instructional services for any child whose learning is 'retarded, interrupted, or impaired by physical or mental handicap.'" (12, p. 183) It seems that the area of social handicap has been neglected here, although it is conceivable that the difficulty is primarily a semantic one, and that social maladjustment is being dealt with in this state but under a different classification.

The City of Chicago is also one of the pioneers in the field of public special education. Frances A. Mullen has outlined its significant achievements in this area:

Among American public school systems, Chicago claims the first class for crippled children (1899), the first child study clinic (1899), the first class for the blind (1900), and the first Parental School for court-committed truants (1902). Public school classes for the deaf were started in 1875. Chicago was an early exponent of the oral method of instruction of the deaf. Classes for the mentally retarded appeared in 1900. Public school teachers were sent into the hospitals to do bedside teaching in 1900; speech therapy began in 1910. (**22**, p. 194)

And today Chicago still holds its place in the vanguard of special education.

The Chicago public schools, in January 1955, make special provision for a large number of handicapped children. . . . Over 17,000 exceptional children are being served by approximately a thousand adults in seven special schools, in classes located in 173 of our 419 elementary and high schools, and in speech services to practically all schools. . . . (**22**, p. 195)

In Chicago, social handicap is officially considered as an integral part of the special education program:

Truancy and other symptoms of maladjustment in the regular grades are problems every school must face. . . . Children will be found whose problems seem insoluble with the resources available to the regular school. Such pupils are given another chance in our day schools for the socially maladjusted. . . .

Pupils who fail to respond to the program of the day school for social adjustment, and pupils who find their way into the courts for other reasons, may be committed to the Parental School. . . . (**22**, p. 197)

New York City takes a somewhat different attitude in its method of coping with similiar problems. In the words of Frank J. O'Brien:

. . . if a child is eventually to take his place with others in the community, he must have experience and help in learning how to associate happily and constructively with them. This can be accomplished best by seeing to it that he is an integral part of his general community during the formative school years.

In harmony with this principle, in New York City all classes for handicapped children, with two exceptions, are organized in regular schools. The two exceptions are the programs for the deaf and the emotionally disturbed. . . . (**24**, p. 210)

The foregoing are merely offered to serve as examples of some of the outstanding state and local programs for the handicapped in this country. Many other areas have equally efficient systems, and still other areas are developing them.

It is obvious that the handicapped child in a large community is going to have a better chance of getting an appropriate education than one in a small community, for the larger community has, first of all, more resources, and, second, is more likely to be able to assemble enough children with the same kind of handicap to make specialized education feasible from the economic point of view.

In speaking of the mentally retarded child, Ingram described a situation that is applicable to virtually all types of handicap as well, namely that many communities are still unable to provide a special-class program—

. . . owing to such conditions as lack of finances, building space, equipment, child study, and trained teachers. Others can provide classes for some of the group only, usually the most outstanding cases. A comparatively small number of towns, villages, and rural communities plan an adapted program for the individual child which can be carried on in the classroom. (9, p. 76)

IDENTIFYING THE EXCEPTIONAL CHILDREN

It is impossible to make more than an extremely rough estimate of the number of handicapped children in the United States today, because the terminology used is so imprecise. Accurately separating the mental deficients from those of normal intelligence has long been known as a difficult problem to solve—and, indeed, to a certain extent, an insoluble one. But, although it is much easier to isolate the physically handicapped from the rest of the school population, physical handicap is not always a matter of simple identification, either. As Mackie has said, with reference to crippled children:

It is not a simple matter to write a clear-cut statement which will define the heterogeneous group of children known as crippled. Factors which tend to complicate the formulation of a clear-cut definition are: Unstandardized classification procedures; the range in severity of cases; and the often-used method of defining the crippled according to available resources and services. . . .

Children with various kinds of orthopedic conditions and those with cerebral damage resulting in cerebral palsy are, without question, crippled children. Some cases not strictly orthopedic or cerebral palsied are classified by various agencies as crippled, in order that they may be included in service programs. Children with cardiac conditions, for example, are quite often classified as crippled. . . . (**14**, p. 1)

She went on to point out that—

Another factor affecting the reported incidence of crippling conditions is the present inadequacy in *case finding*. Most census taking, for example, is done by people who could not be expected to diagnose conditions. As a result, certain types of children have not been reported, because little professional attention has been given to them.

This difficulty of diagnosis is applicable to other areas of handicap. Between blindness and full vision, there is an infinite number of degrees of sightedness. "Hard of hearing" can mean partial as well as total deafness. Speech defects may spring from a hearing defect with which they are associated.

Moreover, a physical defect may not always signify an actual handicap. As Frampton and Rowell have so justly pointed out, "the term 'handicap' implies the *effect* of a mental or physical situation rather than the fact that some disease, malformation, or other marked deviation has existed or does exist in the individual." (3, II, 2) Parents are often reluctant to admit that their children are in any way handicapped and, wherever it is possible to do so, try to conceal them rather than to seek help. This naturally hinders any attempt to determine the number of handicapped individuals extant in this country today.

Many attempts have been made to arrive at least at an estimate of their number, and the results have varied to a considerable degree. It is difficult to compare the individual estimates, because the age groups covered tend to vary from investigation to investigation, and sometimes the precise definition of the handicap as well. Mackie and Dunn have estimated the number of exceptional [1] children of school age in the United States to be between four and five million:

Accepting a minimal estimate of twelve or thirteen per cent (one-eighth) of the school-age population as exception, then this figure can be justified. The Bureau of the Census reported approximately 34,000,000 children between the ages of five and seventeen in the United States for the year 1952. Using the percentage of incidence as 12.70, the number of exceptional children would be 4,318,000. (17, p. 3)

They break down that 4,318,000 as follows:

Areas of exceptionality	Percentage of incidence	Estimated number of school-age children
Visually handicapped	0.20	
Blind		10,000
Partially seeing		58,000
Crippled	1.50	510,000
Special health problems	1.50	510,000
Deaf and hard of hearing	1.50	510,000
Speech-handicapped	2.00	680,000
Socially maladjusted	2.00	680,000
Mentally retarded	2.00	680,000
Gifted [2]	2.00	680,000
	12.70	4,318,000

(17, p. 3)

More definite figures can be given for those children actually enrolled in the special classes of the public elementary and secondary day schools, as shown in the following chart from *Statistics of Special Education for Exceptional Children:*

[1] This includes the gifted as well as the handicapped. The problems of the gifted will be considered separately, in Chapter Three.

1952–53

Type	Enrollment
Mentally retarded	113,565
Speech-defective	306,747
Crippled	17,813
Hard of hearing	11,932
Partially seeing	8,014
Special health problems	11,455
Deaf	3,935
Blind	839
Mentally gifted [2]	22,916
	497,216

(28, p. 19)

It must be borne in mind, however, that the figures are so surprisingly low because the residential and private schools are not included.[3]

Frampton and Gall have made the following estimate of the current incidence of all types of exceptionality in the United States:

All ages (1954)

Blind—both eyes	270,000
Blind—one eye	1,000,000
Sight Saving and Partially Sighted	600,000
Deaf	185,000
Hard-of-Hearing	2,188,000
Poliomyelitis (1953) acute	35,952
Mentally Defective	950,000
Emotionally Disturbed	700,000–800,000
Epileptic	1,500,000
Muscular Dystrophy	100,000
Speech Defective	20% of children under 3
	15% of children 3–18
	7% adults
Cardiac Conditions	5,000,000
Arteriosclerosis and High Blood Pressure	4,600,000
Nephritis	950,000
Cardiovascular (renal)	9,200,000
Tuberculosis	1,200,000
Cancer (under treatment)	700,000
Diabetes	2,000,000
Cerebral Palsy	500,000

(2, pp. 36–37)

[2] The gifted will be considered separately in Chapter Three.

[3] In 1945–46, there were 307 public and 137 private residence schools for exceptional children in the United States.

Some of these estimates will find more universal acceptance, or more nearly coincide with other investigators' estimates, than others. For example, most investigators might consider a figure of seven or eight hundred thousand rather too low to represent the number of emotionally disturbed—even if it is limited to those seriously disturbed—individuals in the United States.

Arthur Lesser and Eleanor Hunt estimated in 1951 that the young people under twenty-one in our population who had had rheumatic fever or its aftereffects numbered 675,000; who had had cerebral palsy, 285,000; who had had epilepsy, 275,000. According to their estimates, the number of children under eighteen suffering from cleft palates or cleft lips was about 64,000. They felt there were 7,500,000 children in need of eye care, 60,000 of them with visual handicaps so serious as to require special educational help, and 6,600 actually blind. The estimate went on to state that from 250,000 to 500,000 young people under twenty-one had hearing handicaps and 2,000,000 from five to twenty years old had severe speech disorders—over half of which derived from functional articulatory defects. Of the children aged five to seventeen, one million had orthopedic defects. (10, pp. 45–46)

The fact that stands out clearly from this diversity of estimates and figures is that there are millions of children in the United States who are severely handicapped and that the question of educating them adequately presents a real problem.

THE NEED FOR SPECIAL EDUCATION
FOR THE HANDICAPPED

There is a serious discrepancy between the 497,216 children actually enrolled in the special classes of the public school system and the 2,811,800 (10 per cent of a total school population of 28,118,000 during 1952–53) estimated by the government authorities to be in need of such services. And, if Arthur Hill is correct in estimating the number of those children served by the residential schools at as few as 45,000, there is no escape from "the conclusion that most children in need of special educational services are not getting them." (**28**, p. 7)

Yet this education is almost *more* important for the handicapped child than the normal one. As Mackie has pointed out:

Many of the limitations in the handicapped adult result directly from inadequate training and care in early years. Good kindergarten and nursery schools, regarded as beneficial for most children, have special values for handicapped children, particularly for the cerebral-palsied, the deaf, the blind, and possibly for the mentally retarded. (**17**, p. 8)

In some schools there has been a tendency to accept handicapped students who might not have been admitted before and then to place them in the regular classes. This is far from being a solution to the problem, for, if the handicapped are placed in regular school classes, they will not only suffer themselves but will deprive the average and better than average students of the education they deserve. As Dr. Harold Michal-Smith has said:

We find that teachers who already feel that their pupils are not offered as much help and individual attention as they would like to give them are asked to accept into the classroom situation a great many children of the type formerly excluded because of disabilities. It would be difficult enough for such teachers if all of these handicapped children were victims of a like disability. . . .

But no, we send into nurseries, kindergartens, special and even non-special classes children with very different afflictions and limitations. Each child of normal capacities presents a special and different problem to a conscientious teacher. Now his situation is vastly complicated by the variety and complexity of the handicaps he must consider in dealing with atypical youngsters. (**20**, p. 203)

Actually, there is a great practical value in organizing special classes from the very start of a child's education, since, in many cases, they may result in a lessened need for these services when the child grows older. Hill wrote:

If the (special) educational services are provided at the nursery school and kindergarten levels, most severely crippled and otherwise physically disabled children may develop improved coordination and better speech habits, and learn to live with their handicaps to the extent that they may be absorbed in the regular schools and classes at a relatively early age (and) it has been demonstrated that both normally intelligent deaf and blind children may achieve well in the regular school classes after they have mastered communicative skills. . . . (28, p. 2)

The Mentally Handicapped

Of all the handicaps, mental deficiency is the hardest to define adequately. One of the problems that face educators and psychologists today is of determining just where the line between mentally deficient and dull normal should be set. Each school system has had to draw up its own statement of requirements for admission to its special classes, as there is still no generally accepted definition of just what does constitute mental deficiency.

As early as the 1890's, researchers at Yale University attempted to develop a numerical measurement of mental deficiency. A little after the turn of the century, Binet and Simon followed up this research in France, working out the idea of intelligence tests, which they saw primarily in terms of a device to identify the mentally retarded. Dr. Goddard, of the Vineland Training School, went to France to study with Binet and Simon, and it was he who brought back their tests to this country, where Louis Terman standardized them according to American norms, thus giving us the IQ, as we know it.

As has been iterated and reiterated throughout the literature, however, dependence on the IQ for determining a child's capacities is dangerous, as that criterion cannot avoid measuring sociological and cultural factors along with the intellectual ones, and so is extremely limited in its applications, whether to the retarded or the gifted. As T. E. Newland has pointed out, it tends to measure only one specific type of intelligence:

Granting that it would be psychologically significant to be able to measure an over-all, all inclusive intelligence either within a given area of exceptionality or among all areas, the bulk of the efforts have been, and probably will continue to be, directed toward the measurement of those aspects of intelligence which are most directly related to the learning of a certain kind of behavior that seems to play a major part both in just living with people and, more specifically, in learning in school situations. Since the provision of school learning situations constitutes the bulk of society's organized efforts in the interests of children, the measurement of the "intelligence" or "mental capacity" of these children becomes largely, if not essentially, the measurement of learning aptitude geared primarily to school situations. . . . (**23**, p. 80)

The IQ system of classification, however, is still used almost indiscriminately. The most commonly used method of dividing the mentally defective group is to consider all those with IQ's under 20 as idiots, those from 25 to 50 as imbeciles, and those from 50 to 70 as morons. This is neat, but it is worse than useless; it is misleading, being in complete conflict with such definitions of amentia as, for example, Tredgold's:

. . . a state of incomplete mental development of such a kind and degree that the individual is incapable of adapting himself to the normal environment of his fellows in such a way as to maintain existence independently of supervision, control, or external support. (**30**, p. 4)

Many other researchers agree that two individuals could have the identical IQ and yet one be mentally deficient and the other dull normal, or that one individual with an IQ under 70 might still be dull normal, while another over 70 essentially a mental deficient. Doll offers a definition of mental deficiency which is more satisfactory than any IQ classification, because it includes six factors rather than one:

. . . six criteria by statement or implication have been generally considered essential to an adequate definition and concept. These are (1) social incompetence, (2) due to mental subnormality, (3) which has been developmentally arrested, (4) which obtains at maturity, (5) is of constitutional origin, and (6) is constitutionally incurable. (1, p. 215)

He later amplified these concepts into his Vineland Social Maturity Scale, which determines social quotient by dividing the social age, as fixed by the scale, by the chronological age.

Of the numerous other definitions that have been suggested, one of the best working ones is that offered by Hegge:

. . . Perhaps the most satisfactory point of view is to regard the mentally retarded group as consisting largely of essentially normal people whose output of mental ability places them at the lower end of a distribution of normal traits. We do, indeed, expect them to grow up and function with *and* as normal people, provided they receive specialized and skilled assistance. . . .
. . . There can be no universally valid single concept of mental retardation. The actual formulation of the concept will vary somewhat with the circumstances and with the purposes which it must serve, and justifiably so. . . . We must encourage the exercise of judgment in applying the concept to the individual case. (6, p. 22)

Even with such systems of classification as are being used, it is difficult to determine how many mental defectives there are in the United States, because only a small number of them are institutionalized, and, wherever possible, families tend to try to conceal the fact that one of their number is mentally inadequate. E. Arthur Whitney said in 1954:

No one knows just how many children are seriously retarded. Estimates range from 3 to 10 per cent. Hungerford's statement that 7 per cent of the school children of New York City are mentally retarded can be used as a reliable figure. Mr. Hungerford was director of special education for New York City when he made his statement. (32, p. 13)

In 1944, Elise Martens estimated that, of the estimated number of children five to nineteen years old in the total population, 2 per cent—or 672,080—were mentally retarded. (18, p. 4) However, the special classes are sometimes organized to include all the "slow-learners"—a group which Ingram estimates as comprising "approximately eighteen to twenty per cent of the school population." (19, p. 4) In 1955, Ernest Roselle estimated that 2½ per cent of the total school population might be considered mentally retarded. He figured that per 100,000 of the children, 1,500 to 2,000 would be mildly retarded, 300 to 450 moderately retarded, and 100 to 150 severely retarded. (26, p. 364)

It is difficult to identify these children before they enter school, and so most of them will have to experience a certain degree of frustration. The earlier they are identified, of course, the better will their later adjustment be.

The Need for Special Education for the Mentally Handicapped

Even close to 700,000 is a substantial number of children, far too large a segment of the population to be allowed to go to waste. If they, plus their 6,000,000 brothers and sisters of slightly higher intelligence, are merely left to vegetate in the backs of classrooms, the amount by which they hold back the optimal functioning of the regular class would, even in terms of expense, be enough to justify the establishment of special classes for them. According to the Council of State Governments' report:

> One of the principal needs in the field of the mentally deficient is to secure the adequate integration of the diagnostic, educational, and industrial aspects of the problem. There is a crying need for, and there are economies to be had in, a better integration of the education of the mentally deficient in the public schools. . . . (19, p. 206)

Obviously, even where the inadequacies of a school system require large classes, the teacher is far better able to cope with the needs of a large class of mental deficients or geniuses or cripples or just plain average children than with a hodgepodge of all three. Wallin has suggested that—

If the cost of maintaining special classes is a deterrent to their establishment, it may be emphasized that for every mentally defective child removed from the grades, from two to four normal children can be substituted without increasing the teaching load. (31, p. 87)

And, finally, special training is needed for the mentally retarded from the vocational point of view, if we expect them ever to earn their own livings rather than become public charges. As Hubbell has said, foremen and managers "have neither the time nor patience to contend with the individual who will require a longer than usual period of training, and it would seem that here is where the institution should step in and help out with the training period." (8, p. 386)

The Socially Handicapped

Socially handicapped children are even more difficult to distinguish from their better-adjusted contemporaries than are the mentally handicapped from those of low average intelligence. The term "socially handicapped" should, as has already been mentioned, not only include children who are delinquent, but also that other and perhaps larger group of children who, although well-behaved and unobtrusive, have not succeeded in making a satisfactory emotional adjustment to society, and may never succeed in doing so without trained assistance.

Teachers in the past have too often made the mistake of considering "the overt types of behavior, such as whispering, disobedience, fighting, using vulgar language, stealing, destroying school property, and lying or cheating" as "very serious, whereas withdrawing tendencies such as unsociableness, shyness, depression, sensitiveness, and daydreaming were looked upon as being of a less serious nature." (4, p. 407) However, they must be made to understand that the purpose of education is to adjust children to the society in which they live, not to make things easier for the teacher. Hence, the problem children with whom teachers are expected to deal as such are not necessarily those who represent a problem to the teacher, but also those who represent or who will, in the future, represent a problem to themselves.

Many delinquents, as Garrison has indicated, are "basically *normal* individuals," whereas the nondelinquent "withdrawn, recessive personality traits may be serious from the viewpoint of mental health." (4, p. 430) He went on to say that—

It is now believed that the timid child shows a definite personality maladjustment, whereas he was formerly considered by his teachers and parents as a model child who was just a little shy. (4, p. 441)

However, the problem of special education for the socially handicapped is a far larger one than the question of the timid or the delinquent child or the blind or the mentally deficient child. Anyone with a physical handicap has a social handicap—in fact, as Frampton and Rowell have pointed out, it is the cosmetic effects of a disease or disability that is the handicapping factor perhaps more often than the disease or disability in itself—and hence this area is all-comprehensive.

More than that, the teacher who is unable to recognize that a child seems "slow" because he cannot hear or see well; the teacher who does not think it "worth while" to organize special classes for students of limited intelligence; the teacher who cannot bring patience and understanding and compassion to the classroom—each of these is suffering from a social handicap himself. And so the total concept of special education must begin from the psychological point of view of social readjustment for all, teacher and student and parent alike, and then branch out in various individual problems.

References

1. DOLL, EDGAR A. "The Essentials of an Inclusive Concept of Mental Deficiency," *American Journal of Mental Deficiency,* XLVI (1941), 214–19.

2. FRAMPTON, MERLE E., and ELENA D. GALL (eds.). *Special Education for the Exceptional.* Boston: Porter Sargent, 1955. Vol. I.

3. FRAMPTON, MERLE E., and HUGH G. ROWELL. *Education of the Handicapped.* New York: World Book Co., 1938.

4. GARRISON, KARL C. *The Psychology of Exceptional Children.* New York: Ronald Press Co., 1950.

5. GARRISON, KARL C., and J. STANLEY GRAY. *Educational Psychology.* New York: Appleton-Century-Crofts, Inc., 1955.

6. HEGGE, T. C. "Psychological Aspects of Mental Retardation," in *Vocational Rehabilitation of the Mentally Retarded,* ed. S. C. DiMichael. Washington, D. C.: Government Printing Office. 1950.

7. HOLLINGWORTH, L. A. *The Psychology of Subnormal Children.* New York: Macmillan Co., 1920.

8. HUBBELL, H. G. "Intensive Training of the Higher-Grade Deficient," *American Journal of Mental Deficiency,* XLVIII (April, 1941), 385–91.

9. INGRAM, CHRISTINE P. *Education of the Slow-Learning Child.* New York: Ronald Press Co., 1953.

10. LESSER, ARTHUR J., and ELEANOR P. HUNT. "The Nation's Handicapped Children," in (2), Pp. 43–46.

11. LOWENFELD, BERTHOLD. "Psychological Problems of Children with Impaired Vision," in William Cruickshank (ed.). *Psychology of Exceptional Children and Youth.* Englewood Cliffs, N. J.: Prentice-Hall, 1955.

12. LYNCH, KATHERINE D., and LOUIS SCHARF. "More Help for the Less Able," *National Education Association Journal,* XLVI (May, 1957), 336–38.

13. McINTIRE, HAZEL C. "A State Program of Special Education," in (3). Pp. 182–93.

14. MACKIE, ROMAINE P. *Crippled Children in School.* (U. S. Department of Health, Education, and Welfare, 1948. Reprint.) Washington, D. C.: Government Printing Office, 1953.

15. ———. *Education of Crippled Children in the United States.* (Federal Security Agency, Office of Education, Leaflet 80.) Washington, D. C.: Government Printing Office, 1952.

16. ———. *Some Problems in the Education of Handicapped Children.* (U. S. Department of Health, Education, and Welfare.

Pamphlet 112.) Washington, D. C.: Government Printing Office, 1954.

17. MACKIE, ROMAINE P., and LLOYD M. DUNN. *College and University Programs for the Preparation of Teachers of Exceptional Children.* (U. S. Department of Health, Education, and Welfare. Bulletin 1954, No. 13). Washington, D. C.: Government Printing Office, 1954.

18. MARTENS, ELISE H. *Needs of Exceptional Children.* (U. S. Office of Education. Leaflet No. 74.) Washington, D. C.: Government Printing Office, 1944.

19. *Mental Health Problem, The.* Chicago: Council of State Governments, 1950.

20. MICHAL-SMITH, H. "Teachers Can Give Too Little Because We Ask Too Much," *Exceptional Children,* XXI (March, 1955), 202–203, 230.

21. MONROE, WALTER S. *Teacher-Learning Theory and Teacher Education, 1930–50.* Urbana, Ill.: University of Illinois Press, 1952.

22. MULLEN, FRANCES A. "A Metropolitan Area Plans for Special Education," in (2). Pp. 194–205.

23. NEWLAND, T. ERNEST, "Psychological Assessment of Exceptional Children and Youth," in William Cruickshank (ed.). *Psychology of Exceptional Children and Youth.* Englewood Cliffs, N. J.: Prentice-Hall, 1955.

24. O'BRIEN, FRANK J. "Special Education in New York City," in (2). Pp. 206–13.

25. *Patients in Mental Institutions.* National Institute of Mental Health. Washington, D. C.: Government Printing Office, 1952.

26. ROSELLE, ERNEST N. "New Horizons for the Mentally Retarded when a State Looks at the Problem as a Whole," *American Journal of Mental Deficiency,* LIX (January, 1955), 359–73.

27. SARASON, SEYMOUR B. *Psychological Problems in Mental Deficiency.* (2nd ed.) New York: Harper and Brothers, 1953.

28. "Statistics of Special Education for Exceptional Children, 1952–1953," *Biennial Survey of Education in the United States, 1952–1954.* (U. S. Department of Health, Education, and Welfare.) Washington, D. C.: Government Printing Office, 1955. Chap. V.

29. "Statistics of Special Schools and Classes for Eceptional Chil-

dren, 1947–1948," *Biennial Survey of Education in the United States, 1946–1948.* (U. S. Department of Health, Education, and Welfare.) Washington, D. C.: Government Printing Office, 1948. Chap. 5.

30. TREDGOLD, A. F. *A Textbook of Mental Deficiency.* (7th ed.) Baltimore: Williams and Wilkins Co., 1947.

31. WALLIN, J. E. WALLACE. *The Education of Mentally Handicapped Children.* New York: Harper and Brothers, 1951.

32. WHITNEY, E. ARTHUR. "The E. T. C. of the Mentally Retarded," *American Journal of Mental Deficiency,* LXI (July, 1954), 13–25.

CHAPTER THREE

The Problem of
Gifted Children

EQUIPPING the gifted child with an education suited to his capacities presents both educators and the public with as much of a problem as securing an appropriate education for the handicapped child. Moreover, it is a problem which has received far less attention than any other area of exceptionality. In 1956, Martin Tonn described the situation as follows:

. . . Thousands of children in America's schoolrooms . . . are frustrated by school, because no provisions are made for their extraordinary capacity to learn. While much creditable work is being done to aid the slow learners and other handicapped children, the gifted child has, until recently, been neglected. . . . (**30**, p. 29)

Educationally speaking, our superior children are grossly underprivileged. So far as being allowed adequate facilities for learning goes, they are among that segment of our school population who seem to be discriminated against most severely. Garrison has estimated that "less than five per cent of the mentally gifted" children in the United States are being given the special education they require (**8**, p. 250), while Ruth Strang has been somewhat more generous in allowing that perhaps as many as 10 per cent are receiving some measure of the individual attention they should rightfully be given. (26, p. 134) Countless other estimates have been suggested by countless other investigators, but there seems to be no doubt among any of them that at least 90 per cent of the superior children in this country are receiving an insufficient education. As Harry Baker has pointed out:

> Society is quite negligent in conserving the talents of gifted children. In many school systems where group mental and educational tests are administered to all pupils, little is done about the gifted who may be identified from the test results. In other systems, gifted children often spend their entire school life without being detected, nor is any particular interest taken in them. (1, p. 294)

WHY SPECIAL EDUCATION FOR THE SUPERIOR?

There has been far greater reluctance from both authorities and public to acknowledge the need for a specialized type of education in the case of the gifted child than in the case of any other kind of exceptional child. According to Frank Wilson, administrators seem to have "little disposition . . . to set aside additional funds to provide special education for gifted children," (32, p. 462), feeling, apparently, that such a utilization of the taxpayers' money would be a virtual painting of the lily.

A major reason for their adhering to such an attitude is, of course, an exaggerated idea of the over-all capabilities of the gifted individual. His superior mentality, they rather naively feel, should automatically give him the ability to derive a profitable educational experience from any kind of classroom situation. Writing in 1950, Garrison observed:

> The past decade has brought with it much consideration by many cities and states of the mentally handicapped child. Very few schools of the nation, however, have given special consideration to the mentally gifted. There has been an almost universal feeling that the gifted will tend to get along all right in school without any special concern or consideration. . . (8, p. 250)

Another factor is that many teachers feel that, if the gifted were to be excluded from their classes, they themselves would thereby be giving up one of the richest rewards to be derived from the teaching profession, and, at the same time, the less gifted children would be deprived of contact with their intellectual superiors—a contact which many feel would be advantageous to both, although it has never been proved that either benefited overmuch from the experience. Finally, just as it is often held that segregating the mentally retarded may induce feelings of inferiority in them, so it is held that isolating the mentally superior in homogeneous groups will tend to produce snobbishness, if not an actual corps of the intellectually elite.

Although there is some slight basis of truth in all these hypotheses, there is a far greater basis of misconception. It is undoubtedly true that the majority of gifted children are able to acquire enough education to enable them "to get through" from any kind of schooling situation. "In school," Garrison and Gray noted, "the bright child is often neglected, since he is able to make satisfactory progress without much assistance or guidance from his teacher." (9, p. 442)

However, satisfactory progress is far from being identical with optimal progress. If the children with superior mental capacities are not given special treatment in the schools, they will not have those superior capacities exploited to the fullest extent possible, and the consequence will be a lamentable waste of this country's badly needed intellectual resources.

The gifted child cannot possibly get an adequate education for his needs in the regular school classes any more than the blind child can receive an adequate education in a class designed for the sighted or a deaf child in a class intended for those who can hear. Just as they deviate from the norm, so does the gifted child differ from the average. It is true that, instead of meaning that he is deprived of any single ability or complex of abilities, his "difference" consists of having superior abilities added to a full complement of normal capacities. As a result, he may not on the surface appear to be undergoing any hardship. However, as Terman and Oden have warned, appearances may be deceiving, and "to compel the gifted child to go through school at the usual rate for average children is fraught with real dangers." (29, p. 43)

The gifted child who is placed with ordinary children and given no special attention is not being allowed to function as a total individual. Furthermore, not only do such children receive only a percentage of the education they are actually capable of absorbing, but they may also become severely maladjusted because of this "straight-jacketing" of their abilities.

At the end of an investigation into the adjustments achieved by a group of gifted children in the regular classroom, James Gallagher and Thora Crowder reported that—

. . . A sizable minority of the present sample (29 percent) seemed to be adjusting as well as could be expected, intellectually, socially, academically, and emotionally. . . . Relatively few members of the . . . group could be considered in serious academic, social, or emotional difficulties. (7, p. 318)

This is not as favorable a conclusion as it might appear to be superficially. Not only does the ambiguity of the phrase "as well as might be expected" seem to imply that the researchers did not anticipate that gifted children could achieve a very satisfactory degree of adjustment under such conditions, but the authors also went on to observe that the children did, as a matter of fact, manifest certain major difficulties, notably "lack of motivation, lack of creativity or originality, and minor personality adjustment problems which tended to sap their total adjustment potential." (7, p. 318)

Segregation of the mentally superior does not, of itself, turn them into social menaces. The concept that when the gifted are set apart educationally they will acquire "superiority complexes" frequently proves to be the very reverse of actual fact. However, in many cases the unsegregated children of superior ability will be afflicted by sensations of inferiority and inadequacy. As a bulletin put out by the Connecticut State Department of Education has suggested:

> . . . It is easy for a gifted child who seems to know all the answers to be misunderstood by his classmates. For this or other reasons he may have feelings of rejection. . . . (6, p. 33)

Such an attitude can extend to the point where the gifted child may begin to feel there is some lack in himself rather than in the others, and this, in its turn, may develop to the extent that he begins to doubt his own abilities. Because the gifted child "does so well in some things," according to the same bulletin, "he is particularly concerned about his inability to be equally outstanding in others." (6, p. 33)

Most studies have shown that there are certain areas in which the superior child is more frequently liable to be "backward," and which can often cost him considerable discomfort when he is called upon to associate with others on a nonintellectual basis. As Ruth Strang observed:

> A gifted child is especially likely to feel inferior in physical skills. One reason is that it takes him so much longer to learn to play baseball or to skate than to master intellectual tasks. It also happens that he is often less interested in physical than in mental activities and consequently does not learn the skills that make young people popular and accepted.
>
> He may also derive a sense of inferiority from associating with older children who have an advantage in active games and sports and in social sophistication. . . . (26, p. 13)

Furthermore, as one group of investigators has suggested, in many situations where the mentally gifted child *does* seem to manifest symptoms of conceit and a superior attitude, in most instances this is merely a defense he has learned to put up against an apparently hostile society.

The queerness, snobbishness, or antisocial behavior sometimes associated with superior intelligence is not a hallmark of giftedness but rather a sign of the antagonism aroused by social rejection or ridicule. (5, p. 13)

Where the child is educated in an environment of his peers, he is far less likely to develop into an intellectual snob than when he is plunged into a situation where, coming to realize that he is by far the mental superior of most of his classmates, he begins also to feel that he is being "held back" in his own educational progress by what he cannot help but come to regard as their "stupidity." Leta Hollingworth reported, as a conclusion of her researches into the value of segregated education for the superior child, that, contrary to much popular opinion—

. . . The special class does not produce as personality handicaps . . . conceit, poor health, or social unadaptability, as is sometimes supposed where there has been no actual experience with special classes. The special class does solve the problem of how to provide both appropriate work and appropriate social contact with classmates. (14, p. 121)

And Heck, although taking great pains to recommend that the utmost care should be given to avoid educating gifted children "in such a way as to make them conceited," at the same time stressed the fact that this unhappy state of affairs has most often resulted "when such children have been taught in regular classes." He went on to point out that children who discover that they are possessed of exceptional abilities "may easily become conceited unless they are helped to realize the responsibilities that their abilities place upon them" (11, p. 375), and thrusting them into the regular class situation certainly does nothing to help solve their problems.

On the other hand, the gifted child who fails to recognize his own abilities and does not have them indicated to him by his teacher, either because she herself is unaware of them or because she is reluctant to let the child know that he is exceptional for fear of "spoiling" him, may stumble into another pitfall, that of never realizing that certain of his capacities are out of the ordinary. The sad result is that, "crippled" by his educational environment, he may be left to "blush unseen and waste his sweetness on the desert air," turning into one of those gifted children whom Garrison and Gray have described as having "educational aspirations . . . far below their capabilities."

. . . The superior child should understand his capabilities and should be guided in setting goals in harmony with his abilities. Failure to do this leads to personal maladjustments and a waste of human resources. (**9,** pp. 468–69)

It should be the function and responsibility of all our schools not only to help the gifted child toward the fullest possible flowering of his capacities, but also to protect him against the adverse environmental factors to which he is so peculiarly vulnerable. It is a shocking commentary upon the state of education in this country today that a group of distinguished educators should have felt moved to make the following statement:

We find that highly gifted children as a group fail to fulfill the extraordinary promise of their early years. It is our belief this failure is due not to inherent instability but to the emotional cost of the acute problems of adjustment they characteristically face in the course of their development. (**36,** p. 105)

Society has certain definite obligations toward its children which it is the community's duty to carry out. There is no question of any privileges being extended toward the exceptional; it is his *right* to receive an adequate education. In Henry Otto's words:

Education in a democracy has a dual commitment, to give each child the opportunity to develop to the fullest those attributes which will make him a happy and successful person and to develop the child's social orientation and sensitivity so that each may acquire an abiding faith in democracy as a way of life and contribute his best toward improving the general welfare of all. We, the educators, must continuously evaluate to determine whether in our sincere efforts to provide for all children we have neglected some of them. Recent educational research indicates that our gifted children constitute an area of neglect. (**23**, p. 7)

Otto then sets forth the threefold responsibility which, he believes, educators bear toward the gifted child:

(1) Identifying (him) at an early age.
(2) Providing an educational environment in which he may reach his maximum potentials in every area.
(3) Providing guidance in personal development. (**23**, p. 7)

HISTORY OF EDUCATING THE MENTALLY SUPERIOR

In the past, the gifted child has never been neglected educationally in the same sense that the child whose exceptionality is a handicap has often been. That is, he would never, as a rule, be completely deprived of an education wherever an education was at all available—for the gifted would always obviously be among those of their particular era and class most likely to receive the benefits of schooling.

Although a strong adherence to the doctrine that all men are created equal meant, during the early years of this country, that attention given to any specialized variety of education for the gifted child would have been considered a highly undemocratic practice, in actual fact our first schools were so small that education was necessarily individual. As a result, those gifted children fortunate enough to have teachers with a sincere love of their profession were very likely to receive an education adjusted to their special needs—and, indeed, in many cases an education far superior to the standard curricula being offered now. However, as classes grew larger, mass-production methods began to take their toll of individuality.

Acceleration

The first official cognizance that the public school system of this country gave to the fact that some children are mentally far superior to others was by adjusting promotion plans to accelerate [1] the progress of the gifted children by allowing them to skip grades. It was in Elizabeth, New Jersey, that this system was first observed in actual use, in 1866, though it may quite conceivably have been utilized earlier in other school systems and merely not have been officially recorded. The following year, a similar system was introduced into the St. Louis, Missouri, schools, from which it spread to the rest of the country.

Although skipping has been recommended by many authorities, including Witty and Wilkins (34, p. 273) and Terman (29, p. 43), it is, in the long run considered an essentially unsatisfactory method of dealing with the gifted by most investigators; and even those who support it qualify their approval, recommending that, where acceleration is used, it should be accompanied by "enrichment of the curriculum." (34, p. 273) One of the most

---

[1] *Accelerate* and *acceleration* are somewhat ambiguous terms. Some writers consider *acceleration* synonymous with *skipping;* others differentiate between the two, as in the following statement:

> . . . Skipping implies that the child skips over the work of one grade and is moved into another one without having completed certain work. Acceleration means the moving of a child from one level of instruction to another, but only after he has mastered the work of the level from which he is moving. Acceleration is possible only when the classroom instruction is sufficiently differentiated to permit one child to proceed ahead of the group. (17, p. 259)

Since this confusion of terms does exist, it has been thought most expedient to use the two words interchangeably in this context, except where they are specifically qualified.

deleterious results of this type of acceleration is that the gifted child who has been skipped one or more times will tend to be considerably younger than the other children in his class, and, as a consequence, he may suffer social maladjustments which will result in isolating him from his classmates just as effectively as his superior intelligence has set him apart from those of his own age. Tonn was one of those who, while not opposed to grade-skipping, found that it was "not a total answer." His suggested remedy was that—

. . . While the child may be advanced a grade, he should remain with the children approximately his own chronological age. The gifted child, while intellectually advanced, is usually not similarly advanced socially and emotionally. It is easy to visualize the personality problems that might evolve from placing an eight-year-old gifted child in a class with twelve-year-old seventh graders. It should be remembered that such a youngster still has the physical development of a third-grade child. (**30**, p. 30)

Otto seemed to be substantially in agreement on this point, saying:

Acceleration . . . does not seem advisable for all gifted children. Many children are not developed physically and socially to the extent that they will be happy in association with older children of a higher grade. Also, acceleration does not assure, and at times it prohibits, the fullest development of the child's creative powers. It is only when mental, physical, emotional, and social development have all been considered and acceleration still seems advisable that this method may be considered wise in individual cases. (**23**, p. 12)

Some school systems have entirely dispensed with skipping, under the theory that its disadvantages far outweigh its merits. For instance, according to Walter Barbe and Dorothy Norris, the Cleveland schools—which have one of the earliest-established and finest intracity systems of education for the gifted—have completely done away with acceleration and double promotion in their program. (2, p. 55) Jack W. Birch has recommended the early admission of gifted children to school as a more satisfactory procedure. (4, p. 84) However, although early admission does have the advantage of keeping the child with the same class throughout his school career, it still means that the smaller, immature children will be grouped with the older, better physically developed ones, unless there are enough gifted children of the same age to form a class by themselves.

Segregation

Acceleration by group rather than by individual is a system which does away with the psychological drawback of placing the child who is mentally superior in a class with children who are his superiors chronologically and developmentally; however, this does require the segregating—whether partial or complete—of the gifted child. Toward the close of the century, more cities began placing pupils in ability groups according to the results they achieved on tests—or whatever modes of identification were then used by the various school system. Perhaps the first instance of the use of this method occurred in 1886, again in Elizabeth, New Jersey, when the pupils in the elementary schools there were organized in relatively homogeneous groups, with each group being allowed to advance at its own rate of speed. (31, p. 8)

Today, there are a number of schools throughout the country with special classes of one kind or another, although there is no really large-scale program for educating gifted children in any of the states. Cleveland, Ohio, has had an excellent system of special classes for children with special ability for over thirty-five years, although the rest of the state has shown no particular distinction in this area. And in the East, in 1922, Leta Hollingworth organized two "special opportunity" classes in New York City "on the premise that there are children with such markedly superior mental ability that no regular classroom can hope to meet their needs." (**14**, p. 123) Of course, her success was in some part owing to the fact that a city as large as New York was an especially favorable site for such an experiment, since the population is so large that it is a rather simple matter to group gifted children into classes which would be relatively homogeneous, not only chronologically and socially, but mentally as well. As a result of their researches, Hollingworth and her coworkers came to the conclusion that—

. . . the advantages to be hoped for from the homogeneous grouping of gifted children lie not so much in the expectation of greater achievement in the tool subjects . . . as in an enrichment of scholastic experience with additional intellectual opportunities. (**10**, p. 261)

Today, the New York City school system continues to offer some of the most superior facilities for gifted children in the United States, with "rapid advance" classes in the junior high schools, "honor" classes in the senior high schools, and even special high schools devoted to those with superior abilities in certain fields.

Enrichment

At the present moment, the most prevalent systems of educating the gifted are the special classes and "enrichment" in regular programs, the latter by far the most popular, partly because it is so much more economical. *Enrichment,* as defined by the Connecticut State Board of Education—

. . . is the use of a variety of resources and experiences which, for the child, give to education a new and richer meaning. This may entail deeper study of topics being summarily discussed by other members of the class, or perhaps study in areas not included in the work for children of average ability. True enrichment comes when the pupil acquires increased understanding of a subject and puts this understanding to use; it is not simply accretion of ideas or isolated facts. . . . (**6**, p. 12)

Current Attitudes

There are adherents and opponents of both systems, with the variations in attitude dictated sometimes by expediency, sometimes by ideology. Horace Mann has summed up the situation in the following paragraph:

Those favoring special classes argue that the special class is most democratic, most effective in challenging the gifted, and most "life-like" in that we tend as adults to select as close friends our intellectual peers. Those favoring the alternate provision of enrichment in regular programs claim that this particular placement is most democratic, most effective in challenging gifted youngsters, and most "life-like" in that the world into which the gifted graduates is not homogeneously grouped. (**20**, p. 199)

Yet it has been proved to be true that adults as well as children do tend to gravitate toward their own kind, wherever they possibly can. In the course of working with gifted pupils in the regular classes, Gallagher and Crowder discovered that those in the group "coming from schools where there were few bright children showed more motivational problems than the children coming from schools where there were many other bright children." (**7**, p. 318) Obviously, therefore, the gifted child does not do his best in a classroom deliberately organized to reproduce a normal, "life-like" atmosphere, and grouping him with average children does not, as Horace Mann's researches underline, train him to accept them as his friends (**20**, p. 206)—nor is the mutual contact, then, especially beneficial for either.

Perhaps the final answer to the question of segregation versus enrichment is to weigh the advantages of the two systems in each case, that is, with respect to each school rather than each individual. As Hunt has said, the only purpose of segregation "is to make special progress possible in order that equality of opportunity may be provided. It has no other justification." (**15**, p. 475)

Naturally, there has been no question of institutionalizing the gifted child except in those instances where he is also physically or socially handicapped. Obviously, the community as a whole is eager to retain the superior child as a functioning part, no matter how its component individuals may reject the gifted members. Furthermore, as Otto has commented, "few school systems are of sufficient size and geographical distribution to make possible an entire school for gifted children" (**23,** p. 11)—a situation which often also precludes the organization of special classes even where they are held to be advantageous.

There have, however, been occasional special schools—generally day schools—organized for children of superior mental attainment, with the first reportedly having been the one established at Worcester, Massachusetts, in 1901. (**21,** p. 99) Outstanding among the present-day ones are the Hunter College Elementary School in New York City and, as has already been mentioned, the same city's specialized high schools for gifted children.

IDENTIFYING THE MENTALLY SUPERIOR

Their Proportions

How many gifted children are there in this country? Hollingworth defined them as the top 1 per cent of the population in general intellectual development, but acknowledged that the setting of this figure was a "quite arbitrary" procedure. (**13,** p. 195) Mackie and Dunn estimated them at about 680,000, or 2 per cent of the total school population. (**19,** p. 3) Ruth Strang has set the figure at the much higher number of 1,500,000. (**27,** p. 514) Again, all these numerical discrepancies probably arise from a semantic rather than factual difference. The question is whether the category of "gifted" is to include the "bright" child as well as the "genius," which gives rise to the semantic problem of precisely how *brightness* and *genius* are to be defined, for the words do not mean the same thing to all men. According to one group of investigators:

> Some authorities define giftedness so rigorously that not more than one out of each hundred persons might be expected to fulfill the requirements. Others, recognizing varying degrees of intelligence, state that ten out of every hundred might qualify for the gifted category provided they were given adequate opportunities for developing their special abilities. (5, p. 11)

Problems of Identification

Ruth Strang has strongly urged "the early identification of . . .{ gifted individuals."

> . . . Unless they are identified, special provision for their needs cannot be made. Worse still, they may be subjected to experiences that discourage the natural use of their abilities. (27, p. 477)

As in the case of any other kind of exceptionality, the basic difference between a gifted child and an average child is qualitative rather than quantitative, being "the *degree* to which the characteristic is present in the individual." This renders identification extremely difficult. Sometimes it is hard to distinguish the gifted children from the average because they have been taught by bitter experience that it is well to conceal their superiority from their fellows. Therefore, scholastic achievement alone is far from being a satisfactory criterion of intelligence, because the gifted do not necessarily make superior grades in school. Garrison has pointed out the unfortunate fact that in most schools there is evidence on file showing "bright students with poor academic records and average students with good or superior ones." (8, p. 267) Sometimes the gifted student's poor record arises from acute maladjustment and is involuntary on his part. At other times, it may be a fully conscious holding back; he is deliberately not exposing the full extent of his ability because he does not want to be "different" from his fellows.

A further reason for the difficulty educators find in defining giftedness in the concrete is the fact that a child may have a specific ability in one particular area without his being necessarily gifted in the sense of having greater intelligence than the ordinary. There have been instances of individuals who owned great artistic or musical or even mathematical faculties and yet were otherwise endowed with average or even meager intellectual powers. This does not mean that the child with specific talents should not be encouraged to develop them but that he does not need extensive special class work. Rather, as the results of the Texas experiment showed—

. . . His needs will be cared for by special opportunities in those areas and by being given the chance to use his special ability to advantage in classroom activities. However, he will, of necessity, spend a major portion of his time on regular class work. (23, p. 9)

There is not even a clear-cut definition of precisely what superior mental ability does constitute. According to Strang:

Giftedness has been defined in many ways. Some writers put the emphasis on superior endowment; others on exceptional performance. Some seek manifestations of giftedness in measurable intelligence; others in a variety of human abilities. Since endowment can only be judged by its products and since modern psychology emphasized the functioning of the organism as a whole, the most acceptable definition should include these two aspects. (27, p. 476)

Although in the nineteenth century numerous researches were made into the problems of the backward child, it was not until the end of the second decade of this century that any attempt was made to undertake a scientific investigation of the gifted child. The idea that there might be a positive correlation between a high IQ and genius came about in connection with the Stanford study to determine the mental, personal, and physical traits of gifted children. This study, started under Lewis Terman's directorship in 1921, is still in operation to a limited extent. (28, p. 5)

After having completed the initial stages of his research, Terman, and, later, Stoke and Lehman, set a minimum IQ for the gifted child, deciding upon 140 as an appropriate figure. (28, p. 43) However, the usual minimum set by later investigators, including Witty and Hildreth (12, p. 20) is 130. Bentley lowered the minimum to 110 to admit the "normally bright child" as well as the gifted (3, p. 19); however, most investigators would regard this as too low. Heck felt that an IQ of 125 "is accepted as the approximate point for determining admission to the special class." (11, p. 39) Using the IQ as a basic determinant, Otto added a further qualification, his definition of the gifted being "any child with a minimum I.Q. of 120 . . . whose performance is consistently outstanding in areas having potential value to the welfare of a society." (23, p. 7)

The use of the IQ might perhaps be considered more valid in identifying the gifted child than in identifying the mentally retarded one, for it is to be presumed that the gifted child is more likely to be possessed of those specific traits which an IQ test can measure, and many investigators hold the IQ tests in high esteem. Hollingworth declared them to be "the only way to identify . . . gifted children with certainty." (13, p. 195) However, so many adjustment factors are involved that there has been considerable objection to the use of the IQ criterion even when applied to superior abilities. Morton warned that—

We may not be able to identify all gifted children with intelligence tests. Expression might have been blocked in some children by insecurity which may be traced to the home. (22, p. 133)

Witty went further, almost completely rejecting the intelligence test as a means of identifying the gifted:

It is evident . . . that an acceptable criterion for giftedness must be sought primarily outside the provinces covered by the intelligence test. For the content of the intelligence test is patently lacking in situations which disclose originality or creativity. . . . The intelligence test neglects the role of feeling and motive and requires only the habituated response of the child to situations which are "set," and which are "low in feeling-tone." (33, p. 504)

Various other criteria were suggested, and the definition of the gifted which the American Association for Gifted Children officially adopted was Witty's "children whose performance is consistently remarkable in music, art, social leadership, and other forms of expression." However, this definition seems to be as open to objection as the intelligence test, since it is so ambiguously phrased as possibly to include the merely talented as well as the genuinely gifted.

The Hartford, Connecticut, board of education has listed nine characteristics by which the gifted child may be identified:

(1) The gifted child can learn rapidly. . . .
(2) Given a chance, he may show an amazing degree of imagination, initiative, originality, resourcefulness, creativity, and inventiveness. . . .
(3) He may have a wide range of interests. . . .
(4) He learns how to search for causes and to draw sound conclusions. . . .
(5) He may have a decided knack of planning and organizing. . . .
(6) He tends to be stronger, taller, and heavier than the average child his own age. . . .
(7) He is usually more stable emotionally than the average child. . . .
(8) He tends to compare his efforts with those of recognized authorities. . . .
(9) He possesses superior power of self-criticism. . . . (6, pp. 7–8)

The board does, of course, stress the fact that it should not be expected that a gifted child would necessarily evidence all of these, though they should all be potentially in him.

Adjustment Factors Hampering Identification

Number seven, that the gifted child "is usually more stable emotionally than the average child," is the one factor that would probably be most highly disputed. Although responsible individuals no longer hold that the greater a person's intellect, the more unstable he must necessarily be—any more than they still believe that the gifted child is an inferior physical specimen—it cannot be denied that the gifted child sometimes can manifest severe psychological disturbances, occasionally to the point where he is so retarded emotionally that he is unable to get on with children of his own age, even those whose mental capacity is fully equal to his. Among the gifted there have appeared not a few instances of what the Pollocks term "dreamers," describing them as—

. . . children who do well in academic work, but who are much less mature emotionally than is normal for their chronological age and who have such poor coordination that they cannot even put on their clothes without help; these youngsters find it difficult to get along with boys and girls of their own age. (24, p. 2)

A mentally gifted child can, of course, be physically handicapped —which is an unfortunate circumstance of fate. He can also become socially handicapped—and this has nothing to do with fate but can come about as a direct result of his own superior abilities, for mental superiority, like any other deviation from the norm, can in itself develop into a prime cause of maladjustment. As Garrison has stated:

The comparison of behavior at various levels of intelligence indicates that children with average mentality are better adjusted than are children who are either brighter or duller than most youngsters. This is to be expected in a world where the environment is adapted to the average level of mentality. (8, p. 216)

Virginia Keehan has agreed that "children with very high I.Q.'s"—which she defines as 150 and up—"are likely to have problems of social adjustment." (16, p. 17) And this social maladjustment can even take the shape of a learning disability. In summarizing May Lazar's speech, "Ten Years of Progress in Remedial Reading," the editorial columns of The Elementary School Journal commented on the fact that "many children who are intellectually gifted" show "retardation in reading, particularly critical reading." (18, p. 416) In large part, this maladjustment can arise as a result of the kind of treatment, ranging from neglect to outright hostility, which the gifted child is often accorded in our society.

. . . The chief hazard [for the gifted child] is the denial of adequate means of expression on the part of adults of the need for satisfactory outlets. Great unhappiness and sometimes serious emotional maladjustment develop when a gifted child's mental tasks are too easy for him or when he invites ridicule or jealousy or even fear because of his manifest superiority. (5, p. 11)

One of the cardinal sins of which our society stands guilty is that, though its need for leaders and scholars and creators is so urgent, it blandly continues to permit the existence of "those with a high potentiality of giftedness whose success was materially limited through the weight of social and emotional maladjustments or poor health or lack of access to suitable raw materials upon which to work." (5, p. 11) Although such a situation is the public's fault to a considerable degree, the greater blame is to be placed at the door of the educators who are the ones who "should know better," and yet, even if they do know better—which is sometimes problematical—fail to act. Still too many of them continue to feel, with Edward Redford, that—

We have no clear-cut evidence to show that genius develops better in a lush environment . . . than it does in an environment of scarcity. Nor that spoon-feeding encourages development of talent more than does a struggle for existence. Nor that segregation in special classes or in a special school has any advantages or disadvantages over integration in heterogeneous groups. Nor as to the advantages or disadvantages of acceleration. Nor as to what type of teacher works best with the gifted. Nor even as to who are the "gifted." . . . (25, p. 144)

It is true that we do not know the answers to many of these questions, but we do know many of the things that are wrong, even if we cannot be sure what is right. Perhaps we cannot identify all of the gifted, but we do know that those whom we have succeeded in identifying are not, in any case, receiving the education they deserve. We know that "a struggle for existence" does not facilitate a liberal education, and, although we may not know all the advantages of segregation or the disadvantages of acceleration or vice versa, we do know a goodly number of them. One thing we do know: that the gifted child, like all other exceptional children, must have a specialized education adjusted to his needs, and, if that is what is meant by "spoon-feeding," then the educational systems in this country need to introduce more spoon-fed courses into their curricula.

References

1. BAKER, HARRY J. *Introduction to Exceptional Children.* (Rev. ed.) New York: Macmillan Co., 1953.
2. BARBE, WALTER B., and DOROTHY N. NORRIS. "Special Classes for Gifted Children in Cleveland," *Exceptional Children,* XXI (November, 1954), 55–57.
3. BENTLY, JOHN E. *Superior Children.* New York: W. W. Norton and Co., 1937.
4. BIRCH, JACK W. "Early School Admission for Mentally Advanced Children," *Exceptional Children,* XXI (December, 1954), 84.
5. BRISTOW, WILLIAM H., MARJORIE L. CRAIG, GRACE T. HALLOCK, and S. R. LAYCOCK. "Identifying Gifted Children," in (34). Pp. 10–19.
6. *Education for Gifted Children and Youth.* Connecticut State Department of Education. Bulletin No. 77. Hartford, Conn.: 1955–56.
7. GALLAGHER, JAMES J., and THORA CROWDER. "The Adjustment of Gifted Children in the Regular Classroom," *Exceptional Children,* XXIII (April, 1957), 306–319.
8. GARRISON, KARL C. *The Psychology of Exceptional Children.* New York: Ronald Press Co., 1950.

9. GARRISON, KARL C., and J. STANLEY GRAY. *Educational Psychology.* New York: Appleton-Century-Crofts, Inc. 1955.

10. GRAY, HOWARD A., and LETA S HOLLINGWORTH. "The Achievements of Gifted Children Enrolled and Not Enrolled in Special Opportunity Classes," *Journal of Educational Research,* XXIV (November, 1931), 255–61.

11. HECK, ARCH O. *The Education of Exceptional Children.* New York: McGraw-Hill Book Co., Inc., 1953.

12. HILDRETH, GERTRUDE H. *Educating Gifted Children.* New York: Harper and Brothers, 1952.

13. HOLLINGWORTH, LETA S. "How Should Gifted Children Be Educated?" *Baltimore Bulletin of Education,* L (May, 1931), 196.

14. HOLLINGWORTH, LETA S., and OTHERS. "The Special Opportunity Class for Gifted Children, Public School 165, Manhattan." *Ungraded,* IX (March, 1923), 195.

15. HUNT, J. T. "Special Education: Segregation," *Education,* LXXVII (April, 1957).

16. KEEHAN, VIRGINIA. *Exceptional Children, a Handbook for Teachers.* Santa Fe, New Mexico: Department of Education. 1954.

17. KRUEGER, LOUISE, E. PAUL ALLEN, ELSA EBELING, and ROBERT H. ROBERTS. "Administrative Problems in Educating Gifted Children," in (34). Pp. 257–66.

18. LAZAR, MAY. "Ten Years of Progress in Remedial Reading," summarized in *The Elementary School Journal,* LVII (May, 1957), 416.

19. MACKIE, ROMAINE P., and LLOYD M. DUNN. *College and University Programs for the Preparation of Teachers of Exceptional Children.* (U. S. Department of Health, Education, and Welfare. Bulletin 1954, No. 13.) Washington, D. C.: Government Printing Office, 1954.

20. MANN, HORACE. "How Real Are Friendships of Gifted and Typical Children in a Program of Partial Segregation?" *Exceptional Children,* XXIII (February, 1957), 199–201, 206.

21. MCDONALD, R. A. F. *Adjustment of School Organization to Various Population Groups.* New York: Teachers College, Columbia University, 1915.

22. MORTON, VELMA YOWELL. "Basic Problems in Guidance in the Field of the Exceptional," in Merle Frampton and Elena Gall

(eds.). *Special Education for the Exceptional.* Boston: Porter Sargent, 1955. Vol. I.

23. OTTO, HENTY J. *Curriculum Adjustment for Gifted Elementary School Children in Regular Classes.* (Bureau of Laboratory Schools. Publication No. 6.) Austin: University of Texas, 1957.

24. POLLOCK, MORRIS P., and MIRIAM. *New Hope for the Retarded.* Boston: Porter Sargent, 1953.

25. REDFORD, EDWARD H., "Special Opportunity Classes for the Gifted," *Bulletin of the National Association of Secondary School Principals,* XLI (February, 1957), 144–53.

26. STRANG, RUTH. "Mental Hygiene of Gifted Children," in (34). Pp. 131–62.

27. ———. "Psychology of Gifted Children and Youth," in William Cruickshank (ed.). *Exceptional Children and Youth.* Englewood Cliffs, N. J.: Prentice-Hall, Inc., 1955.

28. TERMAN, LEWIS M. "Mental and Physical Traits of a Thousand Gifted Children," in *Genetic Studies of Genius.* Stanford: Stanford University Press, 1925. Vol. I.

29. TERMAN, LEWIS M., and MELTA H. ODEN. "The Stanford Studies of the Gifted," in (34). Pp. 20–46.

30. TONN, MARTIN. "The Gifted Child," *American School Board Journal,* CXXXII (June, 1956), 29–30.

31. *Twenty-Third Yearbook,* National Society for the Study of Education. Chicago: University of Chicago Press, 1924. Part I. P. 8.

32. WILSON, FRANK T. "Salvaging Gifted Students in the Regular Classrooms," *Educational Administration and Supervision,* XLI (December, 1955), 462–66.

33. WITTY, PAUL. "Contributions to the I. Q. Controversy from the Study of Superior Deviants," *School and Society,* LI (1940), 503–508.

34. ——— (ed.). *The Gifted Child.* Boston: D. C. Heath and Co., 1951.

35. WITTY, PAUL, and LARRY W. WILKINS. "The Status of Acceleration or Grade Skipping as an Administrative Practice," *Educational Administration and Supervision,* XIX (1933), 321–46.

36. ZORBAUGH, HARVEY, RHEA KAY BOARDMAN, and PAUL SHELDON. "Some Observations of Highly Gifted Children," in (34). Pp. 86–105.

CHAPTER FOUR

The Need for Educational Specialists

THE TEACHER SHORTAGE

One of the greatest difficulties in establishing a sound program of specialized education for exceptional children is the current shortage of adequately trained personnel. "Perhaps the major obstacles confronting school systems in establishing or expanding their institutional programs for the deviating pupil," Dunn has commented, "has been an inability to secure qualified teachers." (8, p. 483) And, of those teachers who constitute the twenty-five thousand which Mackie and Dunn have estimated to be the number currently working in the field, "some . . . are well equipped professionally for service in their area of specialization; some are partially prepared; still others completely lack specialized preparation." (25, p. 4)

Poor Administrative Policies

Many public school administrators, faced with the problem of securing specialists, have resolved it simply by giving their deviant children into the charge of teachers who, however well qualified they may be in the area of general education, have not also re-

82

ceived the precise training designed to equip them to deal with the exceptional child's particular needs. As Burton Gorman observed:

Administrators and school boards since 1946, in their desperate efforts just to keep the schools open and to provide "sitters" if not teachers for all children have been forced to resort to personnel policies of expediency with little regard for their long-range consequences. (**15**, p. 130)

Sometimes, when a teacher is especially inspired, such a makeshift program can work out reasonably well. Too often, however, it negates the entire concept of special education, and, when such a class is given to a teacher who is either incompetent or actually hostile to the deviant—and it must not be overlooked that the hostility can extend to the gifted child as well as the handicapped —the result can be serious emotional damage to the children. Since "the adjustment of the exceptional child in school is often," as Curtis Southard and Mabel Ross have stressed, "dependent upon the attitude of the teacher," it is important that she be as well-adjusted as she is well-educated.

. . . To the teacher who has responsibility for a class partly or entirely made up of exceptional children, the meaning of the various disabilities to her is important in her success. Without intent, pity, revulsion, irritation, anxiety created in the teacher by a particular disability will be felt by the children and affect their relations with the teacher and with each other. (**39**, p. 113)

And sometimes it happens that the teacher is not even well educated in her own area of specialization. Richard Brill called attention to the existence of many classes for deaf children which are currently being taught by "teachers who have had little or no training in how to teach language to the deaf child, speech to the deaf child, reading to the deaf child, and in fact who have never taught any deaf child in the process of their preparation as teachers." (**3**, p. 195)

This situation is known to occur in all the areas of special education, and administrators are frequently to blame for its continued existence, because, according to Frampton and Gall, they do not always insist that the teacher be thoroughly trained for the work he is expected to do. Administrators have also been known to manifest "a tendency toward hurrying teachers into the work before they have had experience instructing non-handicapped children." (13, p. 252)

An even more serious charge against administrators was placed by Wallin, who suggested that principals often placed "maladjusted teachers whom they did not want to dismiss" in charge of special classes. (40, p. 223) This charge was found amply substantiated by this investigator who found that approximately 40 per cent of a representative group of special education classes which he visited were assigned to teachers who were not considered adequate to instruct normal children.

For example, he visited one class for the mentally retarded and found in charge a teacher who appeared to be without a single qualification for her post. Her appearance was slovenly, her manner unprepossessing. She seemed to have nothing but contempt for her pupils and the only way in which she apparently knew how to express herself was by losing her temper, not only in words but by unmerciful beatings—which she seemed to take a great delight in administering to her unfortunate charges. In addition to her personal inadequacy, she obviously knew nothing about the methods, skills, and techniques of teaching the mentally retarded. Later, the principal of her school explained that she had been able to secure and maintain her job because she was related to an influential member of the school board and that now she was on tenure. She had been assigned to him because no other school wanted her, and he was under the complacent impression that he had successfully minimized the danger of retaining such an instructor on his staff by placing her "where she could do the least harm!"

Another principal informed this investigator that he always placed the "dull but extremely nice women" in charge of his classes for the mentally retarded, because he felt that the "slow-witted" teacher would find it easier to get along with children who did not tax her own intellectual faculties too much. Undoubtedly this is true; however, the schools are supposedly organized for the benefit of the children rather than of the teachers. "Anyway," this same principal added, "a nice, easy going, dull woman can at least give them sympathy even if she can't teach them anything!"

Although such attitudes are deplorable, there is no denying the fact that, no matter how well disposed and enlightened the administrator, under current conditions he is bound to have difficulty recruiting skilled personnel. In the words of Mackie and Dunn:

. . . In many communities where public support is excellent and financing assured, school systems are unable to establish progress because they cannot find a teacher with the special competencies essential to effective work with the particular type of exceptional child for whom the service is to be established. . . . (**26**, p. 1)

One Solution

This is, of course, an especially great problem for rural communities, which, in addition to the handicaps faced by the urban communities, have the further difficulty of a diffused school population. It was solved more than adequately in one Wisconsin county which had experienced considerable trouble in securing a fully trained and qualified teacher for its program of special instruction for retarded youth. The problem itself and the procedure used to solve it were described by John Melcher and Kenneth Blessing as follows:

. . . Rural areas frequently experience considerable difficulty in securing a fully trained qualified teacher, so it often becomes necessary to find an especially competent regular teacher who can be retrained in the education of the mentally retarded during summer sessions. A detailed certification requirement listing individually any existing deficiencies is developed for each prospective teacher. If the selected teacher does not fully meet all certification requirements at the time of his evaluation by the certification division, he must reduce his deficiencies in education by taking six semester hours of work prior to his receiving a one-year provisional permit. The special teacher is required to reduce his deficiencies at the rate of six credits per year in order to have his provisional permit renewed. . . . (28, p. 210)

Undoubtedly, there are many who would disagree with such a policy, feeling that the teacher should be qualified from the start of her teaching career; however, it has already proved its efficiency in this particular area and might well be applicable to other rural or even small urban communities.

WHY SPECIAL TRAINING?

For Teachers in the Special Classes

There is little use in segregating the exceptional children from the average ones in special classes unless, as Frampton and Gall state, there are available highly trained special teachers who can understand his needs to head those classes. (11, p. 170) In fact, a system of special education for the exceptional child is worse than useless if the proper personnel is not on hand to carry out its purpose. Mackie has pointed out that "special education cannot be special unless there are people qualified by philosophy, technical knowledge, constructive abilities, and general understanding of the problems to guide properly each individual child for his best advantage. . . ." (23, p. 31) And Baker has agreed that, for the most part, the ordinary teacher, no matter how well trained, is not prepared to cope with the problems of special education:

The teachers of the exceptional must not only have the training and background for teaching average or normal children, but must also be equipped and trained to meet the unique problems of teaching in their specialized fields as well. They have a double burden in this respect and in addition must understand the nature of handicaps together with meeting the needs of every pupil upon an individual basis. Many school systems and states now require special certification and advanced degress to teach exceptional children. Standards are likely to become more rigid as the problems are better understood. . . . (2, p. 18)

In a sense, educating the exceptional child should be a labor of love, to which only the truly dedicated teacher should devote herself, for it requires not only greater time and effort than any other type of teaching but a considerably greater degree of emotional involvement. Only the extremely stable should consider entering this field for, according to I. Ignacy Goldberg:

When an effort is made to promote self understanding, which is the basic principle of mental health in any group of exceptional children, one of the most impressive effects is the emotional impact of such work upon the teacher. . . . the child who is mentally retarded, physically handicapped, or socially maladjusted provides many mental health hazards for the teacher himself. . . . (14, p. 119)

The ideal teacher in this field is the one who, in Mackie's words, finds the handicapped child "extremely fascinating," for "in him she sees a challenge—an opportunity to aid one who might otherwise fail to make normal adjustments. She works day by day with the hope that each child will improve." After several years, some of her hopes may be realized, but, at the same time, she must also be prepared to brace herself for disappointments, because by far the greater number of her hopes not only will not but cannot be realized. (23, p. 31)

For All Teachers

Ideally, of course, it is desirable that *every* teacher should receive some amount of special training in the needs of both handicapped and gifted children, because, first of all, as Mackie and Dunn stressed, "many exceptional children are . . . enrolled for all or part of their schooling in regular classes with so-called normal children." (**23**, p. 6) Second, even where a given school system does include special classes for the exceptional, it is important that the regular classroom teacher should have a certain degree of knowledge of the field, because, Keehan has suggested, it is she who—

. . . is often the key person in discovering handicaps in children which *will* prevent them from making progress or adjusting to the group. Because of her close association with the child, she is in a position to notice deviations from what is generally accepted as "normal" behavior. The teacher, in her concern with the social and emotional adjustments of her group, often notices that a child is having problems in making adjustments to the group. . . . (**20**, p. 3)

Furthermore, since there is no such creature as the completely "normal" individual, a degree of training in this field would be invaluable to every teacher, for it will help him or her to discover those deviations, no matter how slight, that will be present in each one of his pupils and which should be identified if the teacher wishes to obtain a full understanding and a full awareness of their capacities and problems. With the growing improvement in professional attitudes toward special education, the time may soon come, when, as Mackie prophesied—

. . . every teacher will have in her general professional preparation at least one introductory course in education of the exceptional child. This will serve as an orientation to young people entering the profession of special education. It will also give the regular class teacher an understanding of the needs of the handicapped—for back to her will come these children when they no longer require the special class. (**25**, p. 11)

RECRUITING QUALIFIED PERSONNEL

However, granting the premise that special personnel is needed to give instruction in the special classes—and there are few edu cators today who would not at least pay lip service to the validity of this assumption—where are administrators to obtain such highly qualified personnel? Most educators agree that at least a hundred thousand specialists would be needed to satisfy minimal requirements in this area. Yet, according to the Government Office of Education, there were only 14,316 special education teachers in the city school systems in 1952–53. (**35**, p. 15) It is true that Mackie and Dunn have estimated that, in addition to these, there are also—

. . . approximately three thousand teachers working in residential schools for the deaf, blind, and mentally retarded, and at least two thousand five hundred giving hospital or home instruction. Still others not reported are employed by nursery schools and kindergartens, and in private schools. Another group works in small local school systems in rural areas. . . . (**26**, p. 4)

But, if these figures were to be added to the original 14,316, and, even with due "allowance . . . made for the teachers not reported," that would give the total number of teachers working in this field as only twenty-five thousand—a quarter of the figure suggested as the absolute minimum necessary.

The 14,316 represent an increase of about 48.1 per cent over the number of teachers reported in the government's previous study in 1947–48. Since the enrollment increase was 47 per cent, this seems to offer an indication that the situation is changing for the better, especially "in view of current teacher shortages" in all areas of education. Another encouraging fact is that, along with the increase in the number of teachers, has come a diminution in the size of the classes. Although in 1947–48, the average number of pupils per teacher of the deaf was thirteen, in 1952–53 it dwindled to eight. During the same five-year period, "the average number of pupils per teacher of crippled children declined from 14.3 to 11.9," while "for children with special health problems, the pupil-teacher ratio went from 24.4 to 13.2. . . ." (**35**, pp. 15–16)

However, this awareness of the need for special classes only serves to make the recruitment of competent teachers, as Mullen pointed out, in connection with the Chicago program, an even more "crucial problem, except in the field of speech correction." As an example of Chicago's difficulties in recruitment, she mentioned that "although the number of blind babies has been increasing, it has been impossible to find an adequate supply of teachers competent in braille and in teaching the blind." (**30**, p. 201)

One of the factors that seem to make the recruitment of special teachers a thankless task is that it seems almost futile for administrators to hope to secure qualified specialists when they are having so much difficulty in securing competent regular teachers, for whom requirements of ability and training are far less exacting. As a matter of fact, we find included in the teaching profession today too many individuals who, for want of a better term, may be classified as *misfits*—at least so far as pedagogy is concerned.

Among them, for example, is the overly sensitive, shy girl who does not get along well with her peer group. Unable to attract boys and girls of her own age, she turns to teaching children in order to fulfill her personal need for having someone to listen to her and look up to her. Another is the woman who has some ax to grind and turns to teaching as a means of promulgating her own views on social reform or vegetarianism. We also find in the teaching profession the woman who has turned to teaching children as a substitute for the motherhood that has been denied her. Such a person, despite her genuine love for children, may be a degenerating rather than a helpful influence upon them, since, as a rule, she tends to indulge them too freely. Then, too, there is the well-educated neurotic who may have taken up teaching children because they are the only ones who will tolerate her.

There are many other personal reasons which have led a large number of men and women to enter the teaching profession rather than any genuine dedication to pedagogy. This does not mean that the teacher who has taken up that work in order to fulfill her own needs rather than out of a genuine vocation is necessarily a "bad" teacher. Often she can succeed reasonably well in teaching the average child. However, such teachers should never be assigned to teach exceptional children, who have too many unfulfilled needs of their own to be asked to serve as therapeutic instruments for their instructor. If anything, the instructor should be the therapeutic instrument for the child. While many teachers who have taken up that work to fulfill their own needs rather than out of a genuine vocation can succeed reasonably well in teaching the average child, they should never be assigned to teach exceptional children.

Specific Needs

Needs for the various types of special educators vary, not only as a result of the demand, but also of the supply. In 1954, Mackie and Dunn made a statistical survey of the requirements current then, and determined from information contributed by 154 supervisors of special education and 74 college and university instructors training teachers of exceptional children that—

. . . the greatest demand is for teachers of the mentally retarded and for speech-correctionists. Next in order are requests for teachers of the deaf and hard-of-hearing, followed by crippled and emotionally disturbed. The least number of requests is for teachers of the gifted, and teachers of children with special health problems. Requests are relatively few for teachers of the blind, and of the partially seeing. (26, p. 6)

Even if there were some method of guaranteeing a continuous flow of special teachers to the school, under present conditions it is not possible for the teacher training institutes to determine just how many will be needed in each of the areas of specialization and set their sights accordingly:

. . . Because of variability of teaching load, varying degrees of handi-capping conditions, individual community problems, and the many types of specialists needed, no form estimates can be made. However, on the basis of the incidence figures and these factors, it is evident that many more teachers would be required for the mentally retarded, speech-handicapped, or crippled, for example, than for the blind or deaf.

It is particularly difficult to estimate the number of specialists who should be available to work with the gifted and the emotionally dis-turbed. The educational needs of these two types of children are met in various ways, and there are differing points of view concerning the kinds of programs which serve them most effectively. (**26**, p. 45)

Availability

What compounds the difficulty here is that the availability of such personnel does not appear to correlate with the demand for it. For example, even though teachers of the blind and partially seeing are least in demand, they are the type of specialist the ad-ministrator finds extremely difficult to obtain, as Mullen pointed out, standing second in scarcity value. First are teachers of the deaf, and next, teachers of the socially maladjusted, who are seemingly as hard to get as teachers of the blind. After that, only—

. . . moderate difficulty is encountered in locating teachers of the mentally retarded and hard-of-hearing. . . . teachers of the partially seeing, the gifted, and the crippled are not as difficult to secure. Teachers of children with special health problems are in the same category. Speech correctionists seem to be the most available, but even so the demand for speech correctionists far exceeds the supply. (**26**, p. 7)

One of Chicago's solutions to recruiting competent teachers is raising the salary scale, a practice which has much to recommend it from the pragmatic point of view, since teaching is a notoriously ill-paid profession and training in special education generally re-quires more intensive study; therefore, the prospects must be made unusually attractive for the college students to induce them to enter into such a sequence of training. Clearly, the greatest difficulty in obtaining qualified teachers for the special classes is that not enough education majors have chosen to specialize in the field. Frampton and Gall proposed one remedy for this problem. Noting that some teacher-training centers follow the practice of giving work with the exceptional only in the latter part of the graduate training years, they suggested that "consideration should be given to starting some training on an undergraduate level in order to recruit interested and capable students into fields of specialization, and to inform students in general of the problems of the exceptional." (11, p. 253) And Wallin agreed that "effective vocational guidance programs" should be organized at the high school and college levels. (40, p. 239)

However, despite the teacher shortage, any system of mass production of specialists is not the answer to the problems in this pedagogical area, or, indeed, any other. As John Schoff Millis has declared:

. . . I fully recognize that there is a shortage of teachers . . . but the central task is one of providing teachers of quality, for without quality we will never even approach a solution of quantity. (29, p. 181)

REQUIREMENTS FOR THE TEACHER OF EXCEPTIONAL CHILDREN

"One of the greatest difficulties in a discussion of teacher training for work with the exceptional," Frampton and Gall have accurately pointed out, "is that the needs of the field are not clear to the general educator." (11, p. 252) The basic requirements of the teacher's education in this area are, however, in the broadest sense, the same as in any other area of pedagogy, the only difference being that they are considerably intensified. Thus, the fundamentals of teacher education outlined by Joseph Butterwick become particularly apposite when applied to the area of special education:

> If the college . . . pays major attention to the way in which it teaches those ideas and concepts which it associates with liberal arts or general education, it supplies a laboratory in which the prospective teacher acquires a functional attitude toward methods. He still lacks two types of equipment—the intellectual understanding and the skill to do the job himself. The skill can be acquired only through practice. To acquire the understanding, both theoretical instruction and practice are needed. (4, pp. 38–39)

No matter how many education courses, both of a regular and of a specialized nature, the teacher of the exceptional has taken, she has not really finished her education until she has worked directly with the handicapped or gifted children with whom she has been preparing herself to deal. That is not to say that these courses do not represent an essential part of her professional training, but that in themselves they do not represent a *complete* training.

Lindgren has depicted the ideal teacher as the one "who really wants to understand children," and who, in consequence, "should be prepared to learn things which do not fit in with his preconceptions of them and must be prepared to readjust his opinions from time to time as circumstances require." (22, p. 35) This, too, has direct application to the specialized educator, except that she must be even more elastic in her outlook and methodology. Even within the framework of special education, it is important for her to make adjustments in the curriculum to fit the needs of the child and to enrich the curriculum with common everyday experiences that the child has missed. As Joseph Hillyard has observed:

> Teachers cannot grow until they recognize their problems. They cannot move in a new or different direction until they understand and see some validity in a changed procedure. And they can change only within the limits of their background of experience and creative activity. (17, p. 170)

It is unfortunate that there should so often exist in our schools the situation described by Lindgren whereby "much of the communication that could take place in a classroom is blocked by a kind of mutual hostility or resentment. . . . It is as though student and teacher each expected the other to mistrust and misunderstand him." This condition, as Lindgren put it—with remarkable restraint—is "not favorable to learning." (22, p. 195)

It is not favorable to learning of any kind. However, when it comes to the education of either the handicapped or the gifted, such a state of affairs is especially pernicious, for a sound system of mental hygiene is of particular importance in this highly sensitive area.

As a point of departure, we may assume that all teachers, no matter what kind of children they are called upon to instruct, should possess the following ten qualities:

1. Good physical health
2. Excellent mental health
3. A high degree of intelligence
4. A superior command of the mother tongue in both written and oral expression
5. An attractive personality
6. A thorough knowledge of the psychology of the students' age group
7. A high degree of competence in the skills and techniques of the specific teaching area
8. Cultivation and good manners
9. Personal dignity and self-confidence
10. A high moral and spiritual character

However, the specialist should more nearly approach the ideal than the average instructor is required to do, since the teacher represents more to the handicapped child, both as an authority system and as a liaison agent with the community, than to the average child for whom greater direct community contact will fill part of these needs.

Extrapolating from the basic requirements which she has outlined as requisite for the regular classroom teacher, Mackie has developed a series of criteria for the teacher who is planning to make the exceptional child her lifework:

> Every teacher needs certain personality characteristics, plus technical knowledge and abilities, which enable her to do her job well. Good mental and physical health, intelligence, love of children, interest in people and communities, adaptability, resourcefulness, and some of the pioneer spirit will enable her, as a growing personality, to meet the challenge of the young child. To be successful with crippled children (and, by extension, with other deviants) she needs all of these qualities, and she needs them to an even greater degree because of the individual deviations and problems of the children and because of the complicated nature of administering special classes. (**23**, p. 32)

What is of paramount importance in this area is that the teacher should have *faith* in the handicapped child. She must recognize, Richards remarked, that the individual handicapped child, like other human beings, has "hopes, aspirations, and a need to participate creatively in his world, no matter what the temporary or permanent limitations of that world may be." (**36**, p. 417) Gladys Rhodes has further specified that—

> . . . those persons selected as teachers for exceptional children [should be interested] in doing research. . . . The teacher must understand something about the conditions which make the child an exceptional child, his motivations and aspirations and group dynamics. He is one of the team of research workers seeking further understanding of the problems of exceptional children. (**34**, p. 546)

The teacher of the handicapped must learn to help the child to accept his handicap realistically and to mingle freely with other children. And, in order to teach the child to accept himself as he is, the special teacher must be an individual who has learned to accept herself as she is. The special teacher must have an emotional balance and security both inside and outside the classroom.

Furthermore, her presence should radiate an ease and composure that will win the confidence of the children entrusted to her. This is especially important for those who teach children who are overly sensitive or mentally retarded, because often the only warmth and sense of belonging that come into the lives of such children are to be found in the classroom. Thus, it is obvious that the teacher who has taken up her profession largely in order to satisfy her own inadequacies cannot ever be considered the right person to teach classes of mentally retarded or handicapped children, even though she can get along reasonably well in teaching the average—because average children have greater frustration tolerance than the exceptional.

Physical perception proximity plays a significant role in differentiating between the teacher of the normal and the special-education teacher. Poised and well-adjusted individuals, whether adults or children, are emotionally secure. They are never concerned about their feelings of belonging, whether they are in a group or all alone. The overly sensitive and the mentally retarded children, on the other hand, cannot conceptualize a base for their emotional security away from their own immediate presence. Therefore, the teacher must always serve as a source of emotional security for such children, and it is important that the special teacher not only should understand this concept of physical perception proximity but that she should also be aware of her empathetic relationship to the child.

Finally, the special teacher, even more than the regular teacher, must be able to accept the concept of "we learn together." She must be so confident of the abilities and competencies that she does have that she must not hesitate to undertake an experience which is new to her in the presence of the children, if the learning situation demands that a new task be initiated. As an illustration, suppose that it seems desirable that a certain type of table be built in the classroom. The teacher is trained in the practical and industrial arts and knows how to utilize tools and materials adequately. However, she has never in her experience had the occasion to construct that particular kind of table. She should not hesitate to employ the concept, "Let us learn together," even though, at the same time, she will tell the children, "I have never made anything like this before." By making use of this concept the teacher will be able to discover the resources latent in her own classroom, as well as the resources that the children can bring in from the outside, including parental skills, plus materials from all instrumentalities relevant to the particular learning situation—books, magazines, advertising displays, motion pictures, radio, television, and so on. It is obvious that, in order to employ the "We learn together" concept, the teacher must initiate the task without warning, whereas, with average children, she may prefer to take the time to acquire the skill first and then attempt to direct the children, or she may even call in an expert to carry out the task for which she does not feel herself to be too well qualified.

Many teachers of the mentally retarded children, especially, fail to achieve success largely because they are hesitant to learn new skills along with their charges. However, the "We learn together" process has great psychological impact, because it is conducive toward stimulating motivation within the children. While helping the teacher herself to learn, the children not only learn themselves, but derive a great sense of emotional satisfaction from working *with* her.

The teacher who has decided that her vocation is educating the exceptional must understand from the outset the difference between that field and that of general education. In Henry Robinson's words:

Special education . . . is teaching the child subject matter rather than teaching subject matter to the child. It is tailoring general education to fit the needs and capacities of each child. . . . It is not merely a knowledge of mental hygiene, abnormal or clinical psychology, tests and measurements, screenings, counseling, and guidance. It is good stimulative teaching based on individual differences and a knowledge and appreciation of all these things. (**37,** p. 235)

A symposium on education of the exceptional held in 1952 at Hunter College in New York City drew up a rather exhaustive list of qualifications that a candidate for teaching a special class should have, *in addition* to "all the qualifications needed by a regular teacher." Following is a summary of some of the most important requirements the conferees concluded were necessary:

Personal

Integrated and stable personality
Flexibility in adapting the curriculum and procedures to the individual needs of the child
Liking for the individual child
Willingness to experiment
Good judgment
Interest in research
Desire to work in the field
Initiative and leadership
Emotional maturity

Physical

Good health
Good speech and no mouth deformities
Above average intelligence
No serious eye difficulties

Educational

Above average academic achievement
Skill in all needed techniques

Professional

Teaching certificate for the particular level
An accredited A.B. degree
At least 6 semester hours of graduate work in the particular field
3–5 years of teaching in normal classes

Special Abilities

Acquaintance with special services and community resources
Ability to detect medical problem cases
Understanding of family relations
Acquaintance with pertinent legislation
Alertness for child failure or signs of maladjustment
Ability to help educate the community
Capacity to detect cases fit for transfer to regular classes
Ability to teach a handicapped child in normal classes
Knowledge of job possibilities and vocational guidance (5)

Most educators would agree with all of these save for one point—that a BA degree, plus six semester hours of graduate work, is enough. Some might feel that at least a master's degree should be required.

In 1955, Robinson queried a number of instructors and administrators who were working in the field of special education on what, in their opinions, were the "most desirable personality traits and competencies" in teachers of exceptional children. He received responses from 267 teachers and 78 superintendents and college professors, and the conclusions he drew from those responses correlated very well with the Hunter recommendations. Those ten attributes most cited are listed in order of diminishing frequency.

1. A sincere regard and appreciation for the welfare of children, especially those with handicaps.
2. The ability to understand the nature and needs of children and parents.
3. The ability to wait faithfully, to be tolerant to the ungrateful, and to hope graciously for glimpses of even slight improvement in those children with serious limitations.
4. Mastery of subject matter material of the core areas, including proficiency in remedial reading.
5. Prior experience with normal children.
6. Being mature, stable, and wholesomely sound mentally, emotionally, and physically.

7. The ability to master the use of all available resources and materials and a variety of stimulating teaching methods.
8. Being kind, considerate, and cooperative, with initiative in working with everyone interested in exceptional children.
9. Doing the proper thing on time and being courteous, mannerly, and tactful in dealing with children and parents.
10. Having faith in self and recognizing and inspiring into action all the potentialities of children with limitations. (**37**, p. 276)

And Wallin's list of those personality traits which he feels to be "particularly desirable for teachers of the mentally deficient and the slow learners" really would apply to the field of special education as a whole:

Genuine interest in and sympathy for children
Patience and perseverance
Optimism, companionableness, tact
Self-control
Emotional and nervous stability
Emotional maturity
Adaptability, plasticity, resourcefulness
Imaginative insight
Scholarship
Understanding of interpersonal relationships
Loyalty—to lofty personal ideals, to the highest ideals of the profession, and to co-workers, pupils and superior officers (unless they forfeit the right to it) (**40**, p. 224)

In addition to these general requirements for all teachers of the exceptional, there are numerous specific abilities and techniques which have been found desirable and/or necessary in each area of deviant instruction, as well as certain special character traits more important in one area than another.

Crippled and "Delicate" Children

Since nearly one fourth of all exceptional children, according to Mackie and Dunn, are either crippled or have some special health problem, those "teachers who plan to work with either or both of these groups may at different times in their careers find themselves instructing, not only in special day school classes, but also in hospitals, convalescent homes, sanitoria, or in the children's own homes. . . ."

. . . Because these teachers will work with children having many different types of physical deviations, school administrators are seeking persons who have the technical knowledge to understand the problems of each child. In addition, because pupils must be taught under several types of educational organization, such teachers should be equipped to work with allied professional groups and other community agencies involved in each child's care and rehabilitation. (**26**, p. 24)

In order to carry out their duties with optimum effectiveness, the teachers of crippled children should, during their training years, follow a rigid course of instruction. Added to the "general introductory or exploratory courses in the field of exceptional children," which should, of course, be a prerequisite for all teacher education in the entire area, they will need such specialized courses as "surveys of various physical conditions," which a medical staff should present to them in lay terminology, "clinical observations; organization and administration, special adjustments in teaching the crippled; and guidance for the handicapped"— with all these courses conducted by individuals who have actually worked with and had direct experience with crippled children "in schools, in hospitals, in convalescent homes, and in official and private agencies." They will also need—

. . . clinical courses making use of orthopedic and children's hospitals . . . methods courses which include "seeing crippled children at work" and . . . guidance courses which put them in touch with the types of agencies that help crippled children and adults. Only through the acquisition of such technical knowledge will the teacher have sufficient understanding to cooperate fully and effectively with other professional workers. . . . (**23**, p. 33)

Although it is essential that all teachers of the handicapped possess superior ability in classroom management, Mackie considers this talent of paramount importance for the teacher of crippled children.

. . . Many adjustments will have to be made in the curriculum, in daily schedules, and in long-range planning. Certain children will be coming and going from the classrooms all day long and missing class activities, in order that they may get individual treatments, rest periods, and other special services. . . . (23, p. 33)

Those teachers who have to work with children actually in the hospital are, Mackie and Fitzgerald feel, faced with perhaps the most difficult situation of all, since they have to deal with the problem of their surroundings as well as the problem of the handicapped child. Although few teachers today have had such preparation, it would facilitate their work considerably if some arrangement could be made for them to have "training in the education of the physically handicapped with practice teaching in the hospital school," like the other professionals—medical and nonmedical—involved in hospital work, all of whom have had some kind of internship or comparable training for the services they render. This is the only way for the hospital teacher to gain an understanding of "the nature of the work done by the other people in the hospital," and such an understanding is absolutely necessary in order to make her "an effective member of the team working together for the best possible development of the children." (27, p. 15)

Blind Children

A considerable amount of technical training is needed for the instruction of the blind. The teacher in this field must, according to Clarence Athearn, have a thorough knowledge of the "special tools which are required in everyday classes," including "the reading and writing of Braille, the use of the TVL arithmetic type and slate, the manipulation of the Braille writer, the Braille algebraic symbols, and embossed maps," and so on. (1, p. 9)

Yet, despite all the competencies needed for teaching the

blind, fewer institutions, Mackie and Dunn have discovered, offer sequences of preparation for teachers in this area of exceptionality than in any other except the gifted. The explanation for this they believe to be primarily the fact that the blind make up the smallest group of exceptional children numerically speaking. (26, p. 21)

There is one asset that is of particular advantage to a teacher of the blind: that is, either musical ability or a strong interest in, and a knowledge of, music. As Basset Hough has noted:

> Music is . . . a branch of study eminently well-suited to the blind, as its perception depends largely upon the ear. Furthermore, those phases of musical study which are normally carried on by means of the eye are easily made available to the blind through the instrumentality of music notation in Braille. . . . (19, p. 205)

Although it is not true that the blind are more gifted in this field than the normally sighted, it is true that this is the one field in which their blindness does not serve as a handicap, and in which, therefore, their opportunities for proficiency are as great as the sighted individual's. Furthermore, it is the one field in which they can "feel like anyone else."

Education in the psychology of the blind is an important part of the teacher's training, for much of the blind person's handicap is social rather than physical; that is, he is sometimes as much held back by his attitude toward his defect as the defect itself (which, of course, applies to all the other areas, too, though rarely with as much consistency as in the case of the blind). "The teacher's methods," Athearn has noted, depend "upon an understanding of the psychological causes of 'blindisms' and upon personality maladjustments associated with blindness." (1, p. 6)

Speech and Hearing Impediments

Those with deviations of speech and hearing are classified together in this context because there is such a vast area of over-

lap; first, because the deaf are very likely to have speech difficulties; second, because "the main problem in each of these areas
of exceptionality is one of communication." (26, p. 28) As in the
case of the blind, numerous skills and abilities are necessary here,
and "it is generally recognized that speech correctionists, speech
and hearing specialists, teachers of the deaf, and teachers of the
hard-of-hearing will need certain competencies in common." (26
p. 28)

It is in this area that it becomes particularly evident how inadequate the competencies of a teacher trained to instruct the
average child would be if she were called upon to deal with the
exceptional child. As Oliver Kolstoe put it:

> . . . a teacher of deaf children properly recognizes that none of the
> goals of self-realization, human relations, economic efficiency, and civic
> responsibility can be realized by a child who is insulated from
> the world by an inability to communicate with others. . . . (21,
> p. 464)

Brill has outlined in some detail the difficulties that confront
the teacher of the deaf, who has to use an elaborate complex of
psychological and educational techniques in order to achieve
even minimal results:

> . . . a teacher of the deaf must first of all have the technical knowl-
> edge of how to teach the English language to a deaf child who, to
> begin with, has no conception that there is such a thing as the English
> language . . . every hearing teacher of the deaf should be able to
> teach speech to the deaf child. It is a matter of teaching speech to a
> child who has never heard the English language and who, while he
> may be able to hear a small number of sounds on certain frequencies,
> does not have enough hearing to be taught speech through his hear-
> ing. . . .
> A qualified teacher of the deaf must know how to teach reading to
> a deaf child who again has no knowledge of words until he has the
> opportunity to learn them as printed or written symbols. . . . (3,
> p. 195)

Mental Retardation

The Pollocks have given a succint picture of the kind of teacher needed to instruct those of inadequate intellectual powers:

> The teacher of the mentally retarded must have much more patience and understanding (than the regular teacher). She must have a precise knowledge not only of abnormal psychology, but also of the normal achievements of children of all ages and grades, in order to recognize how much the retarded youngster deviates from the normal. (**33**, p. 3)

Heck feels that she will also gain much additional experience in this area that will be of great use to her later if she has training and experience as a clinical examiner and school nurse.

Heck has further stated that the teacher of the mentally retarded must have "an unusual amount of patience," for "the children she must teach learn slowly; explanations must be repeated over and over again." Another qualification he finds necessary is a "high degree" of "contagious enthusiasm," which he believes to be vital "for arousing the interest of children of low I.Q. in the work that they have to do." (**16**, p. 359) The teacher of those of low intelligence must like and understand her students, but she must steer clear of the pitfall against which Wallin has solemnly warned her, that of developing a "morbid sympathy" for her charges—which will do neither them nor herself any good. (**40**, p. 223)

To indicate what qualifications are necessary for the teacher in this sector of specialized education, Wallin has outlined the minimum certification requirements for teachers of the mentally retarded in three widely separated parts of this country:

California (1950)

1. A valid teaching document of the kindergarten-primary, general-elementary, junior-high school, or general-secondary type.

2. Eighteen semester hours of credits in 5 required areas and 7 electives.

Three years of successful experience may be substituted for the course requirements for a maximum of 12 semester hours. Liberal time is allowed for the fulfillment of the requirements.

Missouri (1949)

1. One year of successful teaching experience in a regular school or observation for at least one semester.
2. A baccalaureate degree and valid certificate.
3. Twenty-four semester credits earned in 15 different professional courses, some required, some elective.
4. Unspecified credits in elementary and secondary courses.

Pennsylvania (1950)

For elementary classes for the mentally retarded:
1. An elementary school certificate.
2. Twenty-four semester hours, including 6 in certain basic courses, 9 in courses specifically applicable to teachers of the mentally retarded, and 9 in electives.

Successful experience in teaching, in social service, or in the psychoeducational or psychiatric clinic counts as 6 credits.

The regulations differ somewhat for the secondary field. (**40,** pp. 236–37)

Superior Intelligence

Teaching the gifted, according to a bulletin put out by the Connecticut State Department of Education, "is a complex and challenging process which places great emphasis upon self-direction by the pupil and his acceptance of responsibility." (**9**, p. 31) An instructor in this area must be as carefully chosen and trained as any other specialist, for giftedness is as much a deviation from the norm as retardedness, and the child of high IQ is entitled to individual consideration just as much as the child of low IQ. According to three distinguished educators:

Like other teachers, the person working with the gifted needs to understand human growth and development, with special reference to childhood and youth. He should be able to perceive the potentialities inherent in all kinds of personalities. . . .

The education of gifted children requires gifted teachers who have the ability to recognize giftedness, to create an atmosphere and environment favorable to its development, to provide conditions that give it a chance to emerge and blossom.

The teacher who understands child development and methods of child study is able early to recognize talent or other forms of giftedness in individual children. . . . (38, pp. 112–13)

Moreover, the teacher of the gifted has perhaps the weightiest social responsibility of all, for it is in her hands that the future of our potentially great men and women lie. "Added to her technical knowledge and skills," Otto has said, she must also possess "the ability to understand the great social and ethical integrity demanded in democratic leadership." (32, p. 129) One danger here that is extremely difficult to avoid, and yet which Hollingworth has cited as a very real one, is the possibility that the teacher may be jealous of the child whom she knows to have mental abilities that far transcend hers. This jealousy may be on a subconscious rather than a conscious level, in which case it is more difficult to detect and, hence, even more dangerous. If the teacher herself is of high IQ, this will minimize the hazard of such a situation to some degree, although it is neither a realistic nor a feasible method of dealing with it. (18, p. 195)

Witty conducted a survey of practices regarding gifted children in secondary schools throughout the United States. Of the twenty-nine schools which responded, only five stated that they gave the teacher of gifted children a lighter load than other teachers. As the investigator commented:

. . . Lightened loads are not considered necessary in the remaining schools, since teaching the gifted is regarded by many teachers as a privilege. Intelligence, teaching ability, skill in counseling, good health, pleasing personality, and interest in gifted children are the factors considered important in the selection of the teacher of the gifted. (41, p. 203)

Heck is of the opinion that the most important qualification for the teacher of the gifted is a thorough training in the psychology of the child of high IQ. Teachers in this area, he has declared, must be well-versed in "methods of instruction that take into account the mental make-up of these children," and the technique of making changes in "the materials of instruction if enrichment is to be the goal." (**16,** p. 396)

TEACHER TRAINING IN SPECIAL EDUCATION

The United States Office of Education, feeling "the need for intensive analysis on a nationwide scale of professional standards and opportunities for the preparation of teachers of exceptional children," has been studying the qualifications and type of preparation needed by special-education personnel. (**26,** p. 67) As a corollary study, that same bureau has been endeavoring to discover, at the same time, what opportunities are available in the various specializations to those students who are interested in study in that area. On the whole, such opportunities are relatively limited, for, as Cruickshank has said, "the total facilities of a major university are required" to prepare teachers competently for special education (**6,** p. 283), and, of course, there are few universities today willing or able or even competent to organize such extensive programs. However, it is to be assumed that, with an expansion of student interest, there would be a commensurate expansion of facilities.

According to the National Society for Crippled Children and Adults, a sequence of special preparation in any of the areas of special education would consist of—

. . . three courses of at least 9 to 12 semester hours of specialized preparation made up of (1) a study of the characteristics (physical, mental, and emotional) of the particular condition under consideration; (2) a study of the teaching methods and curriculum adjustment needed; (3) observation and student teaching practices in the specialized area. (31, p. 5)

Currently, according to Mackie's report:

. . . approximately 12 to 15 colleges and universities in the United States offer rather complete curricula of special education. That is, they offer a series of courses in several areas. A number of colleges and universities provide complete training in one or two areas. A still larger group of such institutions give a few courses in areas such as speech correction. (25, p. 11)

Writing in connection with Dunn, she has offered more specific information, namely, that "for the academic year 1953–1954, 122 of the nation's colleges and universities reported sequences of teacher preparation in one or more areas of exceptionality." (25, p. 10)

They broke down the sequences of teacher preparation into the following ten areas which follow here, together with the number of institutions in the United States which offer complete courses on teacher training in each:

Area of Handicap	*Number of Schools Offering Course*
Speech Handicapped	115
Hard-of-Hearing	68
Mentally Retarded	40
Deaf	22
Crippled [1]	18
Socially Maladjusted	10
Partially Sighted	6
Special Health Problems [2]	5
Blind	3
Gifted	2

(26, pp. 12–13)

It is obvious that, in certain areas, facilities are inadequate to an almost shocking degree, and it would be futile to attempt to

[1] The term "crippled" includes palsy, poliomyelitis, amputations, paraplegia, congenital anomalies, and other orthopedic conditions.

[2] The term "special health problems" includes cardiac conditions, epilepsy, endocrine disorders, cosmetic defects, and below par conditions.

arouse undergraduate interest without first securing more extensive opportunities for training. These are for the most part the areas in which there is most need for qualified personnel, and it seems obvious that one of the major reasons for this is that many education students who might be interested in majoring in these areas cannot receive adequate training in their own localities.

As one of the first fruits of its researches, the Office of Education has put out a bulletin entitled *Directors and Supervisors of Special Education in Local School Systems.* The general qualifications it lists for administrators would apply equally well to anyone in the field of special education. They must understand—

(1) The physical, mental, and emotional deviations of handicapped children; (2) the effect of the various deviations on children, their families, and the community; (3) the specific agencies and community services for the various types of handicapped children; (4) current trends in educational programs for them; and (5) major studies about each type of exceptional child (7, p. 46)

COPING WITH THE PROBLEM

The question of obtaining appropriate personnel for special classes is at least a triple one. The first issue is that of getting the right kind of person, the second is seeing that she gets the right kind of training, the third is making sure that such training is available. A fourth part might also be added: that of arousing interest in the right kind of person for undergoing that kind of training.

However, if one aspect of this multiple problem is to be considered as more important than the others, it is the first. The teacher of the handicapped must be a person free of all hostility and rigidity, who has taken up her profession because she wants to help others, not because she wants to help herself. She should be a mature, responsible individual, with a satisfactory personal life outside of school and no need to seek personal compensations through teaching. She should have poise and tolerance, and, while she should be intelligent, it is more important that she have a high functioning IQ than a high paper IQ. If we want happy, well-adjusted children, competent to the limit of their abilities, we must give them happy, well-adjusted teachers, competent to the limit of theirs.

References

1. ATHEARN, CLARENCE R. "Methods of Teaching as Ways of Life," in (10). Pp. 1–14.
2. BAKER, HARRY J. *Introduction to Exceptional Children*. (Rev. ed.) New York: Macmillan Co., 1953.
3. BRILL, RICHARD G. "Education of the Deaf and the Hard of Hearing," *Exceptional Children*, XXIII (February, 1957), 194–98.
4. BUTTERWICK, JOSEPH S. "Whither Teacher Education?" *Educational Administration and Supervision*, XLIV (January, 1957), 33–43.
5. *College Symposium on the Education of the Exceptional*. New York: Hunter College, Department of Special Education, 1953.
6. CRUICKSHANK, WILLIAM M. "Syracuse University Meets the Challenge of the Exceptional Child," in (11). Vol. I.
7. *Directors and Supervisors of Special Education in Local School Systems*. (U. S. Office of Education. Bulletin No. 13) Washington, D. C.: Government Printing Office, 1955.
8. DUNN, LLOYD M. "Teachers of Exceptional Children," *Education*, LXXVII (April, 1957), 483–90.
9. *Education for Gifted Children and Youth*. (Connecticut State Department of Education. Bulletin No. 77.) Hartford: 1955–56.
10. FRAMPTON, MERLE E. (ed.). *Education of the Blind*. Yonkers, N. Y.: World Book Co., 1940.
11. FRAMPTON, MERLE E., and ELENA D. GALL (eds.). *Special Education for the Exception*. Boston: Porter Sargent, 1955.
12. ——— — ———. "Educational and Administrative Problems," in *Special Education for the Exceptional* (9). Pp. 162–81.

13. ———— — ————. "Teacher Training Problems," in (11). Pp. 252–73.

14. GOLDBERG, I. IGNACY. "Mental Health for the Exceptional," in (11). Pp. 116–22.

15. GORMAN, BURTON W. "The Teaching Profession Tomorrow," *School and Society*, XXCII (September 15, 1955), 170–82.

16. HECK, ARCH O. *The Education of Exceptional Children.* New York: McGraw-Hill Book Co., 1953.

17. HILLYARD, JOSEPH B. "The Role of the Supervisor in the Improvement of the Teacher-Learning Situation," *The Social Studies*, XL (May, 1957), 169–76.

18. HOLLINGWORTH, LETA S. "How Should Gifted Children Be Educated?" *Baltimore Bulletin of Education*, IX (May, 1931), 195.

19. HOUGH, BASSET W. "Musical Education of the Blind," in (10). Pp. 205–230.

20. KEEHAN, VIRGINIA R. *Exceptional Children, A Handbook for Teachers.* Santa Fe, New Mexico: Department of Education, 1954.

21. KOLSTOE, OLIVER P. "Nature and Impact of Special Methods," *Education*, LXXVII (April, 1957), 464–67.

22. LINDGREN, HENRY C. *Mental Health in Education.* New York: Henry Holt and Co., 1954.

23. MACKIE, ROMAINE P. *Crippled Children in School.* (U. S. Department of Health, Education, and Welfare, 1948. Reprint.) Washington, D. C.: Government Printing Office, 1953.

24. ————. *Education of Crippled Children in the United States.* (Federal Security Agency, Office of Education. Leaflet 30.) Washington, D. C.: Government Printing Office, 1952.

25. ————. *Some Problems in the Education of Handicapped Children.* (U. S. Department of Health, Education, and Welfare. Pamphlet No. 112.) Washington, D. C.: Government Printing Office, 1954.

26. MACKIE, ROMAINE P., and LLOYD M. DUNN. *College and University Programs for the Preparation of Teachers of Exceptional Children.* (U. S. Department of Health, Education, and Welfare. Bulletin No. 13.) Washington, D. C.: Government Printing Office, 1954.

27. MACKIE, ROMAINE P., and MARGARET FITZGERALD. *School in the*

Hospital. (Federal Security Agency. Bulletin No. 3.) Washington, D. C.: Government Printing Office, 1949.

28. MELCHER, JOHN W., and KENNETH R. BLESSING. "Special Education for Rural Retarded Youth," *Exceptional Child,* XXIII (February, 1957), 207–210, 214.

29. MILLIS, JOHN SCHOFF. "Educating Teachers as Professionals," *Journal of Higher Education,* XXVIII (April, 1957), 179–85.

30. MULLEN, FRANCES A. "A Metropolitan Area Plans for Special Education," in (11). Pp. 194–215.

31. *Opportunities for the Preparation of Teachers of Exceptional Children.* Chicago: National Society for Crippled Children and Adults, 1949.

32. OTTO, HENRY J. *Curriculum Adjustments for Gifted Elementary School Children in Regular Classes.* Austin: University of Texas, 1957.

33. POLLOCK, MORRIS P., and MIRIAM. *New Hope for the Retarded.* Boston: Porter Sargent, 1953.

34. RHODES, GLADYS L. "Improving Education for the Mentally Retarded," *New York State Education,* XLIV (May, 1957), 546–47.

35. RICE, MABEL C., and ARTHUR S. HILL. "Statistics of Special Education for Exceptional Children, 1952–1953," *Biennial Survey of Education In the U. S., 1952–1954.* (U. S. Department of Health, Education, and Welfare.) Washington, D. C.: Government Printing Office, 1955. Chap. V.

36. RICHARDS, EDWARD A. "Children Left Behind at Home, in Hospitals," *Childhood Education,* XXXIII (May, 1957), 415–20.

37. ROBINSON, H. E. "Some Basic Needs for the Education of Teachers and Personnel for Special Education," in (11). Pp. 274–78.

38. RYAN, W. CARSON, RUTH STRANG, and PAUL WITTY. "The Teacher of Gifted Children," in Paul Witty (ed.). *The Gifted Child.* Boston: D. C. Heath and Co., 1951. Pp. 106–130.

39. SOUTHARD, CURTIS G., and MABEL ROSS. "Mental Health of Exceptional Children," in (11). Pp. 105–115.

40. WALLIN, J. E. WALLACE. *The Education of Mentally Handicapped Children.* New York: Harper and Brothers, 1951.

41. WITTY, PAUL. "Nature and Extent of Educational Programs for the Gifted Pupil," in *The Gifted Child.* Boston: D. C. Heath and Co., 1951. Pp. 185–209.

CHAPTER FIVE

Special Classes for the Mentally Retarded

THE concept of special classes for the mentally retarded within the framework of the regular public school system has by no means been universally accepted. Considerable controversy is still raging within the academic world on whether such classes should or should not be organized.

DEMOCRACY THROUGH SEPARATION

Social Adjustments and Maladjustments

Those who are opposed to special classes for the mentally retarded maintain that a well-trained teacher should be capable of instructing every child who is at all educable in her regular classes alongside the other children of normal mentality. It is the contention of those who disapprove of such classes that *all* children—both the mentally retarded or otherwise exceptional and the average—are being educated primarily so that they will be able to take their appropriate places in society—a premise with which no one would quarrel.

However, the opponents of the special-class system go on to state that, since the society in which those children will live as adults will not be divided into homogeneous groups but will be a gallimaufry of all levels of intelligence, it is important that the children receive their training in a milieu which is similarly diversified. Accordingly, these educators believe, not only are special classes wasteful and extravagant, but they stunt the child's personality development by bringing him up in an unrealistic atmosphere.

Setting aside the issue represented by those school boards and administrators who, seemingly placing the cost of education before the welfare of the child, object fundamentally to the special class as such because it costs money, we find many parents and teachers who genuinely do believe that grouping a child chronologically in the regular classes will, of itself, develop his social and personal adequacy. A thoroughly well-meaning teacher not long ago informed this writer that she felt it mattered less that a child should succeed in the academic work that he did in her classes than that he should move along from grade to grade with his group.

Such a naive attitude toward the education of these unfortunate children can result—all sentiment aside—in a degeneration of valuable human resources. It is impossible for a child to develop personal and social adequacy in a vacuum. If it were true that diversified classes would help the mentally retarded child adjust to the society of his mental superiors, and, even more important, help his mental superiors to adjust to him, there would of course be very little reason for segregating the mentally retarded in the public schools. Even the chance to acquire a greater quantity of academic skills would not be of weight against such a desirable end result as this.

However, the truth of the matter is that, under normal social conditions, the mental retardate has nearly always been regarded as an outcast. A visit to an elementary or high school without special classes will readily prove that the child of slower mental output is, as a rule, rejected by the other members of his peer group. He is seldom sought out for games by the other children, and is usually the last to be chosen in almost any activity sponsored by his class. Children develop personally on the basis of talents that they possess, and not on the basis of being thrown with a group by virtue of what has been almost ironically miscalled "social promotion." It is this old-fashioned theory of letting the mental retardate develop as best he may in a society geared for the average that has made "village idiots" out of many children who could, with appropriate care and training, have been developed into useful, productive individuals.

For example, let us take the case of Paul, whom the writer was called in to examine after the boy had become a discipline problem in the high school. According to the school counselor, Paul had previously been a well-behaved pupil, who, despite his poor academic work, had been promoted "socially" all through elementary school and for three years of high school. Then, suddenly, to the consternation of everyone concerned, he had turned into a behavior problem.

At this time, Paul was eighteen years old, about six feet tall, and very healthy and strong. Physically he was a fine specimen, but mentally it was another matter. The boy readily admitted that he felt nobody liked him and that everybody made fun of him. Although he had been able to make some friends in elementary school, the same youngsters had ignored him in junior and senior high school, because they had become sophisticated enough to discover that he was, as they put it with the frank cruelty of youth, "dumb." The only kind of social recognition Paul could get—since acceptance seemed impossible—was by calling attention to himself through misbehavior.

And it could not be said in their defense that the school authorities were unaware of Paul's handicap, because a study of the boy's record cards over the years revealed such comments as:

"Paul is very slow and shy, but should be promoted because he tries his best. . . . This boy is one of the dullest I ever taught, but he should stay in school, since something is bound to rub off on him, anyway. . . . Paul has an I.Q. of 62, but we should send him on to high school to help develop him socially."

His parents had no idea that their son was in any way retarded. They believed that, because he was promoted each term and did not give the teachers any trouble, he was doing well in school. Thus, it can be seen that keeping that boy in regular classes, far from promoting his social adjustment, was actually serving to turn him into a social outcast.

At this point, it became obvious that Paul should no longer be kept in the regular high school, and special training was arranged for him through the state rehabilitation department. Today he is a self-sufficient individual, working in a bicycle-repair shop. Although Paul is retarded, he is by no means deficient. He is socially and personally adequate in terms of his own group and has become one of the best bicycle repairmen in his part of the country. If he had been left to "complete" the regular high school education, he might very possibly have become a community burden. Martens has explicitly stated that "studies of undesirable behavior among pupils show that there is a tendency for disciplinary problems to be concentrated among retarded children who are not given the special educational help they need." (31, p. 7) Joseph Resnick has shown this to be a simple matter of cause and effect:

The child who feels rejected frequently develops antisocial behavior in his effort to release nervous tension due to his unfortunate situation. His behavior is often inclined to be aggressive and rebellious, although he may desire the approval of the individuals whom he aggravates. (39, pp. 352–53)

This is confirmed by Flora Daly and Leo Cain, who point out that "sometimes a student's attempts at social adjustment are so obscured by the overlay of antisocial behavior that he employs in effecting these adjustments that it requires great insight on the part of the teacher to recognize them as a means of meeting his needs." (11, pp. 29–30).

Achieving True Life Adjustment

The concept of education for life adjustment is an entirely admirable one, but such an adjustment must be made in terms of each individual's capacity. When a child is promoted from grade to grade solely on the basis of his age group, no adjustment whatsoever is involved. In a sense the educators are simply taking the "easy way out"—for them, that is, not for the child.

Furthermore, there is a fallacy involved even in terms of those who believe that a school class should reproduce the whole of society in microcosm, because in real-life situations we are not grouped according to our age any more than we are according to our intellectual ability. Therefore, the traditional chronological grouping is just as arbitrary as any other kind of segregation, and a good deal less reasonable.

The case for special classes within our public schools is predicated on the philosophy that, in a highly mechanized, highly urbanized society, all children need an opportunity to develop their talents to the limits of their capacities. Where the child is handicapped or otherwise different from the rest of the children, only special training will enable him to come as near the average as his inherent capacities will permit him to do.

As a result, whenever the school system is large enough to make such a procedure remotely possible, the mental retardates should be placed in special classes. Such classes will be of benefit to the normal pupils by depriving them of certain drawbacks to intellectual advancement as well as of distracting elements in the classroom. It makes the work easier for the teacher of both the average children and the special class, for homogeneously grouped children tend to get along better with each other. It tends to benefit the handicapped negatively because they are no longer forced into impossible competition and its accompanying social rejection; positively, because they will receive more encouragement and successsful experiences when they are called upon to compete only with their peers than they can receive in any other situation—for, in the unspecialized atmosphere of normal society, the cards are quite frankly "stacked against them."

Insofar as it is desirable for the retardate to associate with the total group, any system of special classes that is a part of the regular school system will give the mentally retarded child, as Mary Huesman pointed out, "the benefit of contacts with normal children in the socialization activities of the regular schools."

. . . In some cases, children from special classes are even programmed, for certain subjects, to the regular classes. In this manner, we attempt to avoid as far as possible any stigma which may be attached to residence in special classes and also attempt to teach the mentally handicapped child to adjust better to contacts with the normal child. (**23**, p. 632)

TYPES OF SPECIAL CLASSES

Samuel Kirk and Orville Johnson have identified three major types of special classes, which they describe as follows:

The homogeneous special class . . . which is organized according to a small range of chronological and mental age abilities. . . . This organization has been considered superior to a departmentalized special school since one teacher is in charge of from twelve to eighteen children and is able to correlate activities, establish a mental-hygiene program, and educate children rather than emphasize subjects. . . .

The ungraded special class . . . in which all mentally handicapped children from six to sixteen years of age are enrolled. . . . The ungraded class is not the ideal type of organization, but it is the only practical solution for a small school system which has within the school only twelve to eighteen children who require assignment to a special class.

The modified special class. Many school systems are so small that they do not have a sufficient number of children for either a homogeneous special class or for an ungraded class. The modified special class organization is most commonly found in small school systems. . . . In practice, it takes a number of forms, some of which are: (1) the mentally handicapped children are assigned to a teacher for part of the day and placed in the regular grades the rest of the day. . . . (2) the mentally handicapped children are assigned to a teacher of a regular class who is interested in their problems. . . . (3) the mentally handicapped children are assigned to a regular grade but a special itinerant teacher is provided for tutoring purposes. . . . (4) the mentally handicapped children are sometimes placed in a special class with educationally-retarded children, behavior-problem children, or other kinds of children who are not adjusting to the problem of the regular grade. . . . (**29**, pp. 124–25)

The first group is, of course, considered the optimal one; group two may sometimes be necessary because of local conditions; the educational methodology involved in group three, if it can be dignified by such a phrase, is, by and large, indefensible.

For those children who are "slow-learning," special "opportunity classes" are sometimes established to determine whether they are actually of average intelligence, dull normal, or definitely retarded mentally. A really adequate system of diagnostic techniques, however, should minimize the need for the opportunity class—and, perhaps, do away with it altogether.

ESTABLISHED DEFINITIONS

In order to discuss the question of special classes for the mentally retarded, it is necessary first of all to determine which children, of those generally classed as inferior in intelligence, would be presumed to fall within the scope of such classes. And, in order to make such a determination, the various degrees of mental deficiency and the accompanying social handicaps must be determined to whatever degree is possible.

There is considerable variation in the terminology used in the area of mental handicap. The old classifications of the feeble-minded as *morons* if their IQ's are in the 50–75 range, *imbeciles* if between 25–50, and *idiots* if below 25, has been superseded by more realistic, and, by that very fact, far less precise terms. It is generally accepted that, broadly speaking, the educable mentally retarded will fall into the 50–75 IQ classification, all things being equal.

However, all things are seldom equal in this field. The IQ tests measure only certain types of intelligence; moreover, they can be "contaminated by such conditions as emotional overlay, sensory impairment, motor involvement or abnormal acculturation." Furthermore, the deviant's receptiveness to education is as much a result of his social adjustment as of his measureable IQ. As Wallin noted: "There is no sharp distinction between trainability and educability; there are varying degrees of trainability, just as there are varying degrees of educability." (**46**, p. 65) And neither is dependent entirely upon the IQ, although that is an integral factor.

Amy Allen (**2**, p. 7) and Marion Smith (**42**, p. 165) prefer to use the term "slow-learning" to describe all those who deviate in the direction of intellectual inadequacy. However, in the terms of reference used by other educators, the slow learner is not necessarily of inadequate mental capacity; he is demonstrably retarded only in academic accomplishment. Clyde Curran holds the opinion that slow learners may have potentials at either end of the intelligence scale (**10**, p. 1), while Baker and Martens restrict those so classified to individuals whose mental ability would fall between the average and the actually retarded, according them in general an IQ of 70–90. (**3**, p. 244) Kirk and Johnson consider the slow learner to be "slightly below average in learning ability but . . . not mentally handicapped." (**29,** p. 12) On the other hand, Ingram employs the term "slow-learning" to apply to both the mentally retarded and the mentally handicapped, terms which she uses interchangeably. She also would include in the slow-learning group those of slightly below average intelligence, also known as "dull normal." (**25,** p. 17) Baker simplifies the issue somewhat by devising a further classification to include those who appear to learn slowly, but are not, in fact, of low intelligence, describing them as the "educationally retarded," a category which appears to be similar to Curran's interpretation of "slow-learner." (**3,** p. 206).

In the Detroit psychological clinics, according to Baker, the terms "mentally subnormal" and "mentally retarded" are used "to designate children who are eligible candidates for the special classes provided by the schools. The term "feebleminded" is reserved as a legal definition for children of extremely retarded mental status who are usually committed to state schools for institutional training and permanent care." (**3,** p. 256) And Newland has employed the term "mentally retarded" "to refer to those exceptional children whose intellectual retardation is not so severe as to warrant their falling in the range of mental deficiency nor so slight as to warrant their being regarded as 'slow-learners.' " He accords them IQ's falling between 50 and 80. (**35,** p. 63)

Sarason uses "mental retardation" to refer to individuals who "function intellectually below the average of their peer groups but whose social adequacy is not in question or, if it is . . . there is the likelihood that the individual can learn to function independently and adequately in the community." The same investigator applies the term "mental deficiency" to refer to those individuals who are "socially inadequate as a result of an intellectual defect . . . which is essentially incurable." In his terminology, therefore, "whereas the mentally retarded may require *temporary,* specialized assistance, the mentally defective will *always* require it. (**41**, p. 442) Kirk and Johnson use the term "mentally handicapped" to refer to those children "who can be educated in special classes in the public schools." (**29**, p. 10)

Since there is all this confusion of terminology, the only method of achieving clarity would be to set up a group of arbitrary definitions. In this context, therefore, the terms "feebleminded" and "mentally handicapped" will be used to apply to *all* the intellectually inadequate. The terms "mentally retarded" and "mentally deficient" will substantially follow Sarason's interpretations, that is, the former referring to the educable mentally handicapped and the latter to the uneducable, noting that there is no clear-cut line of demarcation between the two—or, indeed between any of the divisions of intellectual capacity—and that certain of the investigators quoted may be using the terms differently. However, such deviations will always be clarified whenever they are not self-explanatory.

The term "slow-learning" will be used to describe an apparent academic disability in an individual which may result either from severe maladjustment or an underlying mental inadequacy. If the individual's demonstrated abilities and his potentialities prove to correlate, he will generally be classifiable in the group known as "dull normal," although sometimes he may prove actually retarded. If they do not, and he proves to be of average or above ability, he will fall in the group known as "educationally retarded."

No IQ limitations are set for the various categories, because it has been demonstrated not only that the IQ is not the only factor in establishing the quality of the deviation, but also that the original lower limit of 50 set for educability was unrealistic, and that children with IQ's as low as 35 (**46**, p. 153) can be taught. According to Daly and Cain, "some students with I.Q.'s as high as 80 and others with I.Q.'s of 50 or less can profit from the special training classes." (**11**, p. 26)

In general, this chapter will deal with the problems of the mentally retarded, meaning those retardates whose mental and social handicaps are not so severe as to prevent their being educated within the confines of the regular school system. The problems of the educationally retarded will be considered in a later chapter dealing with social maladjustment.

DIAGNOSIS

Problems and Procedures

The initial difficulties of identifying the mental retardate have been indicated to some extent in a previous chapter.[1] Either through a group intelligence test or as a result of his teacher's personal observation, or both, the child suspected of gross mental inadequacy should be referred to the school clinic, or, when there is no clinic, the guidance department. Sometimes a preschool child will be referred to the guidance service by the pediatrician, but this, although a desirable procedure which will spare the child a good deal of frustration in later life, is, unfortunately, not of frequent occurrence.

Under optimal conditions, after referral the child will be examined by a psychologist and given a battery of individual intelligence and achievement tests, plus personality and adjustment tests. In addition to the psychological examination, he should receive a complete physical checkup which will include sensory tests.

It is at this point that every effort should be made to determine whether the child's apparent mental handicap is real or the symptom of some physical or social disability. As Kirk and Johnson have emphasized, the child may be functioning at a low level, not because his intelligence is low, but because of some emotional disturbance or marked physical defect such as cerebral

[1] Chapter Two.

palsy, extremely poor vision, or poor hearing (**29**, p. 39), which is the reason a child must never be "diagnosed as mentally handicapped on the basis of his academic ability or achievement alone."

By the time a child reaches the middle elementary grades, all academic work, except mechanical arithmetic computation, is based upon his ability to read. If a child has a severe reading disability, he . . . may be suspected of being mentally handicapped. (**29**, p. 60)

Again, emotional maladjustment may hold a child back to an extent where he may appear retarded. More involved is the type of retardate known as an "idiot savant," who seems to have one special ability in which he may not only be in advance of his other capacities but may even show above-average talent in abstract terms.

Such a case was Sam, who was brought to the writer for counseling. This boy had been characterized as not only very dull but recalcitrant as well. However, after being placed in a special class, Sam manifested an unusual aptitude for music. He was given the opportunity to study music seriously, and today he is an internationally known composer. Yet, academically speaking, he never completed the equivalent of an ordinary education. Sam was definitely a rather unusual but not unheard of type of exceptional child, who is simultaneously gifted and retarded. If the boy's disability had not been diagnosed before it was too late, he might have grown up to be just another maladjusted, and possibly delinquent, individual. Tredgold has described retardates who were gifted in painting and sculpture as well as music, and others who were mathematical prodigies or who were able to perform amazing feats of memory. (**45**, pp. 310–11) Therefore, the retardate with one talent can still make a major contribution to our society with that talent, whether he becomes a painter like Pissarro or wins the $64,000 Question.

The state of California, in order to minimize the possibility of mistaken diagnosis, has suggested the following careful analysis of information concerning the suspected retardate in at least six areas of inquiry:

(a) Psychometric examination, including at least one verbal and one nonverbal test.

(b) Educational examination. School retardation of more than two or three years is suggestive of mental retardation.

(c) Social history. Persistent play with younger children and with simple games and materials is indicative but not conclusive evidence of mental retardation.

(d) Developmental history. The ages of walking, talking, and dentition, as well as the ages of establishing bowel and bladder control and habits of feeding and dressing, are often delayed in the mentally deficient * child. . . .

(e) Family history . . . evidence of nervous or mental disorders in parents, grandparents, and collaterals or other relatives . . . may serve to indicate the presence of pathological conditions, but strong clinical evidence is necessary to establish this. Limited understanding and slow development among siblings and the parents themselves is suggestive evidence. . . . [However] it is important to understand the family history and socio-economic background of the child in order to understand the degree of cultural deficiency that is contributing to limitations in the child's behavior. . . . severe cultural deficiency may contribute to the impression of pseudo mental deficiency. . . .

(f) Physical examination. A complete examination of physical status is necessary, including health history, nutritional condition, sensory acuity, anatomical abnormalities, and physiological, endochronological, and neurological dysfunction and pathology. . . . (15, pp. 6–7)

Techniques

Limited space precludes a thorough discussion of diagnostic techniques in this context. However, a listing of the most popular tests follows:

The *group intelligence tests* most favored are: Thurstone's Primary Mental Abilities, Detroit General Aptitudes and General Intelligence, Otis Quick-Scoring Mental Ability, Terman-McNemar Mental Ability, Pintner General Intelligence, Kuhlmann-Anderson Intelligence, and the California Mental Maturity.

The most-often used *individual intelligence test* is the Stanford-Binet. Others are: the Detroit Learning Aptitude, the Kuhlmann Mental Development, the Wechsler Intelligence Scale for Children (WISC), also Wechsler Adult Intelligence Scale (WAIS), the Minnesota Mental Development, the Cornell-Coxe Performance-Ability Scale, the Arthur Point Scale of Performance Tests, and the Porteus Maze Test.

The best-known *adjustment tests* are: the California Test of Personality, the Vineland Social Maturity Scale, and such association tests as Rogers' Word Association Test for Children, Schwartz's Social Situation Pictures for Children, the Rorschach, the Murray Thematic Apperception, and Bernreuter's Personality Inventory.

Achievement tests most often used are: the Metropolitan Achievement, the Gates Primary Reading, the Stanford Achievement, and California Achievement Tests.

Various other types of tests that may also be given are classified by Kirk and Johnson under the four headings of "(1) readiness tests, (2) tests of primary mental ability, (3) motor ability tests, and (4) vision and hearing tests. . . ." (**29**, p. 53)

There are other methods of determining mental retardedness besides these standardized tests. Viktor Lowenfeld has suggested creative activity as one means of determining the child's mentality to see if there is a discrepancy between what he produces and the norm for his age. (**30**, p. 304)

Although it is essential to give as many of the tests and test situations as possible for a completely objective evaluation of the child's capacities—or as completely objective an evaluation as can be achieved under prevailing conditions—they should serve primarily to confirm the conclusions drawn by the skilled investigator, for, as Baker says, "a well-trained psychologist is able to form a good estimate of the brightness or dullness of an individual from the type of responses without computing the actual I.Q." (3, p. 259)

PSYCHOLOGY OF THE MENTAL DEVIANT

Psychological Characteristics

Although the general objective of education for the mental retardate is the same as education for any other kind of child, in order to organize an educational program specifically geared to the requirements of the child of low intelligence, it becomes necessary to determine what traits are characteristic of the mental deviant that set him apart as a total individual from the normal child as a total individual—aside from his inferior mentality per se. Undoubtedly these traits arise as a result of his mental retardation, rather than existing alongside it as accompanying handicaps, but they must be considered as factors in themselves in order for an efficient educational methodology to be developed in this area. And it is even more important for the deviant than the normal child that his education should be based on the principle of adjusting him to his environment in terms of the skills and knowledge that can be imparted to him, rather than a stressing of those skills and that knowledge for their own sake. George Devereux has justly observed, in reporting on his own therapeutic methods, that—

. . . Nowhere more than in the case of the defective must we aim at a truly rational and genuinely "person-centered" rather than "problem-centered" education. Nowhere else must we pursue quite so consistently the goal of patterned humanization and ethnicalization rather than brute training in disparate skills. (13, p. 157)

The area in which the deviant comes closest to normalcy is that of physical capability. Even though the mental retardate frequently is somewhat below average in physique and coordination and often tends to suffer from poor hearing and defective eye-sight, nonetheless it is generally agreed, as Ingram has observed, that—

The mentally retarded child approaches nearer to the average child in sensory acuity and motor ability than in more definitely intellectual processes. The majority approximate success at their chronological-age level most nearly in processes which call for eye-hand coordination and for motor response. (25, p. 33)

Most educators also tend to be in accord with the rather obvious proposition that mental retardates as a rule will have a greater comprehension of the concrete rather than the abstract. They are, Wallin has remarked, " 'thing-minded,' 'eye-minded,' and 'ear-minded,' rather than 'word-minded' or 'thought-minded.' " Directly derived from this limitation of theirs is the handicap Devereux has described as looming largest in the disability syndrome of the mental retardate, namely, "his inability to perceive the underlying pattern of things and to relate instrumental values to ultimate goals." (13, p. 157)

Corollary with the subnormal's incompetence in dealing with the abstract is his difficulty in "the use and comprehension of verbal and numerical symbols." In reporting on the subnormal girl, Abel and Kinder have directed attention to the fact that "it is in her restricted vocabulary, her improper use of abstract terms, her inadequate comprehension of verbal instructions, and her poor performance on tests requiring verbal ability" that she "shows her limitations most acutely." (1, p. 10) Irwin Goldstein has described all of these drawbacks to the fact that—

. . . the retardate lacks or possesses but to a superficial degree the ability to draw upon past experiences to solve his immediate problems. Thus the retardate is incapable of logical thought, unable to make generalizations or work with abstractions. (20, p. 209)

Robson has observed that the retardate "may be quick at grasping spatial relations, but only in connection with concrete things,"

(**40**, p. 125), and Kirk and Johnson point out that mentally deficient children are "deficient in quantitative thinking." (**29**, p. 169)

It would follow, therefore, that the reasoning powers of the mentally handicapped would be of an exceedingly limited nature. "They fail to detect errors and absurdities in statements and in commonplace situations." Abel and Kinder have remarked, further, that the subnormal child "has more trouble than the normal in understanding causal relationships." For instance, he believes much more implicitly than the normal child "that if you do something wrong, even unintentionally, you will inevitably be punished by an outside authority." (**1**, p. 10)

The attention spans of mental retardates are short, and their powers of association are small. As might be expected, they are as deficient in imagination as they are in intelligence, but this trait may seem less obvious because of the unrealistic attitude toward society and themselves that so many of them—particularly the lower-intelligence groups—hold. Catherine Chipman describes the mental deviant as one who "lives very much in the present, is childishly egocentric, usually labile emotionally, and, running through the whole syndrome is his inability to learn as easily or usefully as his normal fellow." (**7**, p. 195)

It is the general consensus that mental deficients are lacking in powers of self-criticism, have limited judgment, and lack foresight. Moreover, Morton has amplified the egocentricity concept by stating that "essentially narcissistic in nature," the mental retardate "seldom has very deep feeling toward others." Deviants may completely fail to appreciate the fact that it is necessary to respect the rights of other people. (**34**, p. 133). "Many retardates," Wallin agrees, "are asocial and some are antisocial." (**46**, p. 257) Unable to accept responsibility and extremely immature for their age level, the deviants are given to unpredictable emotional outbursts (**1**, p. 18) which can turn them into serious behavior problems. In fact, Garrison has pointed out that the retarded individual may well tend to amorality, since it requires a mental age of at least ten or twelve, and probably more, to enable an individual to develop the ability to distinguish between the most elementary principles of correct and incorrect behavior. (18, p. 187) However, the mentally retarded should not be considered delinquent per se, for it is as much of a mistake to assume that all individuals of inadequate intelligence are antisocial as to assume that all individuals who are antisocial are inadequate in intelligence. As the Pollocks have commented:

Whether the retarded child is dangerous or not depends to a very large degree on the extent to which he has been neglected or kept in the background. If he has been left to himself too much, he will seek to imitate the most dramatic actions he is aware of, in order to attract attention to himself. (38, p. 5)

The deviant's motivations, according to Daly and Cain, are frequently "inadequate" and their drives "erratic." (11, p. 116) In individual cases, the retardate may show still more marked psychological deviations from the norm than does his group considered as a whole. Wallin has pointed out that the lower-grade deviant may even lack "certain drives of innate tendencies, such as curiosity, playfulness, and constructiveness, which are essential for learning or for mental growth." (46, p. 119)

Mental retardates will have a greater backlog of frustration experiences than the average, partly as a result of societal neglect or inadequacy, partly as a result of what Morton has described as the deviant's "failure to realize his limitations." He does not suffer from a knowledge of his own defect as children with other handicaps do so warpingly, as "the more retarded the child the less he realizes his condition." However, to him, the series of inexplicable failures with which he is faced at every turn "may lead to total personality disintegration." (34, p. 133)

Satisfactory adjustment, even on his own level, is usually not characteristic of the mental retardate, not because he is incapable

of such adjustment, but because, as Marion Smith has mentioned
in connection with her experiences in teaching the retarded—

. . . Almost all the children who come to me have been kicked around.
. . . The average retarded boy or girl is an exile not only in society,
on the street, in the school, but in his own home. . . . (**42**, p. 14)

What is particularly unfortunate is the fact that the high-grade
retardate is far more likely to become maladjusted than the low-
grade, because his deficiences are not so apparent. As Mabel
Elliott and Francis Merrill have pointed out, while "the obvious
imbecilic and idiotic and even the moronic groups are set off from
the rest by their social inadequacies . . . the undetected dul-
lards are expected to live up to the demands of the group." As a
result, when a crisis arises or when their emotions are excessively
disturbed, "they may fail to make the necessary adjustment"; in
consequence, this group, rather than those of the lowest-grade
intelligence, manifests a tendency to become "personally disorganized." (**16**, p. 49)

Applying These Characteristics to Educational Needs

A thorough knowledge of the mental retardate's psychological
problems is necessary in order effectively to develop a sound educational program adapted to his needs. Entirely too many schools
have resolved the difficulty of educating the retarded simply (although they have embraced the principle of special education to
the extent of establishing separate classes for them) by teaching
the contents of standard curricula in these cases until such time
as the children have reached the legal age for dropping out of
the school. The only "special" factor in such instances is that the
work is taught at a lower pace than normal and with an exhaustive amount of repetition. This method, Kirk and Johnson have
observed, "has been known as a 'watered-down curriculum' and
has been frowned upon by most specialists in the field of the education of the mentally handicapped." (**29,** p. 85)

Perhaps the retardate will feel less frustrated in a special class formed of his own intellectual peers, but otherwise he will derive little more profit from classes of this kind than if he were left to vegetate in the back of the regular ones until he is free to leave school, learning little or nothing and probably suffering humiliation, bewilderment, and, if he is not too handicapped to sense it, outright rejection. In effect, those school administrators who refuse to put forth the effort to revise the curricula to meet the needs of the educationally neglected are simply admitting—implicitly, if not explicitly—that they do not attach much credence to the avowed purposes of education in our American democracy.

In order for a really adequate system of education for the mental retardate to be organized and established, due consideration must be given to the retardate's particular differences from the norm, for, as Sarason has stressed—

. . . It is not enough to put a child in a special class. . . . What is required is an analysis and description of (a) the ways in which the retardation has affected the child's conception of himself and others; (b) the way in which the child has defended himself against the recognition of his limitations; and (c) the manner in which his retardation has influenced his handling in crucial areas of functioning: home, school, and play. It is only when the total functioning of the child is considered that one can plan a program adequate to *that* child's needs. . . . (41, pp. 459–60)

Many of the psychological characteristics of the deviant as noted in the aforegoing section may seem so obvious as to be hardly worth drawing to the attention of anyone with the remotest knowledge of the principles upon which educational psychology is based. However, it seems evident from the way many so-called special classes are organized that the educators responsible for the organization of such classes either are unaware of these disability characteristics or have ignored them. The charitable interpretation is that these educators have not consciously isolated these differences in their minds when working out their programs. However, not one subject should be included in the curriculum without having its form, content, and future methods of teaching tested against each aspect of the deficient's total personality.

First of all, the deviant's close-to-average competency in manual skills suggests, according to Ingram, that the majority of them will enjoy "the manipulation of materials and the actual operations in the construction of any product," and that they "can generally be taught to be proficient in hand skills. Practical arts and the 'doing' experiences should, therefore, play a major part in their education." (**25**, p. 33)

From mental retardates' inability to think in abstract terms, it would follow that they must, in Ingram's words, "learn through concrete experiences, that numerous special instances for applying an idea or principle must be provided in directing [them] toward generalization and that desirable concepts, habits, and attitudes must be developed carefully." (**25**, p. 34) Each subject must be taught in the context of its specific application and with as many pertinent examples and situations related to the child's normal living experience as possible. Wallin has observed that—

. . . It is . . . of prime importance, in teaching, to use objects, representations, illustrations, demonstrations, movies, film strips, television, excursions, dramatizations, puppet shows, activity projects and units, and real schoolroom experiences, rather than words, symbols, descriptions, explanations, rules, principles, and abstractions. . . . (**46**, p. 88)

And Ingram has suggested, in regard to the methods that should be used in instructing the mental retardate:

As satisfactory development and adjustment of the mental retardate are so largely dependent upon planned procedures, the child should be carefully guided in learning situations that will develop specific knowledge, skills, attitudes, and habits that will function in life situations. In other words, the desirable choice and organization of materials, of curriculum content and of methods for the slow-learning are those that will aid in making learning specific, concrete, and directly functional in life situations. (**25**, p. 34)

However, this is more difficult of achievement than it may seem on the surface for, as Daly and Cain have pointed out, "a student's range of interests rarely exceeds his range of experience." Since the retardate's range of interests is unusually limited, this factor "presents a serious problem for curriculum planners to solve." (**11**, p. 117) It must be remembered, Birch and Stulcker emphasize, that normal children acquire as a matter of course in their daily lives a good deal of information and habits that the mentally retarded can learn only through specific instructions. (**5**) Therefore, again, care must be taken not to overlook what would be the obvious in the case of normal children.

Although the excessive repetition so often used to the point of abuse in such classes is not recommended, it is undeniable that the mentally retarded child does need considerably more drill and review than does the average one. And the mental retardate is less hostile to monotony than the average child. As a matter of fact, Wallin has reported that—

. . . Many of these children are not averse to doing the same thing again and again; in fact, some delight in it. This, of course, has its fortunate aspect in that mental deficients are willing to stay on routine jobs. . . . Nevertheless, there is little need for purely formal drills in the special classes, except for low-grade children in developing simple skills as a basis for the more complex reaction patterns. (**46**, p. 193)

From the fact that retardates are devoid of judgment and responsibility, Goodenough theorizes that "they are less able to manage their own lives and conduct their own affairs with the prudence and forethought requisite for successful living under the complexities of modern society." In consequence, she feels, "they must be willing to depend more than do their fellows upon the guidance of others." (**21**, p. 245) However, Martens interprets the same characteristics less rigidly, explaining that "many mentally retarded young people . . . while intellectually inadequate have a good deal of common sense and can learn to manage their own affairs fairly well." (**31**, p. 77)

As a result of such children's proneness to emotional outbursts, Goodenough suggests that "the modern stress upon 'self-expression' must be exercised with caution in the case of the mentally deficient child," for "he may express much that would better have been concealed." (**21**, p. 245)

On the whole, however, the mental retardate's emotional make-up is like anyone else's. As Ruth Gegenheimer observed, he "hears the same radio programs that we do, sees the same movies, and it may be that both are really planned for him." (**19**, p. 97) "The three elements of need or purpose, recurrence, and success" are as essential in his education as in educating the average. Of even more importance is "the element of success," for the mentally retarded child has "greater need than the average . . . for special planned opportunities in his school life for achieving some socially recognized success." (**26**, p. 134) In consequence, educators should take great pains not only, as Wallin suggests, to utilize the existing drives and interests of the child "as an entering wedge" to his mind, but to develop whatever capability he may have in the area of those drives and interests. (**46**, p. 149) As Devereux has recommended:

> In most instances, even a minimal talent should be encouraged and fostered, simply because this gratifies the habitually frustrated defective, increases his self-confidence and venturesomeness, and improves his general emotional adjustment. (**13**, p. 152)

In fact, if there is any one principle upon which the education of the mental deficient should be based, it is that of utilizing what he *can* do as a foundation upon which to build all the teaching he will receive. In Clara Middleton's words:

Instructors should think of mentally retarded children as those who are capable of learning something and then try to find out what this "something" is. . . . (**33**, p. 187)

THE CURRICULUM

Broadly speaking, then, the same factors are used as a basis upon which to establish curricula for either the exceptional or the average child. The difference is one of degree rather than kind. As Middleton has pointed out, "in all areas of learning, the normal child deviates from a standard pattern or method of learning." But "the mentally retarded child is even more of a nonconformist." (**33**, p. 188)

Frampton and Gall have further developed this premise by stating that—

If the theory is accepted that the basic philosophy in the education of the exceptional is preparation for living in a world of non-handicapped people, then the same basic principles of curriculum construction apply to both the exceptional and the non-exceptional, except for such changes as are indicated by special needs and the conditions arising therefrom. There must be a core of content of learning and experience; there must be definitely revealed goals at various points; there must be possibilities for enrichment. . . . The curriculum must be flexible enough to be adaptable to the needs of the group and to each individual in it. . . .

With specific reference to the problems of the mentally handicapped, there must be modifications in the direction of a minimum academic week, with the introduction of pre-vocational programs and other means of determining special non-academic abilities and with subsequent change or adjustment to a program better fitted to the individual's abilities and needs. (**17**, pp. 162–63)

The curriculum for the mentally retarded, therefore, should consist primarily of subjects which can be given a practical application to the requirements of his daily living requirements which would include the necessity for self-expression as well as the necessity of making a living. Goals must not be set too high; unless Devereux' principle of setting the "level of aspiration" to comply "with the inescapable demands of reality" is utilized (13, p. 173), the major purpose of the special class is defeated. The acquiring of academic skills should be given some weight as a practical matter, but academic achievement should never be stressed.

The ordinary systems of marking and grading are invalid in this area. "In the education of seriously retarded children," Martens has observed, "grades as such have no place. Age and physical and social maturity are the important determinations in the selection of content." (31, p. 2) Even where the higher-grade retardates are concerned, they should never be judged according to the same criteria as the average student, even within their own peer groups. Isackson and Roessel have pointed out that "the retention of grade standards, competitive marking, and grade repetition are unrealistic attempts at solutions for a problem that is inherent in life itself."

Since life outside the school recognizes and rewards a great variety of aptitudes and combinations of aptitudes, the school should do the same. Just as there are all sorts of people or people with different abilities, so there should be different things in the school for pupils with different abilities to do and learn. (26, p. 344)

"A real program for the retardate," Daniel F. Graham wrote, "is more concerned with functional factors rather than with symbols or vicarious activities. . . . First and primary should be the accomplishment of self-help." (22, p. 38) Acting in accordance with this principle, the state of California has formulated the following goals for the education—or, as Daly and Cain prefer to put it, "training"—of the mentally retarded:

> Begin work without urging
> Finish what is started
> Put away materials
> Depend on themselves

Participate in creative work
Listen to good music
Help others
Protect health
Master tool subjects at ability level
Accept limitations
Communicate

Get along with people
Work co-operatively
Listen while others speak
Participate in school functions, e.g., parties
Make new friends
Understand club procedures
Participate in organized public recreation
Prepare to be homemakers

Develop hand skills
Respect hand work
Develop work habits
Apply for a job
Perform part-time work
Contribute help at home
Save and bank money
Spend money wisely

Become a contributing school citizen
Find information needed
Use basic vocabulary necessary for functioning citizenship
Understand civic processes as they relate to the individual
(11, pp. 105–106)

The curriculum for the mentally retarded child may be sub-divided into four general areas, none of which should be considered as an entity separate in itself. Instead, each should be organized as a coordinative part of each one of the others. These four areas are (1) the social, (2) the physical, (3) the academic, and (4) the occupational. The main emphasis of the curriculum should be placed, as Martens says, "upon planning the best education that can be given over a period of nine or ten years, rather than upon the completion of grade requirements." (31, p. 13)

Social Training

Social training is the most important area of development for the mentally retarded child, who will not, as a rule, learn to get along with other people and adjust to his environment without specific aid. Therefore, as Keehan says, "the development of desirable attitudes should be the major aim in the education of these children rather than the gathering of informational material." (27, p. 5) The other three aspects of the child's training should not only each be correlated with the others, but should also be subordinated to this category wherever it is necessary that one take pre-eminence, for, as Martens has said and most other educators have agreed, teaching these children "to live in a social environment is far more important than to attempt to teach them to read." Insofar as it is possible, they should be given "an appreciation of social and civic values," and every opportunity should be given them to participate in social and civic activities, both in the school and in the community itself. (31, p. 17) Emphasis should be placed upon the acquisition of such desirable attributes as honesty, obedience, and truthfulness, in which the mental retardate is often found sadly lacking, not because he is basically "bad," but because it has occurred to no one to teach them to him.

Kirk and Johnson remarked that the vocational training the retardate will receive—no matter how successful it has been from the mechanical standpoint—is not enough of itself to ensure that the retardate will be able to get and hold a job. Many other factors are involved.

. . . Success on the job is going to depend on getting to the job on time, personal appearance, manners, getting along with other employees and the employer, personal health, ability to handle money wisely, safety on the job, responsibility in following directions and carrying the task through to completion, and many other personal characteristics which are developed from early childhood. The school should attempt from the beginning of the child's school career to establish those habits and attitudes which will develop a responsible, efficient worker, regardless of how unskilled the job is. Even reading, writing, and arithmetic are parts of occupational education, since a child will require a minimum of the academic skills in order to read signs, simple directions, and possibly to communicate by means of writing even at a simple level. (29, p. 119)

As Frances Coakley has so aptly stated, "it is not the mental level which is the primary determinant of an individual's success in a job, but, instead, the personal traits and characteristics which he possesses." (8, p. 304)

One factor in this area that holds true of all children but is especially vital in the case of the retardate is that the child's adjustment to society depends largely upon his parents' adjustment to him. Therefore, wherever it is possible, the school should pay considerable attention to parental education and contact here. As Doyle, Bower, and Daly have written, frequent consultations with parents will have the advantage of providing—

. . . opportunities to explain the advantages to be derived from placement in a special class and to counsel parents who need help in understanding and accepting the limitations of their child. Some parents of mentally retarded children may have hostilities against schools and teachers; others may hold entirely unrealistic conceptions of the learning abilities of their child. . . . (15, p. 20)

The social training applies with equal force to the teachers themselves. "If the retarded pupil is to be really happy he must have guidance and supervision that will help him to face his handicap squarely and to find the avenues in life through which he can give acceptable service." (31, p. 29) Actually, there is one primary goal toward which all education of the handicapped should be directed. In the words of Isacksen and Roessel, "children must be accepted as they are before they can be taught to be different or to improve." (**26**, p. 345)

Physical Training

In its narrowest sense, physical training for the retardate means giving him a system of regular exercises to improve his motor ability and muscular coordination. It is of immense therapeutic value, too, for here he will have the opportunity to enjoy himself through participation in sports and games, and these purely motor aspects of this part of his education may be coordinated very effectively with his music studies.

Such physical training is especially important for mentally handicapped children, since it gives them an opportunity to get rid of a good deal of excess energy that could otherwise be diverted to destructive or, at least, harmful pursuits which might result in delinquency. In general, although the majority of retardates are almost equal to the average child in physical abilities, as has been stated, their physical training programs should be planned and carried out separately from those of the other children because it will take them longer to understand directions and the rules of the game; and any misapprehensions or insufficiencies in this area can prove dangerous not only in terms of social adjustment but from the viewpoint of simple safety. Furthermore, an undifferentiated program will deprive them of their best opportunity to excel.

Many school administrators object to instituting special programs of physical training for the mentally retarded on the grounds that such programs would be an entirely unnecessary expense. These administrators contend that the establishment of special classes for academic work is enough (if, indeed, not too much), but that segregated training in an area where the retardate so nearly approached normal cannot be considered other than a luxury feature of the curriculum.

Yet, the same administrators continue to give enthusiastic support to their schools' football, basketball, baseball, and track teams, all of which, in essence, are established for as small a minority of the students as would be a comparable program for the mentally handicapped. In fact, varsity teams actually comprise a type of special education for the physically superior to the same degree that a planned physical education program for the handicapped is special education for the physically or mentally inferior.

Undoubtedly the varsity teams do provide a vicarious source of satisfaction for the entire student body (as well as prestige for the school), and so they are less limited in scope from the viewpoint of identification than they are from the viewpoint of participation. However, the mental retardates stand far more in need of satisfaction experiences—vicarious or otherwise—than the average child who is far more likely to have made a comparatively satisfactory adjustment to life.

However, a physical training program for the mentally retarded child should involve far more than mere motor activity, important though that assuredly is. It should also involve giving the proper training to his body, so that he knows how to care for his own health and safety. It should involve teaching him to select the right things to eat and to know how to eat them in the proper manner, and it should involve teaching him to stand straight and keep himself as neat and attractive as possible—by bathing and changing his clothing frequently and acquiring agreeable social habits. In short, his physical training should teach him not only to keep himself healthy but to make himself as acceptable as possible to a society whose initial attitude toward him will—regrettable as the fact may be—almost always be hostile.

Academic Training

The individual of low-grade mentality is often able to grasp a sizable amount of the academic subjects—a good deal more than was once thought possible—if the curriculum is a realistic one, geared to the retardate's life experience, beginning with his school and home life, and branching out to include his community experience or potential community experience. Most of the mentally handicapped can acquire a basic education in the tool subjects, if the practical application of each course of instruction is stressed, so that from the very commencement of his studies he can readily grasp the use to which these otherwise apparently meaningless forms and symbols are destined to be put.

As a matter of fact, even in the regular classes, too often the child will be required to absorb a series of concepts which, as far as he can see, are of no earthly use to him. If every school course would include a preliminary orientation in which the teacher explained to the pupils just how the material she is preparing to teach them can be applied practically to their daily lives, either currently or in the future, she will find the learning attitudes in her classes immeasurably improved. Such orientation is desirable for even the average and gifted student; it is absolutely necessary for the mentally handicapped one.

However, in certain cases, notably where the handicap is very great, teaching academic subjects is of such limited value that it is doubtful whether it should even be attempted. Martens has, in fact, recommended flatly that—

. . . For children who have a mental age below six years, regardless of their chronological age, that part of the curriculum dealing with reading, writing, and arithmetic should be wholly omitted. (31, p. 19)

English, of course, is the most important of all the tool subjects, for it is the basic tool of communication. Its component parts—which should be taught as such, rather than as separate studies—are speech, reading, writing, and spelling. Speech is of major importance for the deviant, for he usually has some difficulty with his articulation and very often manifests other speech impediments. He should be shown how necessary clear speech is *to him* in making his needs, aims, and desires known to his fellow students, his teacher, and his family. Later, he may be shown its wider range of uses, as, for example, in talking on the phone, applying for a job, or speaking to a census taker.

Reading should be taught first as a means of understanding such necessary public communications as street signs and directions, telephone directories, and newspapers. Afterward, when the retardate becomes more proficient at this skill, he can be introduced to some of the simpler forms of literature. Unfortunately, as Daly and Cain have pointed out, "there are few reading books on the markets that meet the needs of these students" (11, p. 58), so that the teacher may be forced to resort to the preparation of suitable material herself. The technique of writing should be presented as necessary in order to write a letter or fill out one of the many forms that all citizens are at one time or another called upon to cope with in this well-regimented, well-documented age of ours. Spelling should be taught specifically as an essential part of writing.

Arithmetic can be shown to the deficient as a necessary technique for such indispensable activities as telling time, reading a calendar, making change, paying bills, and shopping. Even in the realm of science, the mental deficient is capable of acquiring a good deal of information. The more complex sciences will be, of course, out of his reach, but he can derive a great deal of profit and pleasure from nature study, and even the rudiments of chemistry can be imparted to him by means of many fascinating daily-life applications. For those boys taking shopwork, the elements of whatever technical science may be involved in that particular kind of shopwork might be profitably given.

As for history and geography, they may be taught in very limited local applications, expanding outward with reference to the retardates' demonstrated capacities for absorbing the material in these areas. It might be most feasible to teach these as part of a general course in social studies which can include a variety of subjects in this area, according to the students' abilities.

The arts, having an emotional as well as an intellectual appeal, offer particularly great opportunities for the development of the mentally retarded. Often such children will find themselves able to express through the medium of one of the arts what they are unable to express verbally. Music is an excellent pursuit for them; most mental retardates can learn to sing, dance, or participate in rhythm groups and even play a simple instrument. Arts and crafts are also splendid, both as a cultural and as an occupational technique. Often it is through exploratory experiences in this area that mentally retarded children can acquire a functional command of the English language and the ability to understand quantities.

Occupational Training

Manual training has, perhaps, sometimes been stressed too much as a suitable pursuit for mentally retarded children at the cost of their academic training. However, it certainly is of the utmost importance, both as an area in which they can develop a certain amount of proficiency and as sound vocational training for the future, because it is here that they are most likely to display those special abilities which will later assist them to earn a living. Richard Hungerford asserted, in fact, that the focal point of the whole curriculum should be here:

. . . the whole program for the mentally retarded must be built around the achieving of vocational and social competence, for here, if anywhere, the retardate will most nearly approach normalcy. (24, p. 2)

Gardening, woodwork, and homemaking are recommended at the start for both boys and girls, with, of course, differing emphases for the two sexes. Later, girls will specialize in cooking, cleaning, taking care of children, sewing, and working in the laundry. The boys will learn shopwork and carpentry plus such special types of training as individual schools may be able to offer, as, for example, tailoring and shoe repairing. Surprisingly enough, Daly and Cain discovered, "typewriting classes have definite possibilities for mentally retarded students" (11, p. 77), and, of course, here the vocational training can be combined with the academic and typewriting tied in with their studies in English. Some special-class programs in California included a course of instruction in driver education which was, Cain and Daly remarked, "the most successful piece of curriculum work" they observed while preparing their study. (11, p. 78)

In 1937, Martens described the types of occupational instruction which the public schools in forty-one cities were offering to the mentally retarded pupils in special classes. The boys were taught brush- and watchmaking, automobile repair, electrical and metal work, pressing, and shoe repair. The girls were taught cooking and household care, table service, child care, and home nursing. Both received instruction in cafeteria, barber, and beauty parlor service; garmentmaking, laundry, "commercial," and repair work; general arts and crafts; so-called industrial training; woodworking; leather tooling; printing; weaving; diversified shop training; and farming. (32, p. 158) Since then the variety of courses offered, as well as the number of schools in which they are offered, has increased.

In addition to the vocational courses, both boys and girls may acquire practical vocational experience within the school environment, as, for example, work in the physical education department, the school cafeteria, nurse's office, or custodial department. It is eminently desirable that a school make such arrangements wherever possible, for, as Daly and Cain have stated, a work experience of this nature yields "dividends far superior to the classroom routines" so far as giving the students "recognition and success in at least one phase of their school work" goes. (11, p. 65) Many mental retardates work part time after school or on Saturdays, and sometimes the schools themselves organize a correlated work-study curriculum, which is an excellent way of preparing the mental retardates for their work lives.

Most educable mental retardates are expected to earn their own livings when they become adults, and, indeed, there is no reason they should not do so, for, owing to the current labor shortage, there are numerous opportunities in industry and service for *well-trained* individuals of lower mental output. Therefore, it is particularly important, according to Marcella Douglas—as well as many other investigators—that the social aspects of jobholding be stressed in the vocational classes along with work efficiency.

We must strive to have the girl or boy accept and be conscious of the individual's importance in a job and to take pride in doing his part to the best of his ability. (14, p. 289)

It has come to be recognized that the aforementioned well-adjusted mental retardate very often can turn out to be a far more stable worker than the person of average intelligence when it comes to low-grade routine jobs. "Frequently," Tiffin wrote, "persons scoring very low in mental ability tasks consistently do better in simple repetitive tasks than do persons whose mental age is average or above." (43, p. 58) Such individuals are able to endure monotony far better than the average individual, and will take pride in a job that no one else would take pride in simply because it gives them a sense of self-sufficiency and personal worth. Some of the best factory operatives, Davies has pointed out, are the mentally handicapped, for "they are the steady, plodding, faithful workers who can best stand the humdrum toil of machine work." (12, p. 373)

There are many occupations where a mental retardate can be employed satisfactorily. Among these are:

General Industry

factory, machine, leather workers
metal polishers
welders
unskilled labor
packers
labelers

Garment Industry

machine operators
finishers
button-hole makers
tailors
milliners

Transport

longshoremen
teamsters
truckdrivers' helpers
loaders

Communications

telephone servicemen
telephone linemen

Building Trades

carpenters
bricklayers
painters, painters' helpers

Retail Stores

sales, shipping, and warehouse
    clerks
elevator operators
packers and wrappers

Restaurants

waiters and waitresses
dishwashers
cooks' helpers
busboys
countermen and girls
soda clerks

Hotels

elevator operators
bus boys

Institutions

porters
matrons
maids
laundry workers

Building Maintenance

janitors
porters
elevator operators
repairmen
furnacemen
doormen
window cleaners

Farm

unskilled labor
animal husbandry
egg candlers

Service

messenger and delivery boys
handymen
bootblacks, shoe repairmen
caddies, bowling alley attendants
bakers, butcher's helpers
newsboys
street cleaners, garbage collectors
barbers and beauty parlor opera-
    tors
laundry and cleaning and dyeing
    workers
domestic servants

Other

gas station attendants
miners

(**4, 28, 36, 46**)

In order to ensure that the mental retardate will find his niche in the working world, it is important that an efficient system of vocational guidance be included in each school's program of occupational training. The handicapped youth himself stands particularly in need of such guidance, because he is "for the most part . . . quite unconcerned" about the kind of job he will get when he leaves school. (11, p. 56) Even though the well-trained retardate is capable of adjusting himself to the community, most of the mentally handicapped would be more successful if they are assisted in finding the job that, Wallin states—

. . . fits the total needs of the individual, compatible with his abilities, disabilities, interests, and mental and physical health needs, and that will result in maximum job performance and job satisfaction. This may mean a therapeutic job for a neuropsychiatric case—e.g., quiet, creative work in a non-irritating environment for a talented neurotic. For a moron, it might mean automatic, repetitive factory work, or directed farm work, or semi-skilled routine. The most important consideration is placement in a job where the handicap is not a disadvantage provided the applicant has the requisite general ability and the technical skill needed for the job. (47, p. 294)

RESULTS OF SPECIAL CLASSES

In a pilot study conducted by the investigator in a city with a population of 175,000, a hundred men and women were chosen at random from the following job titles: hotel porters; elevator operators; highway laborers; barbers; workers in paper-box factories, laundries, and commercial bakeries; wrappers; bricklayers; fishermen; janitors and custodial workers; laborers in a bottling plant; and packers employed in furniture moving. The educational range of these workers was from two years of schooling to completion of the tenth grade in high school, with the average school grade completed the sixth.

Although there was no special effort to limit the study to those of low intelligence, save to confine the job titles to those which did not minimally require more than a low intelligence, a check of school records revealed that the average IQ of the group was 68, the lowest being 48 and the highest 104. However, although most of these workers would fall into the group classified as retarded, only a part of their number had attended special-education classes. A larger number of them, particularly those in the older group, had simply been classified as uneducable and had dropped out of grade school.

This brief study could not attempt to evaluate the effectiveness of the vocational training given these individuals, because obviously those whose training was wholly inadequate would not be employed. Therefore, it was assumed, and, indeed, proved to be the case when the employers were queried, that all the persons included within the scope of this study were satisfactory as far as job performance went. But it was significant that fifteen of the younger workers who had been placed in special classes while they were still attending the public schools also were considered to be the most alert and the most personally adequate workers by their employers. In addition, those who had special-class training appeared to be leading far more stable home lives than those who had not.

On the other hand, approximately 35 per cent of those who had no special education were not judged by their employers to be very stable or reliable. In addition to leading unsatisfactory home lives and being bad credit risks, they tended to have poor records of absenteeism and drinking. Several, in fact, had police records. In other words, although the members of the group that did not have special-class training were able to do their jobs well enough, they did not succeed in acquiring personal and social adequacy.

Harold Phelps studied a group of 163 individuals who had been enrolled in the special classes of the Ohio school system for a median of 3.4 years, and who had entered the classes at a median age of 12.7—which represents relatively late placement. After commenting that, "as would be expected, the vast majority were employed in the semi-skilled, unskilled, and service areas," he went on to state that—

The variables which stood out most clearly in terms of good adjustment on the job were in the areas of attitudes and personal habits. This leads to the conclusion that the school should above all produce in the mental retardate attitudes of wanting to do one's best and a willingness to do his share of every job. He should also be given help in making the most of his appearance and manners so that he will be acceptable to employers and peers. (37, p. 91)

Coakley tabulated the job titles, duties, and wages secured by thirty-seven mental deficients who obtained wartime employment through the United States Employment Service in Ramsey County, Minnesota. All of them did well in war work and earned salaries up to sixty-seven dollar per week. Among the conclusions she drew from the study is the fact that there is no apparent relationship between wages and IQ. (8, p. 306)

Numerous other studies have been made to show that the mental retardate who has been properly trained can fill a functioning place in our own society, which is all that we can ask of any individual. However, proper training means, not only that he be given certain mechanical skills and techniques whereby he can earn a living, but also that he be taught other far more important skills and techniques whereby he can make himself a functioning part of the group to which he belongs, both at work and at home. Even the role of wife and mother is filled more capably by those mentally retarded girls who have received special-class training. (4, p. 428)

The social skills, even more than the vocational ones, cannot be taught to the mentally handicapped in the regular classes, because the needs of average students differ so drastically from those of the handicapped students, especially in the formative years. They must be separated during childhood and adolescence in order that they may live together peaceably during adulthood. Hence, special classes are the only answer.

References

1. ABEL, THEODORA M., and E. F. KINDER. The *Subnormal Adolescent Girl*. New York: Columbia University Press, 1942.
2. ALLEN, AMY. *Let Us Look at the Slow Learning Child*. Columbus, Ohio: Ohio State Department of Education, 1949. Pp. 7–21.
3. BAKER, HARRY J. *Introduction to Exceptional Children*. (Rev. ed.) New York: Macmillan Co., 1953.
4. BIJOU, SIDNEY W., MILDRED H. AINSWORTH, and MERRIT R. STOCKEM. "The Social Adjustment of Mentally Retarded Girls Paroled from the Wayne County Training School," *Journal of Mental Deficiency*, XLVII (April, 1943), 422–28.
5. BIRCH, JACK W., and EDWARD H. STULCKER. *Solving Problems of Problem Children*. Bloomington, Ill.: Public School Publishing Company, 1956.
6. BURTT, HAROLD F. *Principles of Employment Psychology*. New York: Harper and Brothers, 1942.
7. CHIPMAN, CATHERINE. "Psychological Variations Within a Homogeneous Psychometric Group," *Journal of Mental Deficiency*, LI (October, 1946), 195–205.
8. COAKLEY, FRANCES. "Study of Feeble-Minded Wards Employed in War Industries," *Journal of Mental Deficiency*, L (October, 1945), 301–306.
9. CRUICKSHANK, WILLIAM M. *The Psychology of Exceptional Children and Youth*. Englewood Cliffs, N. J.: Prentice-Hall, Inc., 1955.
10. CURRAN, CLYDE E. *The Slow Learner in the Junior High School*. New England School Development Council. Cambridge, Mass.: Harvard University, 1953.
11. DALY, FLORA M., and LEO M. CAIN. "Mentally Retarded Students in California Secondary Schools," *Bulletin of the California State Department of Education*, XXII (October, 1953), No. 7.

12. DAVIES, STANLEY P. *Social Control of the Mentally Deficient.* New York: Thomas Y. Crowell Co., 1930.

13. DEVEREUX, GEORGE. *Therapeutic Education.* New York: Harper and Brothers, 1956.

14. DOUGLAS, MARCELLA E. "Some Concrete Contributions to Occupational Education in the Academic Classroom," *Journal of Mental Deficiency*, XLVIII (January, 1944), 288–91.

15. DOYLE, FRANCIS W., ELI M. BOWER, and FLORA M. DALY. "Information Regarding the Education of Mentally-Retarded Minors in California." *Bulletin of the California State Department of Education*, XXIV (August, 1955), No. 10.

16. ELLIOTT, MABEL, and FRANCIS MERRILL. *Social Disorganization.* New York: Harper and Brothers, 1934.

17. FRAMPTON, MERLE E., and ELENA D. GALL (eds.). *Special Education for the Exceptional.* Boston: Porter Sargent, 1955. Vol. I.

18. GARRISON, KARL C. *The Psychology of Exceptional Children.* New York: Ronald Press Co., 1950.

19. GEGENHEIMER, RUTH. "A Quarter Century of Community Supervision of Mentally Deficient Patients," *Journal of Mental Deficiency*, LIII (July, 1948), 90–108.

20. GOLDSTEIN, IRWIN. "Implications of Mental Deficiency," *American Journal of Mental Deficiency*, LII–LIII (November, 1944), 207–226.

21. GOODENOUGH, FLORENCE. *Exceptional Children.* New York: Appleton-Century-Crofts, 1956.

22. GRAHAM, DANIEL F. "So Johnny Can't Read," *Training School Bulletin*, LIII (April, 1956), 36–37.

23. HUESMAN, MARY. "Psychological Services to the Mentally Handicapped in the Chicago Public Schools," *Journal of Mental Deficiency*, LI (April, 1947), 632–36.

24. HUNGERFORD, RICHARD H., CHRIS DePROSPO, and LOUIS F. ROSENZWEIG. "The Non-Academic Pupil," *Philosophy of Occupational Education.* New York: Association for the New York City Teachers of Special Education, 1948.

25. INGRAM, CHRISTINE R. *Education of the Slow-Learning Child.* New York: Ronald Press Co., 1953.

26. ISACKSON, ROY O., and FRED P. ROESSEL. "Differences in Reading Ability," *The Clearing House*, XXXI (February, 1957), 342–45.

27. KEEHAN, VIRGINIA R. *Exceptional Children: A Handbook for*

Teachers. Santa Fe, New Mexico: Department of Education, 1954.

28. KELLY, ELIZABETH M. "Preparation of the Mentally Handicapped Child for the Post-War World," *Journal of Exceptional Children,* X (March, 1944), 146–50.

29. KIRK, SAMUEL, and ORVILLE JOHNSON. *Educating the Retarded Child.* Boston: Houghton Mifflin Co., 1951.

30. LOWENFELD, VIKTOR. *Creative and Mental Growth.* New York: Macmillan Co., 1954.

31. MARTENS, ELISE H. *Curriculum Adjustments for the Mentally Retarded.* (U. S. Department of Health, Education, and Welfare Bulletin 1950, No. 2. Reprint.) Washington, D. C.: Government Printing Office, 1953.

32. ———. "Occupational Preparation for Mentally-Handicapped Children," *Journal of Psycho-Asthenics,* XLII (1937), 157–65.

33. MIDDLETON, CLARA. "Inter-Personal Relationships Which Affect Learning for the Mentally Retarded Child in Home Economics," *Training School Bulletin,* LIII (November, 1956), 183–91.

34. MORTON, VELMA Y. "Basic Problems in Guidance in the Field of the Exceptional," in *Special Education for the Exceptional* (**17**).

35. NEWLAND, T. ERNEST. "Psychological Assessment of Exceptional Children and Youth," in (**9**).

36. PEARCE, WILLIAM F., and OTHERS. "Workshop in Job Requirements in Occupational Areas of New York City," *Journal of Mental Deficiency,* LIII (April, 1949), 621–44.

37. PHELPS, HAROLD R. "Postschool Adjustment of Mentally Retarded Children in Selected Ohio Cities," *Exceptional Children,* XXIII (November, 1956), 58–62, 91.

38. POLLOCK, MORRIS P., and MIRIAM. *New Hope for the Retarded.* Boston: Porter Sargent, 1953.

39. RESNICK, JOSEPH. "Toward Understanding the Maladjusted Child," *The Clearing House,* XXXI (February, 1957), 352–55.

40. ROBSON, C. M. "Social Factors in Mental Retardation," *British Journal of Psychology,* XXII (October, 1931), 118–35.

41. SARASON, SEYMOUR B. "Mentally Retarded and Mentally Defective Children," in (**9**). Pp. 438–74.

42. SMITH, MARION FUNK, and ARTHUR J. BURKS. *Teaching the Slow-Learning Child.* New York: Harper and Brothers, 1954.

43. TIFFIN, JOSEPH. *Industrial Psychology.* New York: Prentice-Hall, Inc., 1948.
44. TREDGOLD, ALFRED F. *Mental Deficiency.* (8th ed.) Baltimore: Williams and Wilkins Co., 1947.
45. WALLIN, J. E. WALLACE. *The Education of Mentally Handicapped Children.* New York: Harper and Brothers, 1951.
46. ———. "The Psychological Aspects of the Problem of Vocational Preparation and Rehabilitation of Mentally and Physically Handicapped Children," *Journal of Mental Deficiency,* XLIX (January, 1945), 294–95.

CHAPTER SIX

Special Schools and Custodial Classes for the Mentally Handicapped

SPECIAL classes are one way of fulfilling the educational requirements of mentally handicapped children. Special schools are another. These may be of the residential type, involving the complete separation of the child from his home environment; or they may be day schools which the child attends for a set period of hours each day, as in the ordinary school sessions—though the period may be longer, especially in the private schools.

In some large cities where the total enrollment of feebleminded pupils is substantial, special day schools for them have been organized within the framework of the regular school system. However, Heck notes, the current trend in public education is away from the establishment of such centers, since the child tends to be less keenly aware of his handicap when his classes are given in one of the regular schools in his own neighborhood than when he is conspicuously separated from the other children in his school district. Therefore, the majority of the day schools for the mentally handicapped are privately owned and operated.

It is also true that, although there are both state-supported and privately run residential schools, the private institutions far outnumber the public—which should "occasion no surprise," Wallin has observed, "in view of the lucrative returns from an investment in a private school." In fact, some of the private schools, he goes on to comment, "have achieved well-nigh fabulous financial success." (**23**, p. 16)

INCREASE IN SCHOOLS

During the past sixteen years, schools for the mentally handicapped have mushroomed throughout the United States. Some idea of their numbers and distribution is given in the following table, compiled from data gathered by the American Association on Mental Deficiency, which shows the number of public and private schools for the mentally handicapped in each state and territory of the union. Institutions included vary in size from the very small to the very large, and, although most—especially the state schools—are residential, some are day. Institutions housing adults as well as children are included, since it is not feasible to separate the two—indeed, impossible, in the case of primarily custodial institutions.

The data is not complete, since 208 schools did not reply to the questionnaire sent out by the association. However, it is to be presumed that most, if not all, of those schools that did not answer were privately owned, since the public schools are more or less under a compulsion to report to the public. Thus the discrepancy between the number of public and private schools in this country becomes even more marked.

Distribution of Institutions for the Mentally Handicapped
in the United States (5, pp. 9–10)

State	State-owned	Private
Alabama	1	2
Arizona	1	4
Arkansas	0	0
California	3	64
Colorado	1	2
Connecticut	2	5
Delaware	2	3

State	State-owned	Private
District of Columbia	0 [1]	1
Florida	1	12
Georgia	1	2
Idaho	1	–
Illinois	2	19
Indiana	2	1
Iowa	2	1
Kansas	2	2
Kentucky	1	1
Louisiana	1	2
Maine	1	1
Maryland	3 [1]	4
Massachusetts	5	12
Michigan	4	13
Minnesota	6	13
Mississippi	1	0
Missouri	2	5
Montana	1	0
Nebraska	1	1
Nevada	0	0
New Hampshire	1	2
New Jersey	3	11
New Mexico	1	0
New York	7	17
North Carolina	1	2
North Dakota	1	0
Ohio	3	9
Oklahoma	2	3
Oregon	1	2
Pennsylvania	4	27
Rhode Island	1	1
South Carolina	2	0
South Dakota	1	1
Tennessee	0	3
Texas	5	14
Utah	1	0
Vermont	1	2
Virginia	2	6
Washington	2	1
West Virginia	1	2
Wisconsin	2	4
Wyoming	1	0
Hawaii	1	0
Total	90	278

[1] One of the state schools in Maryland is supported by the District of Columbia for the benefit of Washington residents.

Even without taking into account the institutions that did not respond, the total shows that there are more than three times as many private as public institutions in this country. As the table indicates, there does not seem to be any relationship between the size of a state and the scope of its program for the mentally handicapped, although the largest state, New York, leads in the number of public institutions, with seven schools. Minnesota, eighteenth in rank, comes next with six; Massachusetts, and Texas, ninth and sixth respectively, have five each; Michigan and Pennsylvania, seventh and third, have four. The second most populous state, California, has only three; the third most populous, Illinois, only two. Arkansas, Nevada, and Tennessee do not have any state institutions for the retarded, or, at least, did not have any at the time the data was compiled (1956). Currently, twelve states are planning new institutions. Arkansas is organizing the state's first colony for the retarded; Georgia, the state's first for the Negro child. Florida, Illinois, Michigan, Minnesota, New York, Pennsylvania, and Texas are adding one new state training school apiece to their existing facilities; North Carolina, two. (**45**, pp. 9–10)

The proportions are different for the privately owned schools. Here California tops the list with sixty-four; then there is a drop to Pennsylvania's twenty-seven, Illinois's nineteen, New York's seventeen, Texas' nineteen, Michigan and Missouri's thirteen, Massachusetts and Florida's twelve, and New Jersey's eleven. And it is in this area—the privately owned schools—where the growth in number has reached such overwhelming proportions.

Dangers of the Increase

On the surface, such an enormous increase in the number of private schools for the feebleminded appears to be an excellent development in the field of special education, and the parents of those handicapped children who are ineligible for the public school classes, as well as those in localities where such education is unavailable or inadequate, should be very grateful to be offered an opportunity to give their children a suitable education. That is, of course, those parents who can afford it, for, in most cases, such schools are far from inexpensive, running as high as five or six thousand dollars per annum for certain of the private schools. Even the state schools charge fees, which, in some instances, are rather substantial, though in most instances provision is made through the local welfare departments for those who cannot afford to pay.

As a matter of fact, it is important that a distinction should be made in this context between what Walter Jacob has termed the *proprietary* and the *nonprofit* types of private schools. He describes the proprietary school as "a private business enterprise whose profits accrue to its owners or stockholders as in any other business," whereas the nonproprietary schools "have no owners or stockholders," and any excess of funds at the end of the year is "applied to the needs of the school as determined by its board of trustees"—who are, as a rule, unpaid. (11, p. 4) These schools, for the most part, charge according to need and, in general, are very like the state institutions, except that they are not as vulnerable to political pressure, and hence have more freedom of operation.

It is the proprietary schools which tend more often to make fantastic claims as to their potentialities. If these schools *could* carry out the extravagant promises that so many of them make, no tuition fee would be too high, for who can set a price upon a miracle? And miracles are, in essence, what they profess to offer. Unfortunately, a goodly number of the proprietary schools are operated by individuals who are charlatans first and educators second—if at all. Seeking primarily to reap large profits, these operators will promise the parents of the mentally handicapped that, as a result of this particular school's unique system of tutelage, their children—no matter how defective—will be "cured" of their intellectual inadequacies and become individuals of normal intelligence. And it is another unfortunate circumstance that no matter how well-educated and sophisticated the parents may be, they are always very ready to swallow such promises, because they are easier to accept than the far more incredible fact that *their* child is feebleminded.

Irrevocability of Mental Handicap

However, the nature of mental handicap is, of course, such that, by definition, it can never be "cured" through any educational or therapeutic methods. Where there is an apparent cure —i.e., a substantial upward leap in intellectual powers—it usually means that the original diagnosis was mistaken or inadequate—which has happened and will continued to happen as long as the social sciences are inexact and man is fallible. As Devereux pointed out:

. . . We feel that many "surprising" therapeutic results would not seem startling at all had we taken the trouble to ascertain from the beginning not only the patient's handicaps but also all of (his) assets. In fact, we feel that in diagnostic work the correct appraisal of the patient's assets is, if possible, even more important than is the accurate appraisal of his defects. (**6**, p. 171)

It is further known to be of not infrequent occurrence that a mentally handicapped child should, after spending a period of time in an institution or a special class, appear to manifest a decided increase in intelligence. This does not, investigators believe, arise from an originally faulty diagnosis, but from the removal of an emotional block which has been preventing the child from operating at full capacity.

It must be reiterated here that one of the basic advantages the special class has over the institution is that it affords further opportunity for diagnosing and re-evaluating the apparent capabilities of the child without exposing him to the traumatic effects of institutionalization, when there may be no need for it. There is a strong feeling against institutionalizing the feebleminded child not only because it is obviously undesirable to remove him from the home environment but because, should it become known that he had spent any time in a residential school, he will then, in the layman's eyes, always bear the stigma of having been in a "mental institution." Social prejudice is a very real factor, especially in the area of the handicapped, and it should always be taken into account before any plans or programs are arranged, no matter how unjust its basis, since the primary aim of educating the handicapped is adjusting him to society; reforming that society must be left to another branch of education.

The reason emphasis was placed earlier in this chapter upon the fact that a "cure" through *educational* or *therapeutic* methods was impossible is that a considerable amount of research is being done currently with the *medical* treatment of the mentally handicapped. Extreme caution must be used in describing these purely physical methods. In the first place, they are applicable only to certain limited types of mental handicap, and, in the second place, it is by no means certain how effective they are or whether, in fact, they have had any real effect at all. Referring to the treatment of mental handicap by drugs, Abraham Levinson has pointed out that—

It is estimated that 25 per cent of the cases of acquired hypothyroidism can attain normal mentality if treated early enough, during infancy if possible. However, even in older children thyroid extract may be of great benefit. One of our patients, a girl thirteen and a half years of age, showed an increase of fifteen points in her I.Q. after the administration of the thyroid extract. . . .

Mental retardation due to inherited syphilis is treated by penicillin. There is little likelihood of a subnormal child with congenital syphilis becoming normal as the damage to his nervous system is too severe at the outset. In some cases, however, antisyphilitic treatment may be followed by marked improvement in the mentality.

In mental retardation due to lead poisoning, the symptoms accompanying the poisoning grow less severe under treatment. . . . (14, p. 110)

Dr. Levinson goes on to speak about the work that is being done with glumatic acid in the treatment of the feebleminded and that has aroused so much hope—without, so far, too much basis in fact—in those who are concerned with the subject.

. . . Up to date . . . the results have not been uniform. One group of investigators . . . recommends its use very highly on the ground that it raises the I.Q. considerably even in mongolian idiocy. Some found it of benefit in certain cases but not in all. Others report little improvement from its use. The effect of the drug, therefore, is still controversial. . . .

. . . At present, I see no harm in administering glumatic acid provided the parents understand that it is not a cure-all for mental retardation. (14, p. 111)

Careful though Levinson's statements are, still they reflect more optimism than a great many other opinions in the field concerning the use of this drug—which has received far more publicity than is altogether wise at this juncture. Levinson also discusses brain surgery for the treatment of mental handicap, but admits here, too, that, although there is the possibility of effective surgical treatment in at least mitigating certain aspects of the condition, such work is still very much in the research stage.

It cannot be emphasized too strongly that, although medical work with the retarded is a very important and valuable type of research which should be given all possible support, all new developments in the field must be soft-pedaled, lest they arouse false hopes in the breasts of afflicted parents, who are apt to stretch an inch of hope into an ell of actuality. As Wortis stresses, "severe mental retardation is almost invariably due to organic defect," and that "organic defect usually involves the lack or destruction of neural elements which cannot be replaced. . . ."

(**26**, p. 472) Therefore, for practical purposes mental handicap cannot be cured medically, let alone through training or therapy —which is, of course, the basis on which the schools guilty of sharp practices make their outlandish claims, since the laws for medical malpractice are far more stringent than for educational.

This by no means should be construed to imply that the training offered the handicapped child by the special schools is of no value or that his condition cannot be changed for the better. Since few, if any, of us operate under normal conditions at optimum capacity, there is an opportunity for considerable improvement, not only in the handicapped individual's condition, but in the condition of every one of us. However, as the normal individual to a considerable extent educates himself in addition to the formal training he receives in school or elsewhere, the rate of improvement can be more spectacular in the mentally handicapped, both because he will receive, under special education, the type of almost instinctual training, the lack of which appears to the layman as further lack of intelligence, and because his actual capacities tend to be underestimated by the layman in what almost amounts to a reversal of the halo effect. As Sarason has observed, "diagnostic and program planning procedures must take account of the total functioning of the child." (**19**, p. 459) And Devereux agrees, describing the abilities of the mentally handicapped individual—

. . . as a kind of mob, lacking a leader who could coordinate its efforts. This, in turn, leads one to ask whether the segmental abilities of the mentally defective are truly as minimal as current tests make them appear. Indeed, just as . . . no individual can unfold all of his potentialities without the help of society, so no ability may be able to unfold itself with complete functionality unless it is embedded into, and supported by, a well-patterned matrix of other abilities. . . . We suspect that at least in certain types of genuine feeble-mindedness both the jaggedness of the performance profile and the generally low level of performance are not primarily reflections of inherently low mental abilities but, on the contrary, the end products of a lack of patterned coordination of the segmental potentialities. (**6**, p. 145)

Although the goals set for the mentally handicapped individual's education should, of course, exceed the levels expected, in accordance with Browning's dictum that a man's reach should exceed his grasp or what's a heaven for, it must be understood by parent and teacher and physician that the ultimate achievement is bounded by physical factors which no amount of training or aspiration can transcend. Optimistic though he is about the results that can be expected from therapy, Devereux has conceded that—

. . . in the final accounting inherent handicaps do . . . place definite limitations on our efforts. While it is true that a lame man recently became the world's weight-lifting champion, it is quite certain that he could never have become a champion sprinter, no matter how hard he tried. . . . (**6**, p. 170)

Private versus Public Schools

Of course, there are many private schools that are currently doing a splendid job of educating the mentally handicapped and which are, in all ways, equal to or, in many cases, superior to the public schools. And, although these soundly operating private schools would, in the main, tend to be of the nonproprietary type, undoubtedly there are many proprietary schools doing a good job, too. There is no inherent harm, of course, in seeking a profit; it is merely that the possession of such an objective exposes the seeker to temptations that do not exist in the case of the nonprofit institution.

At the same time, the state training schools are often inadequate. In the first place, most of them are carrying a load well in excess of their original, planned capacities. Furthermore, many of them are not allocated sufficient funds to carry on their work properly. As a result, they may have old-fashioned plants and staffs which are inadequate in size, qualifications, or ability, or all three. Cornell Capa and Maya Pines, in animadverting against public custodial institutions, have drawn a hair-raising picture of conditions at one particular state cottage colony, which they take pains to describe as "one of the best institutions in the country, in one of the nation's richest states":

. . . the director of the village (is) a distinguished, conscientious physician who has spent years fighting for more space, more money, more personnel. . . . After succeeding in his efforts to obtain state funds for research, he found it impossible to get trained personnel who might carry it out. He has no control over admissions; the village houses one and a half times as many children as the architects originally planned for. Sometimes there are even shortages of beds. . . .

For the children this may literally mean years with no attention from anyone but the overworked staffs of their particular cottages. . . . Requirements for the position of attendant are low . . . and the pay is low, too. . . .

Education in this institution . . . is made available to only a fraction of the children of school age. Although three-fourths of the children have I.Q.'s under 50, the large majority being in the "trainable" group, only the "educable" are given a chance to go to school—and then only if they have no serious physical handicaps. . . .

In an institution of this size, only the least handicapped students— the small proportion who are upper-level—can be given any real attention or preparation. . . . (3, pp. 111–12)

Undoubtedly, these two investigators are presenting a picture of actual conditions as they see them, but it is to be wondered whether perhaps they might not be unduly emphasizing the dark side of that picture. At any rate, this type of comment, no matter how valid intrinsically, tends to hamper the work of individual diagnosticians and researchers. As Henry C. Schumacher observed: "it is extremely unfortunate, and certainly increases the difficulty of the job of the therapist that there has been so much unfavorable criticism of our state institutions." He does not deny that "some of this criticism in terms of overcrowding in particular is well justified," although he also feels that a good deal "is politically inspired." (**21**, p. 431) Certain sensational charges of mismanagement laid against several of the state institutions during the past few years, even though most were disproved by the courts, still did the residential schools as a whole no good, for there is always an element of popular prejudice that will believe "where there is smoke there must be fire. . . ." Furthermore, even where such criticisms are justified, whatever good they—and their widespread dissemination—may do in terms of correcting conditions at that particular school and in arousing public support in general is counterbalanced by some equally destructive effects, among them being the fact that "there are many parents who in good faith cannot bring themselves, as a result of this publicized criticism, to place their children in a state institution. . . ." (**21**, p. 431) Yet, to attempt to tone down, or even suppress, public criticism of the state residential schools would be just as much a violation of our democratic processes as to deny the mentally handicapped child his right to an education. And so we have still another of the seemingly insoluble problems that seem to arise in this field.

To be sure, some of the nonproprietary private institutions suffer from the same drawbacks as the public ones. As for the proprietary schools, many of them have excellent facilities and do an adequate enough job of training the handicapped—though that is by no means always the case—and yet they, too, are doing more harm than good, by, in this instance, arousing false hopes in the parents' breasts. It is difficult for the local boards of education, to which, in most states, private schools must be accredited, to control such schools, so long as they make sure their hyperbolic promises are both ambiguous and, more important, unwritten—and yet stronger efforts should be made to prevent these unethical operators from victimizing parents with spurious claims.

In all justice to the private schools, it must be remarked that they are not the only ones to delude the parents; the physicians and psychologists are equally guilty, and without even the excuse of seeking a profit. Jensen speaks harshly of those clinicians who encourage the parents of a mentally handicapped child "by holding out false hopes, which naturally results in disillusionment later when the patient is not cordially received in school or becomes a social problem requiring immediate planning for his management." (**12**, p. 830)

According to Israel Zwerling, who made a study that involved the reactions of parents on receiving the diagnosis of mental retardation for the children, too many doctors kept reassuring the anxious parents with words to the effect of "He's just a little slow; he'll catch up"—when, in fact, the child was a retardate or a defective who should have been receiving special training. They are fully as reprehensible as the doctor who, according to Zwerling, told the parent of a defective girl who could not speak that, in the parent's own words, "I should put her away and forget I ever had her, unless I wanted to limit myself to a dog's life. At least a dog could bark, she told me. . . ." (**28**, p. 471)

INSTITUTIONALIZING THE HANDICAPPED

Advantages

There are numerous potential benefits to be derived from institutional placement. Large and well-equipped residential schools, either public or private, which have been organized and are being operated according to the best modern methods (an ideal state which, sad to say, occurs rarely), can offer superior opportunities to the mentally handicapped. As Martens has described an optimal situation in this area:

. . . The possibilities in a residential school of an integrated program in which educational and social values are combined go far beyond the limits achieved by the day school. Through the use of units of experience, classroom activities can be coordinated with activities carried on in the cottage, in the kitchen, in the dining room, and in other phases of institutional life. Experiences during out-of-school hours can become the subject matter of reading, writing, numbers, and language, to an extent not known in the day school. Cottage life gives the best possible opportunity to develop desirable personal and social habits which in turn can become the theme of discussion in the classroom. Social, industrial, academic, and physical development of the child can proceed hand in hand with one another through a complete practical integration of his experience during a twenty-four hour day and during every season of the year. (**17**, p. 90)

Drawbacks

Nonetheless, placing the handicapped individual in a residential school is not recommended if he is mentally retarded, stable, and without egregious physical abnormality, for such a child, as has been pointed out in previous chapters, is ultimately capable of achieving social and economic sufficiency as part of the community *providing that* he is properly trained and educated. Such training and education should include, if it is at all possible, continuing membership in the community, so that, while the child is educated with his peers, at the same time he has sufficient community contact to keep him from developing the false sense of values that may be obtained by living in a segregated school.

In some schools for the handicapped, Devereux alleges, "the child is permitted to adjust to a code of conduct so lax and so much at variance with that obtaining on the outside that it is likely to become grossly maladjusted because of its unpreparedness to meet the demands of the world at large." (**6**, p. 181) Even where every effort is made to reproduce a natural environment, the inmate's surroundings cannot help but be artificial to some degree and, to that degree, psychologically unhealthful. Wallin is of the opinion that, generally speaking, public school classes are better for the mentally handicapped child than the institution for the following reasons:

1. The best place and agency for the care and nurture of any child are his own home and his own parents, if they are fit and responsible. . . .
2. The cost of educating all defective [2] children in colonies would be prohibitive. . . . The educational program . . . can be provided more economically in the public schools than in residential institutions or colonies. . . .
3. Present institutional facilities are wholly inadequate to accommodate the children who would have to be committed and doubtless they will continue to be so for long years to come. . . .
4. Many parents would refuse to send their children to institutions. . . .
5. Institutionalized children would sometimes receive inferior instruction because of the difficulty of staffing many institutional schools with competent, professionally trained teachers. Usually teachers in state institutions for the mentally handicapped are not required to meet the state teacher certificate requirements. . . .
6. Routing young mental defectives [*] into state schools would in some cases be fraught wtih tragic consequences because of mistaken diagnoses. . . . (**25,** p. 168)

WHO SHOULD BE INSTITUTIONALIZED?

The distinction between the *retardate* and the *defective* must be stressed once again at this point, as it is particularly important in any discussion of institutionalization. The retardate is the high-level or "educable" mentally handicapped; the defective, the low-level "uneducable" individual, both distinctions being with respect to social competency as well as intelligence, and both

[2] Wherever the words "retardate," "deficient," etc., are asterisked in this text, they are loosely synonymous with "feebleminded" or "mentally handicapped," rather than with any particular type of handicap.

being very loose in application, since there is no definite line of demarcation between the two types of feebleminded. Of course it is obvious that the institution is a more desirable solution to the problem of the defective than of the retardate, but this does not always hold true, as will be developed in the course of this chapter.

Gale Walker has outlined three broad objectives of the residential school:

. . . An institution may represent a source of training for the individual, a guarantee of permanent asylum . . . or may represent a source of escape for the family and community from the defective *. . . . (24, p. 138)

Although all these reasons for institutionalization are not necessarily optimal solutions with regard to the handicapped child himself, they are often the best solution as far as the community is concerned and so must be given due weight from the purely pragmatic standpoint. They explain why an individual is, or should be—or why people *think* he should be—institutionalized, and, from the *why* of it, we derive the *who* of it. Even so, there are no cut and dried answers to the question of why certain of the mentally handicapped are placed in residential schools and others are not, which is the reason the state of New York is currently undertaking a study to determine "why the mentally retarded are committed to institutions." Research will be done by New York University's Graduate School of Public Administration and social service under a grant from the state's Interdepartmental Health Research Board.

Factors such as degree of retardation; additional physical and physiological handicaps; and attitudes and economic status of families of retardates will be weighed. (5, p. 16)

Retardates

Although, generally speaking, institutionalization is not advised for retardates, there are, as has been mentioned, certain types of retardates who need to be institutionalized. First of all, there are those with special personality problems; those who are psychotic and those who are either already delinquent or who show such a marked tendency toward delinquency that they must be segregrated for the public welfare. As a matter of fact, these troublemakers and potential troublemakers will need to be segregated from the rest even within the institutional environment for, as Martens justly points out, they "are likely to disrupt any curricular program" (**17**, p. 90), as well as be a detrimental influence upon the other children.

Second, there are those whose parents simply cannot cope with the problems involved in keeping them at home. There has been a good deal of emotionally charged talk concerning the parent's "responsibility" toward his offspring, no matter how handicapped that offspring may be, but it is a very unwise procedure to overlay a fundamental issue with unrealistic sentiment. Here, for once, popular prejudice must be discounted, if necessary: no matter what the neighbors think, children should be institutionalized whenever, in Wallin's words, they "are a serious burden to an overworked mother, or menace the tranquility or happiness of their home, or are a hazard to the mental health of parents and siblings because of their eccentricities, pathological behavior, or inordinate demands." (**25**, p. 72) Where institutionalization is not the solution adopted, there is always some amount of conflict. As the National Institute of Mental Health commented in a report published in August, 1957:

. . . The parents and siblings of the retarded child who does not need institutionalization may be traumatized by his deficiency and further hamper his maximum development unless medical facilities, social agency resources, educational programs, and other facilities are available. (**1**, p. 18)

Furthermore, as regards institutionalization of the retardate, some children have an undesirable home environment from

which it is wisest that they be removed, for, as Garrison points
out, "the helplessness of the feeble-minded in poor families ex-
aggerates both the extent and the seriousness of their social
dependency, aggravating existing social and economic problems."
(7, p. 195) The necessity of removing such children from their
environment as early as possible is stressed by Kirk and Johnson's
discovery that, although "idiots and imbeciles are found about as
frequently in families of high intellectual ability as in families
of low intellectual ability . . . the high-grade mental defective,
the mentally handicapped, and the borderline defective child
seem to be found more frequently in families of low socio-
economic, intellectual, and educational level." These investigators
conclude that "the question here is whether the low mental functioning ability of these children is due to inheritance or to the
cultural environment in which they find themselves." (13, p. 33)
And Sarason, too, has suggested that—

. . . An acquired behavioral pattern which has been continually rein-
forced throughout an individual's life cannot be unlearned or markedly
changed. The problem may be put in the form of a question: If a
child has been reared for the first ten years of his life in a Kallikak-like
cultural atmosphere, is one justified in assuming that through psychotherapy (or even marked environmental change) he can become
"normal?" (20, p. 49)

He goes on to quote Freeman, Holzinger, and Mitchell's finding
"that the intelligence level of children of defective parents was
related to the length of time they remained in the family and
emphasizes the deleterious effect that early deprivation may have
on subsequent development." (20, p. 49)

Also recommended for institutionalization are those children
whose environment is adequate per se—that is, so far as physical
conditions go—but whose parents reject them because of their
handicap, often feeling sorry for themselves because they believe
they have been "unjustly treated by providence," rather than feel-

ing sorry for their afflicted children. Such rejection may be overt or covert; in fact, the parent may even evince great reluctance to let the child be placed in the residential school. In Walker's opinion, "parental rejection . . . always exists to some degree even though unexpressed or camouflaged by overconcern and protectiveness. . . ." (**24**, p. 132)

Again it is better for both parent and child that, rather than the parent be adjured that it is his "duty" to love and nurture his child no matter how much he may dislike him, the child be taken away from him and placed in a situation where he has some chance of achieving a degree of emotional adjustment. Obviously, a love that is forced is worse than no love at all, and it takes no great amount of perception to see that it is better for a child to be institutionalized among his peers who will accept him as their equal than continue to be an unwelcome burden at home. The higher the educational attainment of the family, the more likely it is that institutional placement will be desirable for the child. As Devereux commented:

. . . feeble-minded children in rural areas, who are not confronted with tasks and demands beyond their limited abilities, are often relatively well adjusted, while the feeble-minded children of parents belonging to the professional classes frequently become emotionally disturbed because the demands implicit in the style of life of their families are wholly beyond their limited abilities. Surprising results can often be obtained quite rapidly by placing such children in a therapeutic school, whose flexible and individualized demand pattern does not tax them beyond their capacities. In such cases the school must sometimes give the parents a realistic picture of the child's limitations in order to help them reduce their unrealistically high expectations, both as regards the potentialities of the child and as regards the amount of improvement the school can hope to bring about. (**6**, pp. 180–81)

Those who will also probably need permanent custodial care are children who, in addition to their mental handicap, also have a physical handicap which will prevent their ever receiving the degree of education possible for others of their mental level and so will probably never be able to become socially competent. However, before they are permanently committed, Wallin warns (25, p. 73), it must be definitely determined that they are incapable of receiving any education; otherwise, too many of the doubly handicapped may be classified by careless or overworked diagnosticians as ineducable for the sake of expediency. And, finally, those students who live in areas where the public school systems do not offer special classes must unfortunately also be institutionalized.

However, in all cases where the retardate is involved—that is, as opposed to the defective—the children are placed in the institutions with the understanding that they will be released when their training has developed a degree of social competence in them so that they can be returned to their homes, or so that, where the parents do not wish to take them back or where the home environment is unsatisfactory, they can earn their own livings and make their own homes. Thus, although the "stigma" of having been institutionalized cannot be avoided for them, at least the development of false values can be reduced to a minimum and they will live with the constant awareness that their separation from the community is not a permanent one.

It should always be kept in mind that there is a considerable difference between the techniques to be employed in working with the child who has been sent to the institution for permanent asylum than in working with the child who is expected to leave after a period of training or even who will merely maintain familial contact, for, in such case, there must be therapeutic work with the parents as well. Karl Heiser has noted that—

If there is a possibility of a child returning to his family, rather than remain permanently in the institution, or if his parents visit and maintain contact, it is imperative that they be involved in the plans for therapy. . . . It is often as difficult for a parent to conceive of his child's improvement and return home as it was originally to accept the diagnosis of mental deficiency. . . . (**10**, p. 98)

Too many of those connected with the problem of the mentally handicapped—the parent and physician, as well as the psychologist and research worker—do not fully understand what the ultimate purpose and function of the residential schools are, nor do those who work in the schools themselves always realize how far their obligations reach, extending beyond the institute to the community itself. The National Institute of Mental Health has outlined the ideal scope of the residential schools as follows:

> Institutions for the care of retarded [3] children can do more than provide custodial care; they can socialize and train these children and "graduate" some of them back to the community as useful citizens. It is important, therefore, that these institutions . . . . :
>
> Be treatment centers with adequate professional personnel for care and treatment as well as training and educative facilities.
>
> Be as near as possible (which is not always now the case) to the community.
>
> Have as many contacts as possible with the community, increasing the probability that many of the patients will return to outside life. (**1**, p. 19)

The Defectives

The mental deficient poses a substantially different problem than does the retardate. Since, by definition, he can never become socially competent, he must be confined or supervised throughout life; therefore, the objectives of whatever training he is given would be considerably different. Furthermore, he cannot profit from the special classes described in the previous chapter.

In the past, it was generally considered that all of the mental defectives needed custodial care and should be placed in an institution as soon as their condition was established. Sarason

---

[3] Used in this case to embrace the entire concept of mental handicap.

showed statistically that "institutionalization is by far the most frequent recommendation made in the case of defective individuals." (**20**, p. 43) It was argued, with a good deal of truth, that the traumatic effect of separation from the family is always a much less serious factor for the defective than for the retardate. The defective child's sense of rejection at being extruded from the home, although existent, is considerably smaller than the retardate's, for, as Devereux points out, "the grossly defective child's libidinal cathexes are a priori both too tenuous and too unstable to make a transfer from the home to a residential school where it is well treated unduly traumatic. . . ." (**6**, pp. 273–74)

However, with the discovery that, although the defective may not be "educable," he can be "trained," many investigators are coming to agree that defectives need not always be institutionalized. Sarason, for one, commenting that the practice of recommending early institutionalization "is usually based on the assumption that there is nothing one can do for such children," states emphatiscally that "such a recommendation is not necessarily warranted." (**20**, p. 42) And Yepson and Cianci agree that "the idea that every feeble-minded child must be taken out of the community and put into an institution" must be discarded. (**27**, p. 21)

Zwerling found that parents were especially bitter about "the frequency with which the advice to institutionalize the child was given" when they consulted doctors about their children's condition.

One parent felt that, "Medical doctors work with so much sick tissue that they think everything defective should be scrapped." . . . Fifteen parents commented on the attitude of the physician toward institutionalization as one of finding some place to "put away" the child, rather than as a positive procedure in the management of the child. . . . (**28**, p. 474)

However, setting aside the question of whether or not the defective child *should* receive custodial care, the fact remains that a good many *cannot*. Many parents cannot afford the fees asked by the proprietary private schools in their locality, and the nonproprietary and state schools have such long waiting lists that the child may become an adult before there is room for him. Other parents do not want to send their children away, no matter how much more advantageous such an arrangement would be for both parent and child. Where the physician recommends institutionalization and the parents refuse to accept the recommendation, the physician's failure, Jensen—himself a medical doctor—has explained, arises because "we have not fully appreciated the strong emotional ties that most parents center in the mentally handicapped person." (12, p. 830) In some cases, the parents' refusal to send the child away becomes a psychological problem in itself, since it is apparent to the trained investigator that they insist upon keeping this child precisely because they do *not* want him. S. L. Sheimo has observed, concerning this all too prevalent attitude:

. . . To tell parents that they *should* institutionalize the child, should, in a sense, "get rid of him," often tends to increase the guilt and strengthen the defense against this already forbidden impulse [to reject the child]. . . . (22, p. 406)

Therefore, another solution must be found. This would seem to lie in the custodial class, which became a possibility once it was conceded that, as Levinson puts it, "even those who are looked upon as uneducable from the standpoint of formal education can be taught something of practical value and can profit from appropriate training." He mentions that even the mongoloid, who was previously thought to be incapable of absorbing knowledge, can make considerable progress under the right direction.

Although, as Kirk and Johnson point out, in most school systems those children with severe mental handicaps have been excluded from the public schools, some are now beginning to offer training classes and shelter workshops for these children. "This," the investigators state, "is a method sometimes preferred to commitment to a state institution, since it assists those parents who wish to maintain responsibility for the child at home." What these classes attempt to do is—

. . . assist parents in caring for the child at home and . . . supervise the child for several hours during the day at a public school class. It would not be expected that such children could be educated to care for themselves at the adult level, but through training (not education as we usually conceive it) could be taught to function socially at a higher level around the home and neighborhood. (13, p. 9)

On the whole, such classes are relatively rare within the public school system, as many educators—and investigators, too—believe that there is not much point in preparing an individual for community life who can never become an integrated member of the community. On the other hand, the National Association for Retarded Children asserts not only that twenty-five out of every thirty mentally handicapped children are "educable," but that "an additional four . . . are trainable"; that, in fact, only one out of every thirty retarded childred is "totally dependent. . . ." The trainable four—

. . . can learn to take care of their own personal needs even though they may never learn to read or write. They can do simple work at home, or, sometimes, away from home under supervision. As adults, they will be "semi-dependent." They will still need, in order to cope with the complexities of modern living, the benefits of special guidance and sheltered employment. . . . (18, pp. 2–3)

If these children are to be kept at home and not institutionalized, certainly it is desirable that they should receive as much training as they are capable of absorbing, no matter how minimal an amount that may be. Before the formation of the parents' councils, Capa and Pines report, 95 per cent of all parents who had defective children were forced to keep them at home without any training save that which they themselves were able to give them. (3, p. 8) However, starting in the early thirties, groups of parents anxious to improve the status and future of their retarded children began to form throughout the country. In 1951, they consolidated into the National Association for Retarded Children, which has, at the time of writing (1957), some 520 local branches throughout the United States. The organization "is dedicated to improving the general welfare of all mentally retarded persons, regardless of the degree of their handicap" (2, p. 12), and so the word "retarded" in their title is used only in its most general sense, that is, to embrace the entire concept of mental handicap. As a matter of fact, their work is even more valuable in connection with the training of defectives than with the education of the retardates, for it is the defectives who have been most neglected, not only by society as a whole, but even by investigators in the field of special education.

The association works toward its ultimate objective in a variety of ways. One of its first subsidiary aims is the establishment of enough community diagnostic-treatment clinics to give professional counseling to all families who need it, plus the establishment of community centers to take care of the retardate's social needs and help integrate him into society. It also is supporting the organization of systems of home-visiting counselors to help parents train their handicapped children at home, and the setting up of nursery classes for the feebleminded infant.

Not only does the association further special classes for children of school age, the "trainable" as well as the "educable," but it is pressing for the establishment of more residential schools, as well as the improvement of existing facilities. The NARC is also working toward the establishment of vocational training centers and sheltered workshops for the handicapped adults who, although they are capable of earning a living, cannot hold jobs in competitive employment. Because children, as a rule, outlive their parents, the association is demanding that some system of legal protection and guardianship be arranged for those who are outside, as well as inside, the institutions. And, finally, the association has sought to attack the problem at its roots by initiating research into the causes of mental handicap and methods of rehabilitation. (18, p. 8)

Organizing the local branches into a national group has, of course, considerably facilitated the parents councils' endeavors. J. Clifford MacDonald, president of the association, has stated that—

The problem of retardation is not so simple that it can be solved by isolated local groups. In many instances we must seek action at high national levels, such as obtaining social security legislation protecting the retarded youngster and certain tax relief for parents faced with the extra expense of training and educating a retarded child. (5, p. 1)

Many states now have passed laws making special education for the retarded compulsory, and currently six states—Missouri, Massachusetts, New Jersey, Kentucky, Pennsylvania, and Rhode Island—make public school programs for the trainable *defective* child mandatory. (5, p. 16) Of course, many other states have equally good permissive programs. One of the chief troubles the public school systems have in increasing the scope of their special-education programs is—as has been discussed in an earlier chapter—the difficulty of securing qualified personnel. The New York State Department of Education's Bureau of Handicapped Children has, for example, declared that "only the lack of adequately trained teachers" prevents it from "opening many more classes" for mentally handicapped children. (5, p. 16)

The NARC does not overemphasize special classes within the public school system to the exclusion of all other forms of training and education. As Elizabeth Boggs, chairman of the NARC's Educational Committee wrote, the organization is—

. . . plugging neither home care nor institutional care, but *is* plugging for better community facilities for those who are or who might be cared for at home. It *is* plugging for better (which doesn't mean bigger) residential facilities for those who are or may need to be in institutions. It *is* fighting against what one leader has called "institutionalization by attrition"—the phenomenon which occurs when parents who could care for their child at home become convinced that nowhere in the community can they find appropriate training, social activities, or companionship for their youngsters. . . .

And finally, NARC is plugging for the right of parents to determine for themselves, on the basis of competent advice, the course of care, training, and treatment, among those open to them, which they believe best for their family—*and to have their decisions respected by others.* (**4**, p. 12)

WHAT SHOULD THE INSTITUTIONS BE?

Whether or not the child is institutionalized then depends—it is generally agreed—upon the particular factors in his individual case. However, it is as important that the best possible training be given him whether he is sent to the residential institute, the day schools, or the special class.

The problems of establishing a curriculum for the special classes in the public school have already been discussed. Curriculum requirements for the residential and day schools will, broadly speaking, be the same, except that it is generally considered that they should be a good deal more exacting—on the basis that the residential schools are expected to supply much more in the way of educational and environmental advantages to compensate the child for having been separated from home and family. Wallin has summarized this attitude in the following paragraph:

. . . If society is justified in depriving certain individuals of their liberties because of ineradicable handicaps, these individuals have a right to demand that the institutions to which they are committed be organized and conducted wholly in their interest and so as to minimize the detrimental influences that necessarily inhere in institutional regimentation and routinization. The institution should be so conducted as to make its inmates happy, contented, maximally efficient, and useful members of the community. So far as possible, all should be taught self-control, and should learn to conform to the reasonable regulations needed for harmonious community living, and to respect the decencies and proprieties of life and the rights of their asociates. . . . They are entitled to an eminently practical education, with the emphasis always on the development of social skills and occupational competence so that they can contribute toward their own support in the institution. Training for personal and occupational efficiency in a maximally permissive environment must ever be the watchword. No inmate should be allowed to lead a vegetative existence who can be trained to care for himself and to assist in the routine of institutional life. Each should be given opportunities for the kind of job training that will afford therapeutically and vocationally useful outlets for his interests and aptitudes. (**25**, pp. 446–47)

The directors of the Wayne County Training School have described their institution's objectives in similar terms, also stressing the importance of preparing the handicapped individual for return to the community. Summarizing their statements, they say:

. . . The direction of curriculum practice in the School must . . . stem from continuous and informed leadership that enters into the whole gamut of problems: from the clinical question of how to deal with intricate problems of learning process and adjustment occurring in a given child at a given time, through day-by-day administration, to research and evaluation, the creation of materials, and the formulation of general principles and outlines of practice. . . . (**8**, p. 572)

In addition, the residential school will have the further problem of making special provisions for the defective and psychotic delinquents, who will invariably be committed there once they are discovered, because parental sentiment is not given any weight when it is so obviously opposed to the community welfare. According to Martens, these delinquents will—

. . . need a highly specialized type of training, probably in a separate institution, or at least in a separate unit quite apart from the school for the mentally defective.° As long as they remain unclassified in a large institution for the mentally defective,° they complicate the school program by demanding much individual attention and even by demoralizing the general atmosphere of the schoolroom. Because the residential school is likely to receive these difficult cases, it must make the needed provision for careful diagnosis, treatment, and individual instruction of each one in accordance with the needs revealed. (**17,** p. 92)

The institutions will also have to pay more attention to the problems of the deficient than some of them have been doing. Custodial care is not enough. They must be trained, now that it has been proved they are capable of receiving training, and, indeed, in the long run, whatever tasks previously performed for them by others that they will be able to learn to do for themselves will provide an economy for the institution that has them in custodial care.

In addition to these diverse operations, the residential institute has still another significant function, one to which Martens described it as being "peculiarly suited," and that is in "the use of experimental methods and research."

. . . Many of [the institutions] are under the direction of medical men or other highly trained persons who are especially interested in the fields of pathology, biology, and eugenics, as applied to the mentally defective.° In some, there are clinical laboratories, which have been the battleground of intensive research, designed to increase knowledge and to develop possibilities of training. The activities of the classroom may make a valuable contribution to this program of research through the use and evaluation of experimental methods of instruction. Only controlled experimentation will ultimately prove the value of desirable procedures, and it is to the scientific laboratories of residential schools that one must look for a large contribution in certain phases of needed investigation. (**17,** p. 93)

In short, the residential institution has a valuable and necessary place in our society. It should not be regarded as a catchall for human waste, but as a dynamic force for converting that wasted humanity into useful and responsible citizens. The NARC has appropriately outlined the ideal aims and functions of an institute for the retarded in the following words:

> . . . Some retarded children need temporary care away from home; a few may require it all their lives. Such centers should be staffed by skilled and sympathetic professional workers. They should offer pleasant surroundings and opportunities for the retarded to progress at their own speed. They should be designed to help as many of these children as possible to go back into the community and make their own way. Finally, our dire need for more training and research facilities suggests that such residential centers develop a close and continuing relationship with an institution of higher learning which is training professional staff in the field of mental retardation. (18, p. 9)

References

1. "A Research Report," *Children Limited.* (National Association for Retarded Children.) Vol. VI (August, 1957).
2. Boggs, Elizabeth. "The Editor Talks Things Over," in (4). P. 12.
3. Capa, Cornell, and Maya Pines. *Retarded Children Can Be Helped.* Great Neck, N. Y.: Channel Press, 1957.
4. *Children Limited.* (National Association for Retarded Children.) Vol. V (October, 1956).
5. *Children Limited.* (National Association for Retarded Children.) Vol. VI (August, 1957).
6. Devereux, George. *Therapeutic Education.* New York: Harper and Brothers, 1956.
7. Garrison, Karl C. *The Psychology of Exceptional Children.* New York: Ronald Press Co., 1950.
8. Heck, Arch O. *The Education of Exceptional Children.* (2nd ed.) New York: McGraw-Hill Book Co., 1953.
9. Hegge, Thorleif G., and Bluma B. Weiner. "Problems and Procedures in Curriculum Development in a Special Residential School," *American Journal of Mental Deficiency,* LVII (April, 1953), 563–72.
10. Heiser, Karl. "Psychotherapy in a Residential School for Men-

tally Retarded Children," in *Counselling and Psychotherapy with the Mentally Retarded* (**23**). Pp. 94–101.

11. JACOB, WALTER. *New Hope for the Retarded Child.* New York: Public Affairs Committee, Inc., 1954.

12. JENSEN, REYNOLD A. "The Clinical Management of the Mentally Retarded Child and the Parents," *American Journal of Psychiatry*, CVI (May, 1950), 830–33.

13. KIRK, SAMUEL, and ORVILLE JOHNSON. *Educating the Retarded Child.* Boston: Houghton, Mifflin Co., 1951.

14. LEVINSON, ABRAHAM. *The Mentally Retarded Child.* New York: John Day Co., 1952.

15. *Listings of Public and Private Schools and Homes for the Retarded.* Mansfield Depot, Conn.: American Association on Mental Deficiency, 1956.

16. MACDONALD, J. CLIFFORD. "Let's Talk Things Over," in (**5**). P. 3.

17. MARTENS, ELISE H. *Curriculum Adjustments for the Mentally Retarded.* (U. S. Department of Health, Education, and Welfare Bulletin 1950, No. 2.) Washington, D. C.: Government Printing Office, 1953.

18. *Now There Is Hope.* New York: National Association for Retarded Children, n. d.

19. SARASON, SEYMOUR B. "Psychosocial Problems of the Mentally Retarded," in William Cruickshank (ed.). *Psychology of Exceptional Children and Youth.* Englewood Cliffs, N. J.: Prentice-Hall, 1955.

20. ———. "Psychotherapy," in (**23**). Pp. 42–55.

21. SCHUMACHER, HENRY C. "Contribution of the Child Guidance Clinic to the Problem of Mental Deficiency," in (**23**). Pp. 426–34.

22. SHEIMO, S. L. "Problems in Helping Parents of Mental Defectives and Handicapped Children," in (**23**). Pp. 403–11.

23. STACEY, CHALMERS L., and F. MANFRED. *Counseling and Psychotherapy with the Mentally Retarded.* Glencoe, Ill.: Free Press, 1957.

24. WALKER, GALE. "Social and Emotional Problems of the Mentally Retarded Chilld," *American Journal of Mental Deficiency*, LIV (June, 1950), 132–38.

25. WALLIN, J. E. WALLACE. *Education of Mentally Handicapped Children.* New York: Harper and Brothers, 1951.

26. WORTIS, JOSEPH. "Toward the Establishment of Special Clinics for Retarded Children," *American Journal of Mental Deficiency*, LVIII (January, 1954), 472–78.
27. YEPSON, L. N., and V. CIANCI. "Home Training for Mentally Deficient Children in New Jersey," *Training School Bulletin*, XLII (1942), 21–26.
28. ZWERLING, ISRAEL. "Initial Counseling of Parents with Mentally Retarded Children," *Journal of Pediatrics of St. Louis*, XLIV (April, 1954), 469–79.

CHAPTER SEVEN

The Psychology of Teaching
the Gifted

HOWEVER much the mental abilities of the intellectual retardates in our population may be developed and accentuated by training, it cannot be reasonably expected that—except under the most unusual of circumstances—they will ever become leaders in the art and science and industry of our nation. It is, rather, from that small proportion of our populace comprising the intellectually gifted—a group which is, at the most generous estimate, less than 3 per cent—that our great men and women will be drawn.

DISSIPATION OF OUR INTELLECTUAL CAPITAL

Unfortunately, not only is this resource of valuable human capital so limited in size to begin with, but a large part is wantonly wasted, either because our gifted individuals are not recognized as such, or, worse still, having been recognized, are not given sufficient opportunities to develop their latent powers. This waste is regrettable as regards the individual's welfare, but, as regards the nation's welfare, it is appalling. "We cannot afford such waste," Witty has declared, "from the standpoint of sheer selfishness. . . . We need every ounce of talent, every spark of brilliance, every flare of ingenuity if we are to continue to maintain our place in the modern world. . . ." (**22**, p. 4)

Results of the Waste

This failure of ours to capitalize on the intellectual resources potentially available to us has been thrown into sharp focus by Russia's recent and humiliating victory over us in the race to put up an earth satellite. Yet the handwriting was on the wall for all to read: For years, authorities in various fields had been warning us that a technological disaster like this was bound to happen unless we altered our educational policies drastically.

A year or two before our shortcomings were put on display before the entire world, Norma Cutts and Nicholas Moseley, two investigators who were discussing this particular field—i.e., special education for the gifted—wrote that one of the most important reasons for educators to emphasize the necessity of identifying all bright pupils and seeing that they continue their education resulted from "acute and growing shortages of professional personnel," and warned that—

. . . if we are to win the conflict between democracy and communism, we require great numbers of highly trained professional people and technicians not only for defense but also to serve the backward nations of the world and thus incline them to our point of view. (**4**, p. 3)

To which they added in a burst of what seems now like uncannily accurate prophecy: "We have apparently been overconfident of our leadership in technology." (**4**, p. 3)

It is not only for military and tactical reasons that this country needs those "scientists, mathematicians, engineers, and technicians." They are equally necessary for our own personal needs—to feed our population, maintain its health, and develop our industry. (**4**, p. 3) And, although "the importance of scientists

and engineers . . . tends to obscure shortages in other fields,"
we do have equally great—and often greater—shortages elsewhere,
including, of course, a serious shortage of teachers in the field of
special education. (4, p. 4)

Causes of the Waste

Why is it that we are so prodigal of our human resources? The
reasons, therefore, can be classified under three headings: economic, psychological, and social.

Economic Factors. Lack of financial resources is the principal
reason why many gifted individuals are unable to acquire the
education they need to develop their abilities to completion.
America is said to be "a rich country," but only a small proportion of its families are sufficiently well off to be able to send their
children through college and graduate or professional school. The
school's fees are by no means the paramount consideration. Even
where advanced study is possible at no cost for tuition, the poor
family must then undertake to support its gifted member through
at least four unproductive years during which he might otherwise be filling the role of a breadwinner himself.

America is also said to be "a land of opportunity," but the opportunities it offers are limited. It is true, as a bulletin put out
by the Educational Policies Commission of the National Education Association observes, that—

. . . the barrier of poverty is not insurmountable. One of the glories
of American democracy is the extent to which the ideal of "careers
open to talent" has been realized. Public education, from kindergarten
through graduate school; private philanthropy; scholarships for the
gifted; merit systems for employment . . . —all have helped to pry
open doors of opportunity for young men and women of superior
ability. . . .

"But the ideal," the bulletin goes on to admit, "is still incom-
pletely realized." (5, p. 25) Too many young people of college
caliber do not get to college.

To give an example of what we may be losing, Pritchard has pointed out that, as a result of the educational provisions of the GI Bill of Rights, many young men and women who had served in the armed forces of this country were given an opportunity to go to college at the end of their service. As a result, numerous young people for whom "further educational advantages would have been out of the question" went to college and proved to be "outstanding" students. Yet, if it had not been for those veterans' benefits, the potentialities of these young men and women might forever have lain dormant, and the contributions they are now making to the welfare of this country might never have come to be. (**14**, p. 80)

Economic factors can extend beyond mere individual privation. A poor community often cannot afford to develop and support adequate programs of special education for its gifted children, no matter how fully its educational administrators might recognize the potential value of such programs. Often it cannot even offer sufficient scholarships so that the community's intellectually best and brightest can, at least, continue their studies elsewhere.

Psychological Factors. Under this heading will be discussed only those waste-causing psychological factors which concern the individual and the stresses and strains arising from *inside* him. The community psychology and its often debilitating effects upon intellectualism in general and the gifted individual in particular will be dealt with separately in the following section on social attitudes.

To return to the psychology of the individual, although the gifted are certainly not the "mad geniuses" of popular legend—and actually possess a physical and emotional potential that is quite "normal" in terms of the average population—still, without proper guidance, they are as subject to emotional maladjustments as any other type of exceptionality. As the NEA bulletin justly observed, an intellect cannot "function fully or efficiently" if the individual's "social and emotional aspects are not well developed." Although it cannot be denied that substantial achievement can be made without "personal integration"—as has been amply evidenced by the numerous instances of acknowledged geniuses who have manifested markedly neurotic, and even psychopathic, tendencies—the fact remains that "no one knows how many others with great endowments have failed to achieve because of mental illness." (5, pp. 27–28)

Martens has confirmed this point of view, stating that—

It is true that some gifted adults performed poorly as children in school, seeking solitude or other experiences which the classroom did not provide. Many of the works that are ageless have come out of cruel and bitter hardships, out of poverty and want, social and spiritual deprivation, rather than out of an abundance of material with which to work. Despite the most adverse conditions, the persistence of giftedness has conquered, and the genius is revealed by his works.

At the same time, no one knows to what extent giftedness has been *un*used or *mis*used in adulthood, because no one was at hand to detect its possibilities or to give it kindly guidance in childhood. . . . (11, p. 5)

Very often the symptoms of emotional maladjustment can be such that they actually serve to conceal the child's superior qualities, particularly when he is placed in the charge of a somewhat diagnostically naive or not-too-well-trained or, in fact, not-too-bright teacher. Cutts and Moseley observed, from their personal experience, that—

Our collection of case histories of bright children has many examples of pupils who were so given either to daydreaming or to aggressive disorder in school that their teacher thought them stupid. When their high intellect was discovered and they were given work which challenged their power, the change in behavior was often miraculous. But there are many cases where the discovery came only after the pupil had developed such faulty habits of work and such an antisocial attitude that the school could do little or nothing to help. (4, p. 8)

Social Attitudes. Broadly speaking, social attitudes are the most significant factor in inhibiting the development of our national intelligence. They stem from both home and community sources, and are far more potent in effect than economic insufficiency or psychological maladjustment (which often has adverse social attitudes and background as a causative factor, for all three causative groups are, of course, closely interwoven).

Often gifted children of low-economic backgrounds do not receive the education they are capable of absorbing less because their families are unable to afford such an education for them than because they are not likely to think in terms of going on to college after finishing high school. In their circles, young people do not accept the idea of a college education matter of factly, and the child, the NEA bulletin states, "tends to accept the values that predominate among his family and playmates." (5, p. 26) With this premise, Nicholas Hobbs tends to be substantially in agreement, commenting further that—

Significant factors in the development of talented children are the attitudes toward such people which are held by members of the community. These feelings are subtle and varied. Is it somehow un-American to provide special opportunities for the gifted? Are geniuses rude and unpredictable people, just a little queer? Are art, poetry, music, dramatics, the dance, literature, really practical? . . . These questions . . . reveal attitudes which are largely unfavorable to the gifted child. But they are, nonetheless, decisive factors in determining a child's behavior. A boy in a slum area aspires to be a gang leader because of community approval of a notorious racketeer. A promising scholar finally accepts a family-and-community imposed role of business man, an activity in which he is successful but not too happy. (8, p. 166)

Although he attempts to lessen the black light in which he has painted community thinking by adding that "there are certainly positive attitudes as well, attitudes which favor the development of outstanding ability," Hobbs is forced to admit that communities are, at best, capricious in their relations with the gifted among them.

> The attitudes of a community are varied; they are favorable to talent and unfavorable; they are sometimes consistent, sometimes contradictory, sometimes even whimsical. . . . (8, p. 166)

Lamentably, it is these community attitudes and opinions—ill-founded and arbitrary as they may be, as they so often are—that influence the child's total orientation. "There can be no question," the NEA bulletin declares, "that socially conditioned attitudes toward intellectual and aesthetic values play a significant role in the extent to which an individual develops his intellectual and artistic gifts." (5, p. 27) And, as a whole, the current climate of America is decidedly an anti-intellectual one.

Furthermore, it is all too often an unfavorable community attitude that prevents local school systems from organizing special programs for the gifted children, even where there are sufficient funds to support such programs. If the community, as represented by its leaders, chooses to express the fear and animosity it holds toward those with superior intelligence by declaring that there is no "necessity" for giving individual attention to the gifted, it can—particularly in the case of the smaller community—very well block any attempts to improve educational facilities for those whom they have reason to believe will, unless checked, grow up to be "eggheads."

A more personal social factor instrumental in holding back the gifted child is that, if he derives from a low economic background, he is likely in school to feel excluded from the activities of the groups whose families are in more fortunate financial circumstances. "Being rejected socially, [the gifted child] in turn rejects not only the 'snobs' but also the values that they espouse—including respect for education," which does not necessarily imply a corresponding respect for intellectualism, as education, to our middle and upper classes today, has come to represent a "polishing" rather than a "learning" process, with the colleges becoming, to a great extent, finishing schools instead of institutions of higher learning.

In this area a diagnostic difficulty can again present itself: the mental attitudes of a child whose cultural background is substandard may not be as readily apparent as those of a child from a more favorable background, who already may have some appreciation of intellectual values, and, generally, if he is not defective in intelligence, a greater facility for expressing them. Other adverse background factors, such as poor family relationships, broken homes, and so on, can also retard the development of the gifted—or, in fact, any—child.

The gifted child who comes from a minority group is additionally handicapped by two more factors: (1) it is initially more difficult for him to secure recognition and appreciation of his gifts; and (2) he is continually tormented by awareness of the fact that opportunities are not easily available to him—or, in fact, available at all—that are freely offered to the other children. There is, of course, no sound reason for such biases; they merely represent prejudice of the worst sort. As Pritchard pointed out: "Belonging to one racial group or another has not been found to be an all-important factor in the later achievement of the identified gifted." To blast two old wives' tales, the Jew has not been found to be intellectually superior or the Negro intellectually inferior—although, curiously enough, both have been persecuted in large part because of these legendary opposite deviations from the norm.

Pritchard goes on to speak of the adjustments made by gifted minority group members who have come within the scope of various programs with which she has been associated.

Most of those with whom we are acquainted show an eminently satisfactory college record; most of them report general life happiness

and satisfaction with vocational status. However, when in addition
to superior intelligence there are many negative factors such as sub-
marginal economic status, a broken home, or a home having undesirable interpersonal relationships, plus membership in a minority racial
group with real or fancied persecution and discrimination, there are
ingredients either for the development of performance that is potentially dangerous to our society, or for becoming a burden to society.
(**15**, p. 109)

Cutts and Moseley have confirmed these observations, mentioning
that "many recruits to communism (and many clever criminals)
are young people who know that they have the ability to excel in
a profession but feel that they have been discriminated against
because of poverty or because of racial background." (**4**, p. 8)

All these factors—economic, psychological, and social—can be
attacked by a sound program of education, not only for the gifted,
but for the community and the parents as well. The schools cannot carry the full burden of such a program; the state and the
nation and private institutions must do their share as well. However, the primary concern of this chapter is to define the role of
the school, with the roles of the family and the community
touched on only as they become necessarily involved with the
school's program.

CHARACTERIZING THE GIFTED

Before arrangements can be made for setting up an appropriate
training program, the schools must determine just who their
gifted children are. Methods of identifying them have been discussed in some detail in Chapter Three. Because the current identification techniques are so unsatisfactory and seem likely to
remain so for a long time, it will have to be taken for granted that,
no matter how extensive a program of identification any given
public school system may undertake, it will, unavoidably, miss a
certain number of the gifted. However, it is useless to cry over

milk that we cannot keep from being spilled. If the program is really an honestly conceived and thoroughly executed one, it should succeed in ferreting out most of the children whose superior mental aptitudes establish them as suitable candidates for this kind of special education.

In order to make these students into appropriate raw material for an educational program, they will need to be categorized, for schools tend to operate according to categories. It is at this juncture that the much-abused but still much used IQ becomes useful—to separate the near-sheep from the almost-goats. Expediency plays a large part in drawing the admittedly arbitrary lines of demarcation. Although most educators would agree that the minimum IQ for the gifted child should range from 135 to 140—sometimes as high as 150—for the purposes of special education it is often placed somewhat lower. Otto, for one, has explained the very practical reasons that led him to select a minimum of 120 for his program in Texas—and his reasons are probably similar to the factors that have influenced other educators in setting their minima.

. . . First, we have concluded from personal experience and from case studies that a child whose I.Q. is 120 is capable of completing the regular assignments in an average class in less than the allotted time. He, therefore, has more free time. This free time will be more profitably spent through proper guidance. Also, if only children of 130 I.Q. and over are considered, they would comprise only one per cent of the school population. . . . If all children of 125 I.Q. and over are classified as gifted, only three per cent of the enrollment would be included. Using 120 I.Q. as the approximate lower limit of general intelligence makes it possible to anticipate six per cent of the enrollment in the "gifted children" category. . . . (13, p. 9)

The first factor quoted is, of course, largely a bow to idealism. It is the second that is of pragmatic importance. Obviously, the more children that can be included in plans for a particular program of special education, the more likely that program is to appeal to administrators as an economically sound one; hence, the more likely it is to be adopted as part of a regular public school system.

In order for a suitable program to be planned, it becomes necessary to know, first of all, wherein the gifted children differ qualitatively and quantitatively from the others in their own age and class group.

Background

There seems to be some feeling that superior capacities can be inherited. Certainly, authorities of the stature of Terman and Oden have agreed that, "despite many exceptions to the rule, the typical gifted child is the product of superior parentage— superior not only in cultural and educational background but apparently also in heredity." (18, p. 55) As far as the hereditarily superior parentage goes, there has not, so far, been any conclusive evidence to support the thesis that there is some genetic base for intellectual superiority. Bristow and his collaborators seem to offer qualified support to the balance of Terman and Oden's statement when they suggest that there is a "high but by no means perfect correlation between the gifted child's economic and cultural environment and the emergence of his giftedness," but ascribe this datum to "the influence of early environmental factors." (2, p. 11) It is probably also true that the gifted child of superior—in all the different senses but especially the cultural—parentage is the one whose abilities are the more likely to be discovered. Otherwise, as Otto has declared, gifted children can be found anywhere:

. . . in cities, in small towns, and in the country. They are found among the rich, those of moderate income, among the poor, and in all races and religions. . . . (13, p. 7)

Intellectual and Personality Traits

There is considerably more agreement among educators as to the specific traits of intellect and personality which distinguish gifted children from the average. Most typical is their superior ability in abstract thinking, which involves a correspondingly greater power to make generalizations, to reason, and to see "logical relationships" and draw "correct inferences." (**4**, p. 18) They also possess greater critical judgment than average. Cutts and Moseley would further give them "insight into problems," with what they consider to be its "connotation of sympathetic understanding" which "helps individuals to discover the essentials of a problem and so to reach a sound solution quickly." (**4**, p. 19) The gifted child will tend, moreover, to have greater insight into himself. As Witty has said:

> Because of their greater sensitivity, gifted children tend to be more self-analytical than average children; hence they tend to work through their problems more swiftly and more successfully than others. . . . (**22**, p. 26)

Bristow *et al.* have described "the mentally gifted" as being "characterized by 'power'—that is, they are able to do mental tasks of a high degree of difficulty." (**2**, p. 14) The gifted child's memory and attention span are also said to be better than average—though this is an area where maladjustment can do much to inhibit capability—and, according to Witty and Bloom, he has "an extremely rapid rate of learning." (**23**, p. 115) He will, as a rule, read a good deal faster than average, and the range of his vocabulary, plus his ability to use the words, will generally tend to be much greater than the run-of-the-mill child's vocabulary. In fact, Cutts and Moseley point out that "language ability is so often said to be the best single indicator of brightness" that one must guard against giving it too much weight and be careful to "remember that children with limited backgrounds are under a handicap in learning words." (**4**, p. 18)

The gifted child is much more likely to possess a well-developed sense of humor than the average—although the NEA bulletin sternly decries "whimsy" as part of the inefficiency pattern of "lazy" gifted students who have failed to learn good work habits (a subject which will be discussed in full later in this chapter). (**5,** p. 24) "Given a chance," a bulletin circulated by the Connecticut State Board of Education declares, the gifted child "may show an amazing degree of imagination, initiative, originality, resourcefulness, creativity, and inventiveness." (**6,** p. 7) According to Terman and Oden, the gifted child also manifests more enthusiasms than the control child. As an instance of this trait, he is far more likely to engage in making collections of objects—and even ideas—which interest him. (**18,** p. 32) And, finally, gifted children may also display a considerable degree of organizational ability.

Interests

The gifted child will, on the whole, have a greater range of interests than the average child, and a far greater intellectual curiosity. After undertaking a detailed investigation of his scholastic interests, Terman and Oden discovered that—

. . . in general, the gifted children were more interested than were unselected children in school subjects which are most abstract and somewhat less interested in the more "practical" subjects. However, the two groups express about the same degree of interest in games and sports. Literature, debating, dramatics, and ancient history were rated as much more interesting by the gifted, while penmanship, manual training, drawing, and painting were rated somewhat higher by the control group. (**18,** p. 30)

As was to be expected, the majority of gifted children studied by Terman and Oden proved to be "inveterate readers," with reading tastes that were not only more catholic than the control child's but also appreciably different in nature.

. . . the gifted children . . . read more science, history, biography, travel, folk tales, informational fiction, poetry, and drama. On the other hand, in proportion to the total number of books read, the gifted read fewer books of adventure or mystery, and far less emotional fiction. (**18,** p. 30)

Queried as to what they hoped to be when they grew up, again their selections showed marked divergencies from the choices made by the average child, although, if the allegations concerning the gifted child's superior background have any foundation in fact, this might account in part for the difference in their selections:

. . . analysis of the data revealed that gifted subjects showed greater preference for professional and semiprofessional occupations, for various kinds of public service, and for the arts. The control group expressed greater preference for mechanical and clerical occupations, transportation, and athletics. . . . (18, p. 31)

Limitations

The one factor in which the gifted child does not seem to rate well—at least in comparison with his other traits—is sociability. Although Terman and Oden make a strong effort to prove that gifted children get along with others just as well as, if not better than, the average, they are forced to admit that their researches show that—

. . . On sociability nearly 45 per cent of the gifted . . . fell within the lowest quartile of the respective sex norm for the control group. The superiority of the control on activity scores is hardly less marked. (18, pp. 36–37)

They attempt to explain these data in terms of their contention that the gifted child has optimal capacity in all areas by maintaining that—

. . . These discrepancies are in part accounted for by the fact that several of the very mildly social games which appeal to gifted children are unpopular with average children because of the demands they make on intelligence. . . . Another explanation is the fact that the gifted child is usually a year or two younger than his classmates and is therefore handicapped in the more strenuous competitive sports. . . . (18, p. 37)

And, undoubtedly, these reasons are valid enough, as far as they go. However, social adjustment is a result of outside forces working on a capacity, not a capacity in itself, and Terman and Oden tend to minimize the fact that, although gifted children are, certainly, *capable* of more than satisfactory adjustment with others, they frequently fail to achieve such an adjustment because of outside pressures.

It is also true that Terman and Oden's group, having been identified as gifted individuals from the beginning, and, having received superior education, training, and guidance by virtue of their experimental status, if for no other reason, certainly were more likely to have achieved a higher degree of adjustment than the unselected superior child. Therefore, insofar as the two investigators' findings regard only that particular group of gifted children which they specifically studied, their findings are undoubtedly valid; the question is how far those findings can be applied generally to the gifted child as a whole.

Cutts and Moseley follow in Terman's footsteps to the extent that they declare that "bright children as a group are superior in physical and emotional and social adjustment." However, they qualify that statement by admitting in their next sentence that maintaining that superiority necessitates these children's being "granted a good start," (4, p. 18) which is equivalent to the Connecticut bulletin's "given a chance."

In summing up their picture of the gifted child, Terman and Oden are again perhaps overenthusiastically applying the traits they found to be true of their group of gifted (which seem a little too good to be true of even such a select group) to gifted children as a whole:

. . . seven character tests showed gifted children above average on every one. As compared with unselected children, they are less inclined to boast or to overstate their knowledge; they are more trustworthy when under temptation to cheat; their reading preferences, character preferences, and social attitudes are more wholesome; and they score higher in emotional stability. . . . (**18**, p. 56)

Intellectual superiority, it must be remembered, by no means ensures moral superiority. The one is inherent; the other is learned. And learned behavior is the province of the school, even more than it is of the home and the community, despite the major role they play. One of the purposes of a sound program of special education is an attempt to build the gifted child's character up to resemble the glowing portrait Terman and Oden have drawn of it, and which, if it has done nothing else, has set up a worthy ideal toward which the educator may strive.

PSYCHOLOGY OF THE GIFTED

What causes the gifted child to fail to come up to the ideal in so many cases is his failure to make adequate adjustments. Despite his high IQ, the gifted child is just a child, without the maturity to make the best use of his own advantages. No child can cope singlehanded with an adverse environment; therefore, psychological disturbances can handicap the development of his full resources just as much as they can handicap the retarded.

Work Habits

First of all, and most frequently, emotional upsets can affect the gifted child's work habits. Superior mental abilities do not of themselves necessarily involve superior work habits. As Terman and Oden have pointed out:

Because he is usually able to accomplish the ordinary school tasks without serious effort, the gifted child runs the risk of developing habits of intellectual slackness. He may come to take a certain pride in getting his lessons quickly or in making plausible recitations without adequate preparation. (**19**, p. 41)

Or, he might equally well go to the opposite extreme entirely and acquire what the NEA bulletin describes as "inefficiency patterns marked by *meticulousness,* overorganization, discursiveness, and inability to bring a job to conclusion." (**5**, p. 4)

Both patterns of behavior represent equally reprehensible habits of study; both are potential causes of the gifted child's failure, later, to make a satisfactory achievement in college—which, according to Terman and Oden, did happen, even to the members of their select group. There had, however, been no error of diagnosis in the majority of these cases:

> Real lack of intellectual ability . . . was rarely the source of the trouble unless some form of definite mental breakdown had occurred. . . . More important were habits of idleness, unwillingness to do routine assigned tasks, excessive amount of work for self-support, or the deliberate choice to give preference to social and extracurricular activities. (**18**, p. 157)

Poor work and study habits tend to be the psychological handicap most typical of gifted children as a group, and this characteristic is manifested even by those who have otherwise achieved a fair-to-good degree of adjustment. As a result, their status is such as to prompt Bristow and his collaborators to make the remark that "few gifted children are as educationally advanced as their ability warrants." (**2**, p. 16)

Drive

However, these study habits can also be a manifestation of a far more serious type of emotional maladjustment to which the gifted child is often prone and which is the chief basis of his failure to achieve optimum potential in life as well as school. The fact that a child has superior intelligence does not prevent him from being a problem child—often quite the reverse—although the problem is not necessarily one of discipline but the equally frustrating—to the genuinely dedicated teacher—one of apathy. Zorbaugh and others have observed in this connection that—

. . . highly gifted children are likely to present difficult problems from the time they enter school. Typically we have found highly gifted children working far below their potential capacity.

At best, the result is flagging of interest and restiveness. Too frequently it is frustration and resentment, resentment that may be returned by contemporaries and teachers. . . . (**24**, pp. 101–102)

Apparent lack of ambition is the most common sign of disturbance in the gifted child. Some gifted children seem to be almost without any motivation or desire to accomplish, but are content to drift along on a mere minimum of effort, apparently, in spite of the foresight that is supposed to be one of their characteristics, not caring what the future holds for them.

These children need help. As Bristow has put it, "the foremost" factor in the "full growth and expression of the gifted child's abilities . . . is the drive to accomplish, the urge or motivation to use exceptional abilities, which most but not all gifted persons possess. . . . When that drive is lacking," these investigators conclude, the individual's chance of "reaching eminence" is remote. Yet, although "the possession of exceptional abilities is usually in itself a powerful spur," this is not invariably true. Still, it cannot be that lack of drive is an inherent trait in one kind of gifted child and not in another. Something has happened to the motiveless child—perhaps rather early in childhood—to make him lose his ambition. He may have met with—

. . . denial of adequate means of expression or a lack of understanding on the part of adults of the need for satisfactory outlets. Great unhappiness and sometimes serious emotional maladjustment develop when a gifted child's mental tasks are too easy for him or when he invites ridicule or jealousy or even fear because of his manifest superiority. (**2**, p. 11)

"Inferiority" versus "Superiority" Complexes

It must be remembered that the gifted child has another trait in common with all exceptional children; he, too suffers from being "different." And the fact that this difference lies in superiority rather than inferiority may be a compensation but rarely a consolation, especially in a society so anti-intellectually oriented as ours is today. By and large, the bright child has much more social difficulty than the average, for he is buffeted from all sides. First of all, he finds that "he develops at different rates physically, intellectually, socially, and emotionally." (5, p. 160) As a result, where he can meet the average child on one level, he will find that he is either lesser or greater than he on another. This means that in a heterogeneous situation he will often have trouble in making friends, and, as a result of numerous rebuffs and defeats, may become shy and uncommunicative. Cutts and Moseley have made the following observations concerning this phenomenon:

> Exaggerated shyness in a bright child is sometimes a result of being younger or smaller than the other children in the class. Sometimes it seems both the result and the cause of an undue amount of solitary activity. The child finds reading more pleasant than group play and so does not have much experience in give-and-take with other children. When he discovers that he does not know how to get along with them, even though he may be eager to, he withdraws into a world of his own. (4, p. 164)

Another response the gifted child may make to social disapproval or outright rejection is to become a "show-off." Unable to secure the approval of his age-mates, he deliberately demonstrates his superiority over them, as if to indicate to the outside world, and, also, to himself, that he "doesn't care"—that, in fact, it is from choice that he, the superior one, eschews the society of these inferior creatures. But the truth of the matter is that he really does want their society and may at times feel he would give up all his vaunted intellectual powers to be like the others. "What they can easily have," Strang has commented of the gifted children, "they do not want."

. . . When they have failed to make friends of their own age, they may find some solace in scholastic achievement—a certain satisfaction in demonstrating their intellectual superiority and winning some admiration from students and teachers. They use their mental ability to gain affection and to win the limited security that comes from intellectual achievement. (**17**, p. 151)

The gifted child's social difficulty is often compounded by the fact that the community is incapable of understanding the true reason for his withdrawal or "showing off," as they would more readily in the case of the mentally or physically handicapped. They cannot comprehend that he can be insecure and frightened, and so they feel that his behavior is deliberately antisocial, that he genuinely does not want to be a part of their society. Witty has underlined the perils of this situation, both from the community's and the child's viewpoint:

It may seem odd to us that a gifted child should feel "inferior," but often this is exactly the case. A gifted youngster realizes he is "different," and to most children there is no greater evil. . . .

The gifted child's abilities often cut him off from others, make him feel different, and, as a result, inferior. One of the gifted child's most difficult personal problems is that of adjusting himself to his differences. . . . (**22**, p. 25)

There is a third solution which has been adopted by many gifted children and which—though reprehensible in itself—seems to be the most socially acceptable so far as the community is concerned. Strang speaks of certain high-IQ-children who deliberately "do poorly in their school work in order to identify more closely with their friends. They would rather be popular with their own age group than with the academically minded teacher." (**17**, p. 151)

And so we have the withdrawn individual, the "show-off," and the conformist. To these the NEA bulletin would offer a fourth psychological handicap which it considers as a corollary of egotism:

. . . infantilism, fostered by doting parents in the gifted child perhaps more frequently than in others. Although both of these difficulties tend to arise from causes outside of school, teachers sometimes permit them to become aggravated in school situations by showing favoritism to their bright pupils or by showing them off or by oversolicitous concern. (5, p. 79)

Various educators have suggested various broad patterns of dealing with these problems. Cutts and Moseley warn that "sarcasm, toning down, and pressure for conformity" are not ways of dealing with the confirmed egotist. "He will not be conceited," they maintain, reflecting the rather rosy tone of optimism that permeates their entire volume, "if you let him know that much is expected of him because he has much to give." (5, p. 179) Such a measure will certainly do no harm; however, the NEA bulletin advocates a rather more objective, even if less concrete, method of dealing with all these psychological malfunctionings.

With respect to promoting the emotional maturity and personal integration of gifted students in school and college, the first rule is: *let them grow up,* and the second rule is: help them grow up into well-rounded personalities by aiding them in the achievement of self-understanding and by nurturing the development of the other-than-intellectual aspects of their lives. (5, p. 79)

Effects of Outside Attitudes

Correctly balancing all factors so that the gifted individual should have as normal a childhood as possible, while still developing his powers to the utmost, is not an easy task for either home or school. Overcultivation of the child's talents can be as disastrous in effect as undercultivation. Strang has noted that—

. . . In certain cases, the child's physical and social development has been hindered by forced cultivation of his mental ability. This is pathetically true of some so-called child geniuses whose overambitious parents have drilled them to perform memory feats. . . .

Both school and home may overdo the enriched program idea; they may forget that the child has the right to be a child—to live normally through each stage of his development. . . .

Gifted children may be under such pressure to achieve that they feel their gifts are being used against them. . . . (**17**, p. 150)

Witty has agreed that the kind of "parents who overemphasize a child's talents pose as serious a problem as indifferent parents. They are always pushing the child toward more and more intellectual or artistic accomplishments. . . ." And yet, he goes on to charge that "this type of exploitation is mild compared to that of the parent who attempts to use his child to satisfy his own frustrated vocational, social, or intellectual ambitions." (**22**, p. 19)

At the same time, in seeking to avoid overcultivation of the child's abilities, it is difficult for the home and school to avoid swinging back in the opposite direction, arriving at—

. . . the other extreme . . . homes and schools that do not provide sufficient intellectual stimulation for gifted children. These children are bored by the school work offered them. . . . Those who do adapt to these conditions tend to regress into mediocrity. . . . (**17**, p. 151)

It is especially hard for parents to stick to a middle-of-the-road course, since, unless they have received the right kind and degree of education—which, of course, is unlikely in most cases—they are not equipped to deal with the problem. The most unfortunate factor here is that, with the best will in the world, they may be starving the child intellectually.

Parents may be indifferent to a child's gifts—and still love him deeply. Their indifference often is due not to lack of affection and love, but to their own limited backgrounds which give them little understanding of the "bright" members of their family. . . . (**22**, p. 18)

THE NEED FOR GUIDANCE

For the Child

As Pauline Williamson observed, in an article describing the work and objectives of the American Association for Gifted Children:

> Health educators point out that with increased tension, frustrations, sensitivity, and loneliness of the rejected and misunderstood gifted, obvious major needs are for mental and emotional as well as physical health. A philosophy . . . that satisfies the inquiring mind and provides stability among the many complexities and adjustments must be basic for the development of the gifted as well as all others. (20, p. 124)

Hence, the school's responsibility in educating the gifted child goes beyond simply giving him skills and information. Guidance, not only to show him how to use this knowledge, but to show him how to use himself, is also of vital importance. In a sound program for the gifted, the class lessons should only be a part of an over-all plan which will also include, in the words of the Connecticut bulletin—

> . . . working with each gifted child to help him understand himself and others, as well as to plan a career which will enable him to make a significant contribution to mankind's knowledge and social welfare. Gifted children, like all children, need help in making educational and vocational decisions. Many of them have abilities in so many fields that it is especially important that they have skilled help in planning for the future. (6, p. 33)

Unlike the retarded child, the gifted child *can* acquire a considerable amount of book learning in the regular classroom without any special adaptations having been made to the standard curriculum for his benefit (which does not mean that he necessarily *does* acquire that learning; merely that it has been known to happen). This is, of course, the basis on which those who

allege that the gifted child does not need special education—
he can "get along" in the ordinary classroom situation—rest their
claim. Or, in other words, "if he's so smart, why does he need
a special class?"

However, if the gifted child is left to his own devices, there
is an ever-present danger that his intelligence and ability will be
developed without a corresponding development of character—
an especially dangerous possibility in the case of the gifted for,
as the NEA bulletin has warned—

Leaders in a democracy need more than intelligence and knowledge
and skills. They also need character, of which perhaps the principal
ingredients are personal integrity, human sympathy, and a sense of
social responsibility. Able and educated leaders who lack character are
dangerous, for they may use their abilities for selfish or anti-social ends.
Qualities of character develop from the habits and attitudes that one
acquires from the totality of life experiences. The portion of such experiences that is subject to the influence of school and college can contribute significantly, if not decisively, to the development of character
for potential leaders as well as for others. (5, p. 9)

Strang agrees that the importance of maintaining mental health
among the gifted goes beyond the fact that such undeveloped
talent is expensive to society. It must also be remembered that
"intelligence and talent can be misused for aggressive, destructive
purposes," and "misdirected ability or talent, as in the case of a
criminal or the mentally disturbed leader, constitutes a social
menace."

At one time it was thought that mental deficiency and criminal
tendency went hand in hand. Subsequently, it was discovered
that the evidence on which that hypothesis was based—namely,
the low average mentality of inmates in penal institutions—could
also be used to prove another premise and one which is now held
to be more accurate: that the clever criminals are not often
caught. Accordingly, it follows that it is essential that we de-

velop the gifts of our talented youth to our own advantage, lest they be turned against us.

For the Community

A program of guidance for the gifted child must also include a program of guidance for the whole community. Just as he must be adjusted to them, so must they learn to overcome their irrational prejudice toward him—and trying to pretend that such a prejudice does not exist is merely closing one's eyes to a very real problem. Even though the persecution is, to a great extent, covert, the gifted form a real minority group which, like most minorities, is vigorously persecuted by the ignorant.

Curiously enough, this attitude of anti-intellectualism did not always prevail. Terman and Oden mention that, prior to the middle of the nineteenth century—

. . . the youthful prodigy was generally regarded with a mixture of admiration, awe, and hopeful expectation. His parents were envied, and the child was likely to be made the protégé of a prince or king.

Then, after 1850 or thereabouts, one finds an increasing number of treatises, written chiefly by doctors and educational theorists, in which the "precocious" child was classed with the abnormals, depicted as a neurotic, and alleged, if he survived at all, to be headed for post-adolescent stupidity or insanity. Gradually the view came to prevail that a rich and well-balanced maturity demands the prolongation of infancy and the fullest living-out of each developmental stage. Not only should the bright child be protected from intellectual stimulation; any tendency toward early cleverness should be positively discouraged. "Early ripe, early rot" was the slogan of those who favored slow maturation. . . . (18, p. 1)

The American Association for Gifted Children attempted to determine the nature and origin of this prejudice as it exists today, first by asking: "Is this prejudice directed toward gifted children as individuals or toward a stereotype in the public mind?" And then they went on to wonder whether the educators and investigators themselves had not perhaps inadvertently contributed to this prejudice:

> Is there a possible semantic basis for some of the resentment toward the gifted child and toward special provisions for his education? Have we used the terms "gifted" and "superior" as professional terms and attached to them a whole conceptual framework of meanings quite different from the meanings assigned to them by laymen? It is an interesting fact that the word "gift" means "poison" in German. The inference is clear; what may be one man's gift may be another man's poison. . . . (**15,** p. 110)

The theme of the children's novel, *Prince Prigio,* written by the nineteenth-century British scholar Andrew Lang, is, in essence, the problem of the gifted child's adjustment to society. The hero—the prince of the title—is the unfortunate victim of his parent's traditional failure to invite the wicked fairy to his christening. After all the good fairies have presented the baby with their gifts, the wicked fairy bestows her curse upon him, and that is: "My child, you shall be too clever!"

At the end of the book, the prince, after having spent a lifetime being disliked by everybody because he knows so much more than they, is asked by his wife to put on his wishing cap and "wish to be no cleverer than other people. . . . Then everybody would like you."

However, the prince cannot quite bring himself to do this, and so what he actually says when he puts on the cap is: "I wish to *seem* no cleverer than other people." And, although, he "remained as clever as ever he had been . . . as nobody observed it, he became the most popular prince, and finally the best-beloved king who had ever sat on the throne. . . ." (**9,** p. 75)

The moral of the story should serve as a guide to all who are interested in improving traditional community attitudes toward the gifted child. Since it is the gifted individual who is the superior, it is he who must make the greater effort. He does not have to "*be* less clever," but sometimes, his teacher may advise him, it is more discreet to "*seem* less clever."

For the Parents

A program of guidance for the parents is also indicated, for they can do even more to hinder the work of a school's program of special education than to help it, and so their support—or, at least, neutrality—must be enlisted.

Parents tend to fall into two camps. Witty has described one group as the kind who—

. . . may be fearful of admitting that their child has special talents and of helping him develop them. They may fear that if the child is too extraordinary in his abilities, he will have difficulty in his relationship with other people. Perhaps, they think, he will not be able to make friends. Some parents, too, are still frightened by the old wives' tale which holds that genius is related closely to insanity—that the highly talented are more likely to develop emotional illness than more average individuals. And a few parents actually discourage the child's developing his abilities because they are jealous of his special gifts. (**22**, p. 17)

Pritchard has made some observations concerning the more sophisticated echelons of this same division—who tend to be very emphatic about their smattering of child psychology. She reports that a principal of a school enrolling a high proportion of gifted children told her—

. . . that some of the younger parents, usually those with college backgrounds, have been taught to place maximum value on social adjustment, on being liked by one's peers, on being one of a group. Therefore, these young parents are reluctant to have a child's gift or talent developed for fear it will be a social barrier that will set the child apart as being different from his classmates. Such parents need the reassurance that neither giftedness nor talent, properly developed, need result in eccentric behavior, egocentrism, or any kind of queerness. (**15**, p. 174)

The other group of parents is delighted to discover that their child is classified as "a genius," for no other word will satisfy them. They are, Witty says—

. . . so impressed with the special gifts of their offspring that they lose sight of the child as a total personality. It is as though such parents saw their children solely as brains capable of advanced mathematical calculations or as hands able to draw beautiful music from a violin. . . . (**22**, p. 20)

And Witty warns against their pursuing such a course, stating that—

. . . If the gifted are not to become distorted, one-sided personalities, it is important that we remember they are much like other children with the same needs to act like children and to be cared for and loved just because they are themselves. . . .

It is important for parents to understand that their gifted child may not be growing up as rapidly emotionally and socially as he is intellectually. . . . (**22**, p. 20)

PLANNING THE SPECIAL PROGRAM

The three educational methods that have been developed to cope with the problems of the gifted have already been discussed in Chapter Three. The one still most prevalent is acceleration, which, together with its variant, early admission, has fallen out of favor with most educators. Since acceleration and early admission are purely mechanical procedures, and their lack of desirability has already been pointed out, they need no further explanation in this context.

The second most prevalent form of special education for the gifted—and the one ranking next to acceleration as far as lower cost goes—is that of curriculum enrichment, which, in substance, means developing a program for the gifted child within the framework of the regular classes. The purpose of an enriched program should be to add that wider and deeper meaning to the gifted child's learning experiences in the regular classes that, if he were more mature, he would be able, in theory at least, to obtain for himself. In Martens' words, such an enrichment program should lead a child—

of unusual promise . . . on to an ever-widening circle of interests, a higher level of achievement and service, and a greater appreciation of problems which have little or no appeal for less able children in his own age group. Whether the field which eventually claims him be that of research, of technical execution, of creative expression, or of social leadership among men, the program of enrichment should lay the foundation for a well-rounded life experience in later years, as well as for specialized attainment in the field of his choice. . . . (**11**, p. 9)

Establishing the Basic Skills

The immediate aim of such a program should be to deal with the academic handicaps of the gifted child. Paradoxically enough, there are areas in which he may even be *behind* the average students in his own class. These deficiencies, Cutts and Moseley remark, may not be readily apparent in the case of the child of recognized ability.

A bright child's deficiencies may escape detection, even by himself. He is likely to be glib in his use of words and give the impression . . . that he knows more than he does. (**4**, p. 21)

Although Otto is less troubled by the child's lack of awareness of his own deficiencies, he, too, is concerned with the fact that a gifted child may, because of his superiority, be sadly lacking in the fundamentals on which a sound education needs to be based.

. . . All too often the ease with which the child of superior ability learns to read, write, and spell influences the teacher to let him forge ahead on his own without checking to see that he is developing the necessary skills and understandings in the proper sequence. Such unevaluated progress often leaves serious gaps that cause confusion and frustration at a higher level. . . . (**13**, p. 30)

And the Connecticut bulletin agrees that sometimes the simple is more difficult for the gifted to master than the complex, and, since the teacher will suffer from the same handicap—being superior in relation to the total class by reason of age, experience, and training, if not in actual mentality—she "may be tempted to overestimate the extent to which basic facts and skills have been mastered." (**13**, p. 30)

Reading is one area where the gifted child's drawbacks are especially likely to go undetected, because it is so commonly taken for granted that superior reading ability is concomitant of high intelligence, and so, Cutts and Moseley say:

Many bright children have never learned to read as efficiently as they should. Above-average speed and comprehension should not be accepted as sufficient when there is a potential for more rapid or more efficient reading, or for better adaptation of reading techniques to various types of material and various objectives in reading. (**4**, p. 121)

Another one of the areas in which the gifted child is prone to manifest deficiencies is handwriting. This handicap is logical enough, for Otto comments, "since the child of superior mental ability can think more rapidly than he can write, he is prone to become satisfied with less than his best in this area. . . ." (**13**, p. 3)

Although spelling is allied to intelligence, it, too, does not necessarily bear a correlation with it, for the artistically minded child and many otherwise intelligent individuals are sometimes exceedingly inept at this skill. Arithmetic is still another *bête noir* for the gifted, possibly the most prevalent deficiency in all the academic studies. There is a popular tendency among gifted children who have reached the high school and college level of articulateness to fancy that arithmetical ability varies in inverse relationship to intellectual capacity. This kind of snobbishness should be sternly dealt with by the teacher; anyone who is above average in intelligence should have no difficulty in mastering the fundamentals of arithmetic.

Physical education is another skill where the gifted child frequently falls below his usual high standards. Even more than arithmetic, physical education—particularly the way it is taught in our schools—can become an absolute nightmare to him. Otto has described many of the reasons for the child's failure in this area, and the disastrous consequences such failure may lead to.

. . . Since he learned to read easily, the chances are that he has spent a greater proportion of his time than other children in intellectual rather than physical pursuits. Consequently, he may have made relatively poor development of motor skills when his potential is considered.

He discovers that he is unable to acquire physical accomplishments with the speed that he is able to master intellectual tasks. He may be less interested in learning the motor skills. . . .

So it is in the physical education period that the very gifted may experience some of his first feelings of inferiority, as he finds himself excelled and cast in the role of follower or even outcast. . . . (**13**, p. 103)

None of these technical handicaps should, by any manner of means, be considered a support for the "law of compensation," whereby the intellectual superiority of the gifted is fancied (by the ungifted) "to be offset by inferiorities along nonintellectual lines." Terman and Oden state that if "in school achievement the superiority is greatest in the abstract subjects and least in penmanship, spelling, and routine arithmetical computations," that is because "the gifted are at their best in the 'thought' subjects, average children are at their best in subjects that make least demands upon concept manipulation." (**18**, p. 57)

Expanding the Horizons

Correcting the blind spots in the gifted child's education is, of course, just the preliminary step in a program for his education. In most subjects, the gifted child will be in advance of his age-mates in the ability to grasp essentials, and, sometimes, in already acquired knowledge. Hence, he will need more advanced study in the same areas as his regular class group is studying, plus additional courses in related or enriching fields. In any case, he needs productive work to fill the spare time which might otherwise lead him to develop habits of indolence or worse. Therefore, other roles must be found for him—roles which will depend largely upon the capacities and resources of the school he attends.

Most educators have a tendency to suggest that the roles offered him be leadership roles. However, as the Connecticut bulletin wisely points out, "high intelligence alone does not necessarily indicate that a person can become an effective leader." (6, p. 14) And many gifted children will never, despite training and coaxing, develop talent along those lines; they simply do not possess that particular talent. There is only one way to find out whether or not they have it, however, and so "teachers and parents should provide the challenge and the opportunity for pupils of superior aptitude to develop latent leadership abilities." (6, p. 14)

Classroom and school management offer the most obviously feasible opportunities for the gifted child to develop his leadership potentials. Various roles have been suggested that he can play in this area. As a teacher's aide, he can lead the class in special programs, as well as in committee work and group discussion. He will also be of assistance to the teacher by helping the slower pupils or those who have missed school sessions to catch up with the others. In addition, the gifted child can also function in all-over school activities, working as an office or library assistant, acting as a playground or cafeteria monitor, serving on the school council and working on student publications, and—to develop his social as well as his organizational ability—he might also be entrusted with the arrangements of such extracurricular activities as class parties and assembly programs.

Where the executive aspect of classroom management is minimized, gifted children might make their contribution and enhance their development by becoming research aides, helping the teacher to discover resource materials, and also—where these resource materials are of a difficult nature—to prepare interpretations of them for the other, less able students. Theirs also might be the task of organizing classroom displays and collections.

However, even these roles within the regular classroom will not provide sufficient outlet for the gifted children's excess of mental energy. In addition to their regular classroom work, then, the gifted may also be provided with special interest groups— organized, according to the schools' capacities, as hobby groups, workshops, or actual classes—in such fields as language, creative writing, dramatics, music, science, painting, ceramics, civics, and so on—wherever they manifest a particular facility or wherever they should, as the hoped-for leaders of tomorrow, acquire a deeper understanding of the subject.

Although the gifted as a rule tend to have many interests, generally each will have one particular talent. For the sake of our country's future welfare, the school should endeavor to foster this talent. On the other hand, for the sake of the individual's social adjustment, the school should take care that he does not develop that talent at the expense of his all-round development. Moreover, it is not advisable for the teacher to attempt to determine what the child's particular talent is too early in his life, even when its identity seems obvious. The Connecticut bulletin stresses the fact that—

> Although most gifted children have a wide range of interests, some may need help in broadening their activities. It is important not to encourage the cultivation of one talent to the exclusion of others, particularly while young children are in the most formative years. . . . (6, p. 15)

The confines of the school will not be adequate to satiate the enormous intellectual thirst of the gifted child. He needs to derive the benefits that are to be obtained from direct community experience. Hence, numerous extraschool activities should supplement his intraschool assignments. However, these field trips would also be of benefit to the average child; optimally, therefore, most of them should be for the entire class, with the gifted child's role perhaps being in the selection and organization of such trips. Certain field trips, of a more limited or specialized nature, would have to be for the gifted children alone.

The scope of the gifted child's excursions and extraschool interests depends to a great extent upon the cooperation of the community. As Hobbs has observed, "many worthy members of a community may be reluctant to sponsor any program that offers special opportunities to relatively few children in the community." (8, p. 170) On the other hand, some enlightened communities have done much to provide enriching experiences outside the school. Their museums have offered courses in arts and crafts and science to those with aptitudes along those directions; their clubs have given similar opportunities in music and the theater. One community has a theater especially for children. Industry and local government have offered opportunities for participation in their activities, as well as scholarships for the gifted.

Again, the teacher must try to make sure that all these extra opportunities do not, by seeming to put the gifted child in a privileged group—not only in the eyes of his classmates but in his own eyes—hamper his emotional adjustment and so vitiate many of the benefits of the program, for—

. . . gifted children need especially to learn the techniques of sharing and working together in class on common problems. As part of their preparation for successful adult living, they need opportunities for their deviations from the average to serve as aids rather than handicaps in learning how to get along with others. (**6**, p. 15)

If gifted children who know they are gifted sometimes become snobs, it is because this role has, in a sense, been thrust upon them. Gifted children suffer from a tendency to become detached from their environment, either, as has already been stated, by withdrawing or transcending (i.e., acquiring a "superiority" complex). Although this may result largely from the attitudes of hostility held by their classmates, these classmates—the average children—are no more to blame for their immature behavior patterns than are the gifted for theirs. It is the teacher's responsibility to see that the gifted are helped with their social adjustments.

Preoccupation with books should not be allowed to cut the child off from contacts with reality. Interest in every aspect of the material environment should be encouraged. . . .

In every possible way the child should be encouraged to associate in play and other activities with children who are not too far from his own age. . . . (**19**, p. 40)

The teacher should be trained to recognize the point at which the child's social handicap goes beyond her ability to cope with it. Where the maladjustment is severe, she should seek outside help without delay.

The habitually shy pupil, the one who continues to withdraw from contacts with others despite [the teacher's] cautious and continued efforts to help him, may be in great need of skilled psychological assistance. Excessive withdrawal is often a symptom of incipient mental illness. . . . (**4**, p. 165)

ENRICHMENT VERSUS THE SPECIAL CLASS

Drawbacks of the Enrichment Program

As a matter of strict truth, the enrichment program is not, basically, calculated to further the happiness or emotional adjustment of the gifted child, because it enhances rather than minimizes his differences by setting him apart from the rest of his class far more flagrantly than if he and his mental equals had been discreetly segregated in another class, where they competed only with one another. As it is, his superiority is continually being "flaunted" before the average children who, intelligent enough for invidious self-comparison, will be jealous of the gifted children's talent and resentful at their own exclusion from extra privilege—no matter how little they are capable of taking advantage of the same opportunities. To the administrator, a gifted child undergoing an enrichment program is being given opportunities to develop leadership characteristics and broaden the scope of his intellectual attainments; to the average child he will simply appear as "teacher's pet." Thus, a good deal of the social hostility that the gifted children engender may be, as the American Association for Gifted Children has suggested, of the school's own making.

Cutts and Moseley have proposed one method of operation which they feel will help ensure acceptance for the gifted child placed in a heterogeneous environment:

Class discussion and group planning are the best basis for setting up and maintaining an enrichment program. You can explain your ideas about why and how pupils might go beyond the curriculum and give the class a chance to criticize and make suggestions. Accept their suggestions whenever you can. If you are proposing a specific project and ask, "Who would be a good person to . . . ?" the class will probably pick the most able candidate. If not, you can easily add to that committee by asking for volunteers or making suggestions of your own. When you talk over interesting individual projects and books for reviews and give the students free choice, the bright and gifted will probably pick the more challenging. . . . (4, p. 69)

However, other investigators fail to share this optimistic approach to a possible solution. Zorbaugh and his collaborators do not speak only for themselves, but have summarized the results of a great many studies when they state that "in the typical elementary school we find . . . that highly gifted children have little chance of achieving group leadership. . . . Indeed . . . the highly gifted are more likely to be followers than leaders. . . ." (**24**, p. 104) These investigators observed a group of children in nursery school, when they are at an age, it is to be presumed where the average children have not yet had time to acquire prejudice against the gifted:

> . . . After having been accepted with the group, [the gifted children] attempt to alter the group's activities. An analysis shows that the changes they propose are in the direction of more complex patterns with more remote goals. Although these new goals afford the gifted children greater enjoyment in their pursuit and greater satisfaction in their attainment, the rest of the group loses interest and drifts away. Repeating this attempt at reorganization of activities, the highly gifted child finds himself marginal, if not isolated. (**24**, p. 102)

Another reason why the enriched regular class program for the gifted is inadequate is that the regular class programs are growing to be inadequate even for the average child. In a false spirit of democracy, many schools, Arthur Bestor has written in the *New York Times*, are beginning to pay proportionately less attention to the necessary intellectual disciplines, and, by conducting their programs along those lines, are building for their pupils "a high-walled playground within which the realities of modern intellectual life are forbidden to intrude." This, Bestor goes on to say, so far from being democratic, is committing "the ultimate treason against democracy":

> . . . The free educational system of the United States was born of the realization that every increase in democracy means an increase in the intellectual responsibilities that the ordinary citizen is called upon to assume. Democracy rests upon the conviction that the common man possesses the intellectual capacity to discharge such responsibilities. The function of the public school is to convert this potential capacity into actual intellectual power.

I do not minimize the difficulty of giving to the children of all the people the intellectual and cultural background which in the past was acquired chiefly by a minority in the upper economic and cultural brackets. I am simply saying that this task was precisely the one that a democratic educational system was created to perform. It involves, of course, a resolute facing of the problem of individual differences in individual ability. (1, p. 25)

So far, the disadvantages of the enrichment program have been considered here solely as regards the gifted child's welfare. But is the average child's emotional adjustment not to be given due consideration? What are his emotions when he finds himself in the same class with other students who, singled out because of their alleged superior mental abilities—alleged because, in many cases, the average child cannot see that superiority for himself, nor could he be expected to when trained investigators sometimes cannot—are not only receiving privileges that are not accorded him, but sometimes are allowed to assume a role tantamount to the teacher's?

And it is difficult to conceal the existence of an enrichment program from the average children—whereas the special class need never be officially identified as such. So, to the average child, enrichment will seem like an active flouting of the democratic ideal. Indeed, one cannot blame the child who sees his age- and classmates placed in so many favored positions from regarding the whole situation as flagrant injustice and regarding the gifted child himself with outright hostility.

Furthermore, the average child's work habits may also be affected adversely by this circumstance. He may feel that there is no use in his studying hard, for his achievements will always seem pale beside those of the gifted children with whom he is competing; hence, it appears futile for him to do any work, and so both groups will suffer psychologically.

There is still another extremely practical reason why educators should consider the average child's feelings—that is, if considerations of humanity alone do not have sufficient weight—and that is: Who are the members of the community who prove today to be so uncooperative toward the gifted children in their midst? Are they not the adult versions of the average children, and is it not likely that they did or will acquire some of their suspicions of intellect and intellectualism from their classroom experiences?

A program of community guidance and education, therefore, can best be started in the classroom, where the school has the future members of the community more under its influence than it will ever again find possible. In consequence, a program of guiding the gifted child toward getting on with the average should be juxtaposed with a program of guiding the average toward getting on with the gifted—to make each understand that the other has his place of worth in the world. Unfortunately, an enrichment program too often has precisely the opposite effect, bringing the two into such direct competition that mutual hostility can and usually does develop, leading to the anti-intellectual atmosphere which has placed us in the unfortunate political position we find ourselves today.

Aside from psychological factors, there are numerous operative drawbacks to an enrichment program. Even from the purely technical standpoint, it is not an efficiently functioning method when applied to current school practices. Cutts and Moseley comment that, the way our school systems are run—

> Strict departmentalization tends to reduce opportunities for enrichment. . . . Periods are generally short, so there is not much time left when students have finished their regular work. . . . The teachers are subject-matter specialists who think of a student's progress mainly in terms of their own subjects. . . . (4, p. 40)

Another objection to this kind of program is that the gifted child's "rights" under an enrichment program can seldom be clearly delimited. Sometimes the harassed and overburdened teacher, no matter how well meaning, cannot devote extra time to the gifted child—even if, theoretically, he is supposed to be following an enriched program—when her average pupils stand so sorely in need of aid. Furthermore, as the NEA bulletin has pointed out—

. . . even when a teacher knows the individual differences of his pupils, he may fail to act on that knowledge in his teaching. Perhaps he does not know what to do about it; perhaps he lacks suitable instructional materials; but most likely he lacks the time and energy that he knows he ought to give to individualizing his instruction for the few gifted members of his classes. . . . (5, p. 30)

Many teachers are willing enough to take on the extra task of helping the gifted child to develop his intelligence at its own rate, for—except to those small-minded pedagogues who are jealous of the child's superior IQ—most teachers are inclined to find the concept of helping those whose gifts may some day make them great an inspiring one. However, even such high-principled teachers may become a trifle disgusted at the discovery that, before they can broaden their little geniuses' horizons, first they must drill them in arithmetic and handwriting—in which they may well be rather worse than the rest of the class. The teachers are glad to teach them now to run, but feel they should have learned how to walk before being placed under their tutelage.

Advantages of the Special Class

No kind of educational program can be planned in the abstract. It has to be worked out in relation to current school conditions or it becomes simply an elaborate intellectual exercise. Today most public school classes, especially in the larger cities, are grossly overcrowded, both because of lack of space and lack of staff. As a result, a teacher is seldom if ever able to devote sufficient time to each of her pupils.

Where the class is both crowded and heterogeneous, the gifted children are the ones who will suffer by far the most deprivation, since the class will then follow a program scaled down to the average student's capacity—and, of course, rightly so, since the average children are in the majority, and there is no suggestion that democratic practices should not be followed in the school. However, under these circumstances, an enrichment program, even if it exists on paper, would have to go by the board.

Where the class is homogeneous, however, no matter how crowded it may be, at least the program will then be geared to the gifted child's intellectual level. Consequently, his deprivations—for there are always deprivations when there is overcrowding in the classroom—will, at least, be as minimal as circumstances permit.

A further argument in favor of the special class is that intellect stimulates intellect. Gifted children, when grouped, tend to have a salutory effect upon each other. According to Cutts and Moseley:

> Bright students who work together stimulate each other to greater intellectual activity than is ordinarily found in a regular class. They give and take criticism, exchange ideas, and share research in a way that is hardly possible between pupils of unlike abilities. And, because all are able to do a great deal of work and are expected to do it, there is no feeling of discrimination. . . . (4, p. 91)

Among many other educators, David Moskowitz has come out strongly in favor of the "honors" school, which, in substance, differs from the "honors" class only geographically . . . although he feels that the schools are of far greater value than the classes (but is forced to concede that except in a very large city like New York, with a vast reservoir of pupils to draw from, they might be impossible). It is his contention that—

> The honor school organization based upon the principle of general ability provides for continuity, total curricular modification and enrichment, the determination of unified, cumulative, long-range objectives, encourages correlation and integrative experiences by cooperative

effort, stimulates continual revaluation, and affords administrative flexibility for individual work. (**12,** p. 5)

And Cornog has declared that a school cannot really initiate a "working educational program for able students" unless those who are superior in ability be "segregated in special groups," adding that, in his opinion, "these intensive courses cannot best be given . . . by way of individual enrichment and private arrangements in a heterogeneous class." (**3,** p. 53)

Numerous intermediary provisions have been suggested by different educators. Martens has described a variant halfway between enrichment and special classes, which, she says, is operating reasonably well in some school systems. It is the practice in these schools—

. . . to form separate groups of gifted pupils for some curricular activities and to assign them to heterogeneous groups for other activities. In some cities it is the so-called tool subjects in which special groups are formed . . . while the more diversified activities like music, art, science, physical education, and shopwork appear to lend themselves more readily to treatment in heterogeneous groups. In other cities . . . attention is given to the organization of special groups for pupils talented in music, art, dramatics, or other creative fields, while classes in the subjects considered fundamental for all pupils may or may not be formed on the basis of homogeneous grouping. (**11,** p. 11)

However, the lack of agreement in the instances cited as to whether it is the "tool" or the creative subjects that should be taught homogeneously seems in itself to imply that this method is at best a groping, with results still too indefinite to warrant even qualified recommendation of the method.

ENSURING AN EDUCATION FOR THE GIFTED

Futility of Classifications

As a matter of fact, none of the programs that have been suggested is absolutely clear-cut. Unlike the issue of class versus school for the mentally retarded, there is no sharp line of demarcation among the enriched regular class, the special "honors" class, and the special school for the gifted. One blends into the other; it is difficult to say where the enriched program with workshop adjuncts leaves off and the special class begins. Perhaps there is no need to pursue the question exhaustively—at least not at this time when a more pressing issue is—or has been—the problem of getting *any* kind of special education at all for the gifted, let alone one particularly desirable type of program. As Pritchard commented:

> . . . much useless energy has been dissipated and . . . progress toward the successful implementing of an effective program for special education for the gifted has been severely hampered by too great indulgence in useless controversy over such questions as nature versus nurture, homogeneous grouping, acceleration versus enrichment, and the like. These are questions to which there may not be any definite all-inclusive answers. In the face of the present great need to use all of the country's outstanding ability, planning activities should not be delayed nor energies dissipated by undue preoccupation with such matters. . . . (**15**, pp. 107–108)

Current Activities

Up until now, the gifted child has not received his just dues in the matter of special education. Witty and Bloom, writing in 1953, mentioned that "surveys made during the past decade have revealed that gifted children are the most neglected of all groups in special education. Funds have sometimes been appropriated for the very slow or retarded pupil; seldom have they been made available for the gifted pupil. . . ." (**23**, p. 119)

Even at that time, however, more efforts were being made to help the gifted than could be concretely surveyed. Due weight could not be given, because of the very nebulousness of the practice, to the fact that, although organized programs of special education were lacking, the gifted children were getting considerable individual attention from various sources—erratic and unpredictable though it might be—for the gifted, more than any other kind of exceptional child, is likely to inspire the teacher as an individual to efforts on his behalf. Then, too, as Witty and Bloom pointed out further, since its beginning in 1946, the American Association for Gifted Children "stimulated wide interest in constructive endeavor on behalf of the gifted." (23, p. 119) At the same time, a factor that stood in the way of appropriate programing was not only the anti-intellectualism of the community, with which educators had at least prepared themselves to cope, but, far more shocking, what Bestor has described as "the anti-intellectual assumptions that underlie the thinking of substantial groups of professional educationists today. . . ." (1, p. 25)

Outlook

As of this moment, the future for our gifted children looks brighter than it had previously. Terry Ferrer, education editor of the New York *Herald Tribune* writes: "The public is awakening to education as never before . . ." (7, p. 3) but for a reason that does us as little credit morally as it does technologically. The Soviet Union's Sputnik has, more effectively than a thousand articles by perturbed educators, underscored to the general public what vast potentials we have failed to exploit, what extensive resources of intellect we have dissipated.

Right after the satellite's existence was made known, column after column of newsprint was filled with invidious comparisons between the Russian system of education and our own, mentioning the Soviet educational system's attention to seeking out the gifted, and stressing its making educational opportunities available to all who could take advantage of them (although, it was emphasized, because of the totalitarian nature of the Soviet government, not always in the areas the students themselves might have chosen). Terry Ferrer has quoted Dr. Lee A. DuBridge, president of the California Institute of Technology, as saying:

The Russians have launched an earth satellite because they can mobilize their best brains to the service of the state at will. Our best brains are as likely to be found developing television sets, doing research in medicine . . . or pursuing a thousand other opportunities which are available in a free society. We prefer a free society . . . and an important part of keeping it free is to feed a tiny fraction of our great wealth back into a first-class educational system which will give all Americans the opportunity to develop their intellectual abilities to the fullest. (7, p. 3)

Dana A. Schmidt, writing in the *New York Times,* declared, more critically, that our "lag" in the earth satellite and guided missile programs "is symptomatic of a disequilibrium in our national life." One reason for this imbalance, he declares, is "the American lack of respect for the learned professions, including research in pure science," and points out that "the Russians suffer from no such disability. Among them all practitioners of the arts and sciences enjoy high prestige and proportionately high income." (16, p. E3)

Still another *New York Times* writer, William L. Laurence, commented that, although

Russia is training scientists and technological personnel at a pace four times that of our own . . . the problem confronting American science is not solely that of training large numbers of scientists and engineers. In a free society such as ours it is not possible "to channel human efforts" without the individual's consent and wholehearted willingness. To attract able and promising young men and women into the fields of science and engineering it is necessary first to offer them better inducements than are presently offered.

In this respect we are behind Russia. In Russia a scientist is not only a highly honored member of society, he also is one of the most highly paid. . . . Furthermore, (scientists) are not stinted on funds with which to carry on their researches, as is often the case in this country. (10, p. E11)

The conclusion to be drawn from this debacle is clear: If we want to keep up with Russia, let alone exceed her, we must train our leaders almost from the cradle. And, unless the current leaders of our national and local governments show themselves to be completely impractical, it seems likely that programs for identifying and training gifted children will now be accelerated and receive more community support—at least in the sciences; it will be harder to get the community to accept the fact that leaders in the arts can be of equal importance.

However, this must not result in an attitude of "we do this because we *need* you, not because we *like* you." Nothing would be more conducive to the development of an intellectual caste which, in essence, is what the community fears. The gifted individuals must be made to feel that they are *wanted* members of the community, and that their contributions are appreciated, rather than worshipped . . . and hated. Otherwise, why should they not look down on those who are trying to cast them out?

Our attitude must be that everyone gets all the education necessary to enable him to give as much as he is capable of giving. Only then will our democracy be strong, not just militarily but intellectually and, most important of all, spiritually.

References

1. BESTOR, ARTHUR. "Progressive Education," *New York Times Magazine,* September 8, 1957. P. 25.
2. BRISTOW, WILLIAM H., M. L. CRAIG, G. T. HALLOCK, and S. R. LAYCOCK. "Identifying Gifted Children," in (**21**). Pp. 10–19.
3. CORNOG, WILLIAM H. "Initiating an Educational Program for Able Students in the Secondary School," *The School Review,* LII (Spring, 1957), 49–59.
4. CUTTS, NORMA, and NICOLAS MOSELEY. *Teaching the Bright and Gifted Child.* Englewood Cliffs, N. J.: Prentice-Hall, Inc., 1957.
5. *Education of the Gifted.* Washington, D. C.: National Education Association, Educational Policies Commission, 1950.

6. *Education for Gifted Children and Youth, 1955–56.* (Connecticut State Department of Education. Bulletin No. 77. June, 1956.) Hartford, Conn.: State Department of Education.
7. FERRER, TERRY. "At Last: Public Wakes up to United States Education," New York *Herald Tribune,* October 20, 1957. P. 3.
8. HOBBS, NICHOLAS. "Community Recognition of the Gifted," in (**21**). Pp. 163–84.
9. LANG, ANDREW. *Prince Prigio.* New York: A. L. Burt, n.d.
10. LAURENCE, WILLIAM L. "Science in Review," *New York Times,* October 13, 1957. P. E11.
11. MARTENS, ELISE H. *Curriculum Adjustment for Gifted Children.* (U. S. Department of Health, Education, and Welfare. Bulletin 46, No. 1. Reprint.) Washington, D. C.: Government Printing Office, 1953.
12. MOSKOWITZ, DAVID H. "Educating Superior Students," *High Points,* XXVIII (June, 1946), 5–9.
13. OTTO, HENRY J. *Curriculum Adjustment for Gifted Elementary School Children in Regular Classes.* (Bureau of Laboratory Schools. Publication No. 6). Austin: University of Texas, 1957.
14. PRITCHARD, MIRIAM C. "The Contributions of Leta S. Hollingworth to the Study of Gifted Children," in (**21**). Pp. 47–85.
√15. ———. "Total School Planning for the Gifted Child," *Exceptional Children,* XVIII (January, February, March, 1952), 107–110, 128, 143–47, 174–80.
16. SCHMIDT, DANA A. "U. S. Foreign Policy: Outlook for the Future," *New York Times,* October 13, 1957. P. E3.
17. STRANG, RUTH. "Mental Health of Gifted Children," in (**21**). Pp. 131–62.
18. TERMAN, LEWIS M., and MELITA H. ODEN. *The Gifted Child Grows Up.* Stanford, Calif.: Stanford University Press, 1947.
19. ——— ———. "The Stanford Studies of the Gifted," in (**21**). Pp. 20–46.
20. WILLIAMSON, PAULINE B. "The American Association for Gifted Children: Objectives and Growth," *Understanding the Child,* XXII (October, 1953), 121–24.
21. WITTY, PAUL (ed.). *The Gifted Child.* Boston: D. C. Heath & Co., 1951.
22. ———. *Helping the Gifted Child.* Chicago: Science Research Association, 1952.

23. WITTY, PAUL, and SAMUEL W. BLOOM. "Education of the Gifted," *School and Society*, LXXVIII (October 17, 1953), 113–19.
24. ZORBAUGH, HARVEY, R. K. BOARDMAN, and PAUL SHELDON. "Some Observations of Highly Gifted Children," in (21), Pp. 86–105.

CHAPTER EIGHT

The Psychology of Teaching
the Socially Handicapped

NATURE OF SOCIAL HANDICAP

A socially maladjusted person is one who has failed to come to terms with his environment. As far as the individual himself is concerned, the problem is not an intellectual but an emotional one; that is, no matter how intelligent he may be, his reasoning powers will not be of much use to him in solving it—or sometimes, in fact, in letting him know that he has such a problem. All social maladjustments or handicaps, therefore, spring from some basic emotional disturbance within the individual. Generally speaking—and especially in the case of the delinquent—that emotional disturbance appears to stem from environmental causes. Although some investigators are inclined to place part of the blame on heredity, its significance in this area, even as a predisposition, is doubtful. However, the individual's maladjustment is caused not by the environmental forces themselves working directly upon him, but by his emotional interpretation of those environmental forces—which is one reason why two children may hail from what seems like precisely the same background, yet one evidences severe behavior problems, and the other seems quite well adjusted.

238

Manifestations

Social maladjustment is evidenced by a variety of deviant behavior patterns, which may be as pronounced as outright delinquency or as relatively inconspicuous as faulty or insufficient response to normal environmental stimuli. The more serious disturbances, verging upon the psychotic, are generally more obvious, but not necessarily so; even a seriously disturbed individual can often do an excellent job of "covering up," particularly if he is of superior intelligence. This by no means is intended to imply that he understands on a conscious level *what* he is doing "wrong," or *why* he is doing it. As Norman Fenton has commented:

> It is evident that abnormal or mentally ill persons are often found to be in the throes of impulsive behavior whose origin or meaning is beyond their comprehension. . . . Why he does many things the pupil himself cannot fully explain. . . . (**12**, p. 103)

Although the emotionally disturbed child unquestionably is a handicapped child—a psychological cripple—he is, nonetheless, far from being, in any real sense of the word, "different" from other children. Marshall Clinard has pointed out that—

> . . . *all deviant behavior is human behavior.* By this is meant that the same fundamental processes which produce the "normal" person also produce the "abnormal," for both of them are human beings. If certain basic processes underlie the personality development of the normal person, those same processes and structure must be sought in the deviant. . . . (**5**, p. 29)

Lowell Carr has carried the same theme further, observing that "the important thing to remember is that most unsuccessful methods of adjustment are simply normal, everyday methods *carried to extremes.*" And he cites the following as the principal type of what he terms "adjustment by exaggeration":

. . . *repression;* . . . *defense* (defense mechanisms are developed by practically all personalities in some degree at some time to reduce the suffering caused by feelings of inferiority. . . . certain forms of anti-social behavior such as lying and stealing frequently have their roots in efforts to compensate for feelings of inferiority. . . .); *emotional indulgence;* . . . *withdrawing;* . . . (children who are too quiet, too shy, too willing to crawl away into a corner by themselves are with-drawing from something. Frequently they need help more than any other type. But they disturb no one); *regression* . . . (and) *hysteria* and *worry.* . . . (3, p. 140)

The socially maladjusted child is extremely difficult to cate-gorize, because he may represent one or a combination of a num-ber of different and sometimes overlapping types of personality disturbance. It is possible to give a very general over-all picture of the gifted or retarded child, but not of the disturbed child. Intelligence, certainly, is no criterion here: his mind may be in-adequate, average, even superior—but often, until his emotional disturbance is alleviated, it may not be possible to determine precisely what his mental abilities are. Of course, the fact that his mental ability may be readily apparent still does not mean that the child cannot be a clear case of social handicap, for, as the bulletin put out by the Connecticut State Board of Education points out—"sometimes emotional blocks keep able children from achieving in accordance with their high potential"—yet, at the same time, the existence of that high potential can definitely be recognized. (11, p. 15)

Not only the gifted, but all exceptional children, to the degree that their deviation from the norm has not been recognized and/or accepted, may tend to develop emotional instability. And, in addition to the gifted and the handicapped, the under-privileged child, the overprivileged child, the rootless child and the too deeply rooted child, the child whose parents do not love him enough and the child whose parents love him far too much, the child whose parents are too strict and the child whose parents are too permissive—all can develop psychological disturbances that may result in social maladjustment.

In essence, the maladjusted child may be compared to a machine that does not function properly. He may be such a complex and high-powered mechanism that it may not be apparent to the untrained observer that he is working at only a fraction of his total maximum output. Unless he is actively delinquent or has some outstanding eccentricity (or is notably psychotic), he is often hard to identify in the average classroom. Yet potentially his talents, like those of the gifted child, are being sadly wasted if nothing is done to help him. As the National Education Association bulletin has pointed out: "Ability embodied in a disorganized personality tends to be either undeveloped or paralyzed at the very threshold of production." (**10, p. 27**)

Delinquency as a Manifestation

To many, the term "socially maladjusted" is synonymous with the term "delinquent." This is far from being an accurate understanding of the total problem of maladjustment, for there are many of our children who have serious socioemotional disturbances, and yet not only are they far from evincing any criminal tendencies, but there is no reason to suppose that they will ever develop any. Yet they stand just as much in need of outside help as the youthful thief or vandal, conspicuous in his deviation from the accepted social norms.

In short, social maladjustment is the over-all problem of which delinquency is but one manifestation, albeit the most dangerous, so far as the community is concerned. As Strang has put it:

Delinquent behavior is only one of a number of poor ways in which young people try to solve their problems. Some daydream constantly; they imagine themselves successful, beautiful, popular, all the things they want to be and are not. They are happy as long as they stay in their dream world. This makes reality still harder to face. Some try to avoid or evade problems; they just let things slide. A few blame other people for their difficulties and take no responsibility themselves. None of these are satisfactory solutions to life's problems; in every case, the individual risks his own chances for happiness. However, the delinquent's way out is more likely to hurt other people as well as himself. (**34**, p. 22)

And Fenton agrees that "in the field of juvenile delinquency . . . many of the undesirable activities of children are explosions of impulse or desires which in other more fortunate children are being satisfied in wholesome ways." (**12**, p. 143)

The person who is socially maladjusted is not only in conflict with himself but with society. Fundamentally, he is *hostile* to society, and, whether he manifests that hostility in the form of attacking society or its component parts, or by holding himself aloof from them, the basic cause of both types of maladjustment is the same. A bulletin put out by the state of New York as part of a program to prevent juvenile delinquency describes as the two types of predelinquent behavior that should be noted by the diagnostician—or the teacher, when functioning in that capacity:

. . . *aggressive* behavior . . . considered to mean that the child was working out his problems of adjustment through contacts with his immediate environment in which disciplinary action was required. *Withdrawn* behavior . . . used to describe the working out of problems by "turning inward" and avoiding contact with the environment. It should be noted that the same child may show both aggressive and withdrawn behavior: the generally withdrawn child, for example, might have explosive reactions of an aggressive nature when forced to participate in social activities, but such aggressiveness would usually be of short duration. (**30**, p. 5)

It is the tendency to think of the aggressive child as the one more likely to be delinquent, but this does not necessarily hold good—although it *is* true to the extent that the nonaggressive child is less likely to indulge in the more overt types of delinquency. As a matter of fact, social handicap could be defined to characterize individuals who *could* potentially be delinquent *were* circumstances different (and who may yet be delinquent, since delinquency is not, of course, confined to the juvenile). In a sense, all maladjusted children are delinquent, if we consider the term "delinquent" in the sense of failing in one's duty or responsibility. The "quiet delinquent" is failing in his duty to society by refusing to become a part of it, by refusing to give all that is in him, just as the aggressive delinquent is failing in more obvious ways. Both the "quiet" and the aggressive delinquent are failing in their duty toward themselves. And society, by having allowed them to fall into such poor behavior patterns, has failed in its duty toward them.

Although conceding the basic affinity between general maladjustment and out and out delinquency, Harry Shulman feels that a clear line should be drawn between them:

What differentiates juvenile delinquency from personality disorders is that, in addition to a similar set of interpersonal maladjustments, delinquency involves deviation from an officially stated value system. Actually, all deviations in conduct are at the same time deviations in interpersonal relationships; that is, disagreements as to what constitutes proper behavior toward other persons in a defined situation. But in juvenile delinquency, treatment involves not only a series of adjustments in interpersonal relations to ease the tensions that underlie breaks in communication and understanding, but the development of a sharpened sensitivity to the rights and welfare of other persons as officially defined within the culture. . . . (33, p. 26)

In the early stages, however, that line cannot be drawn. Since the discovery, cited by Carr as "one of the most important that has been made in the whole field of crime control in recent years," that "overt delinquency is frequently preceded during a period ranging from months to years by less serious deviant behavior" (3, p. 264), it has come to be recognized by all those concerned with the problem of crime prevention, as well as all those concerned with the behavior problems of youth, that the two problems are inextricably interrelated, and that any program designed to prevent juvenile delinquency must be aimed at preventing all maladjustment, or it is destined to failure. As the New York State bulletin declares:

. . . The patterns of difficulty and the bases of difficulty may be as varied in number as the cases of children involved. No one can say with certainty in what particular case, or against what background of a particular causal complex of tensions, emotional, social and personality needs this boy or that girl may express his or her maladjustment in the ways we label "delinquent." (**30**, p. 15)

And Carr fully supports this viewpoint, stating that, "in order to prevent delinquency, society will somehow have to . . . discover emotionally disturbed children and remove the causes of their disturbances early, i.e., before they can develop antisocial attitudes and habits. . . ." (**3**, p. 130)

It is true then that any predelinquency program will of necessity include a number of children who, although standing in need of guidance, will never become an active threat to the community, and, therefore, that the community which is interested only in preventing crime and not in ensuring the future welfare of its members may feel that its resources are being "squandered" on these "harmless" deviants. However, *no deviant is ever entirely harmless.* Anyone who is maladjusted, and who is in consequence hostile to society, is capable of engaging in a destructive act against that society, even though he may not manifest his hostility until he is an adult. Furthermore, as Carr emphasizes, although "only a minor fraction of the maladjusted children and the children in danger at any time attain sufficient 'nuisance value' in the community to reach the juvenile court . . . that fraction, just because its deviations have attained such a high nuisance value, contains a relatively high percentage of children so badly maladjusted or so seriously endangered that further deviations are inevitable." (**3**, p. 216)

The Gluecks held that it was possible to prognosticate delinquency at an age as early as six (15, p. 144), and T. C. Russell, in a speech made in his capacity as chairman of the Commonwealth Club of California's delinquency prevention program, went so far as to declare that "child delinquency often begins prior to the time of going to school. Bad traits show up early in a child's life." (31, p. 75) However, Clinard argues very rationally that "it seems unlikely that delinquency, which involves social definitions, could be predicted at an age when the child has not participated much in the wider community." (5, p. 191) And so, generally speaking, if the child's behavior problems are identified as such at the time he enters school, that should be early enough to start a remedial program, providing that the necessary corrective techniques have been already established.

Diagnosis

Even when the child is already attending school and well in the educator's grasp, it is still not so easy to determine the existence and the extent of his personality disorders. How is it possible, for example, to determine when an apparently normal child is not operating at full potential? How can the lay teacher be expected to determine what part of a blind or deaf student's inadequacy results from the disability itself, and what part from the frustrations and rejections incident upon the disability? For, as Chamberlain and Moss have remarked, "the child senses the feelings of the parent who rejects him because of his handicap, even though that parent may feel he has successfully hidden his feelings of guilt and rejection" (4, p. 5), and, although they were referring specifically to retardates, the same principle applies to all handicaps. Even the gifted child can feel rejected by parents who are jealous of, or frightened by, his superior abilities.

Adjunctively, how can that teacher distinguish an hysterical handicap from a genuine—in the physical sense—one? Certain types of handicap which may seem clearly organic often turn out to be psychological in origin. Pseudo feeblemindedness is, of course, the classic example—although this case of mistaken identification sometimes results less from the child's being actually considered defective in mentality than from the practice which Frampton and Rowell find "distinctly to be deplored," namely, that of "using classes for the mentally handicapped as . . . dumping grounds for children whose chief deviation is behavior." (13, p. 331) Although that practice has been minimized in the seventeen years since their text appeared, it still does exist to a considerable degree and can, in itself, become a further factor in the increasing maladjustment of the child concerned.

Stuttering is another handicap presumed to stem from some kind of emotional disturbance. In fact, today most speech defects are considered to have psychological bases, with the exception of such clearly organic causes as cleft palate, harelip, and so on. However, all speech defects will be dealt with, in this volume, in Chapter Nine, together with the physical handicaps, because, whether they are psychological or organic, the greater part of the treatment involved will be physical in nature.

In the same connection, Frampton and Gall have observed that "impairments of speech may exist simultaneously with or arise secondarily in practically all types among the exceptional" (13, p. 167)—such impairment, again, being often symptomatic of severe emotional maladjustment. And furthermore, according to the New York State bulletin, "undetected or uncorrected physical handicaps or defects, particularly those of vision and hearing" can be a considerable causative factor in psychological disturbances. Therefore, in cases of maladjustment, the teacher should always, in addition to whatever other diagnostic techniques and procedures she employs, check to see whether there is present in the child some slight, easily remedied physical handicap—such as, for example, the need for glasses—which she can immediately take steps to remedy. Thus, although she cannot undo the emotional damage that has already occurred, she can prevent its further increase.

Another basis of emotional conflict for a child may be "mixed dominance," wherein the child cannot seem to commit himself either to right-handedness or left-handedness. This indecisive state may, according to Chamberlain and Moss, result in his being "subject to emotional problems" and "convulsions," and may slow him down mentally as well as affect his speech development. (4, p. 7)

It may be taken as a rule of thumb then that all exceptional individuals will suffer from some degree of emotional maladjustment. Generally speaking, in this text, the specific maladjustments connected with the specific handicap (or gift) will be or have been taken up in the section dealing with that handicap. Still, it should be pointed out here that often the emotional disturbance has transcended the actual physical handicap—as, for example, in the case of the child who has exaggerated a slight orthopedic defect into what he fancies to be a monstrosity.

Emotional maladjustment can also be manifested in various academic disabilities, among which reading lag has been most widely publicized. According to Fenton, "many cases of reading retardation . . . illustrate the dynamic aftereffects of earlier, long-forgotten emotional disturbances associated with school in general and reading in particular." This is one of those involved types of disturbance that compound their own maladjustive influences, for, he goes on to say, "the child who fails initially to learn to read with his class group is handicapped not merely by this retardation in reading but also by the carry-over of feelings and attitudes of failure and discouragement." (12, p. 121)

Intelligence tests, subject to the usual warning, are useful, though even less conclusive than usual, as a diagnostic technique in this area. They are, furthermore, subordinate here to the personality and adjustment tests, which, in their turn, have their dangers also. Corrigan points out that—

. . . The highly subjective and personal nature of the questions or items of a test may lead the subject to "fake" his answers in order to give a socially acceptable picture of himself. . . . (7, p. 157)

To which Fenton has appended very bluntly his diction that "the accurate appraisal of the potentialities of any individual for personality development is not obtainable by means of present scientific technique." (12, p. 116)

Carr has outlined six very general methods for discovering problem behavior in the classroom:

(1) direct observation of "symptoms"; (2) ratings by teachers; (3) ratings based on a child's reputation with his playmates . . . ; (4) questionnaires; (5) information or conduct tests; and (6) appraisal of correlated conditions. (3, p. 265)

He has also listed a series of specific behavior traits that *may* be symptomatic of psychological maladjustment in some degree, and, consequently, which are characteristics the teacher or diagnostician should constantly be on the watch for:

What behavior is indicative of an inadequate adjustment situation? Police suggest *unusual* behavior—sudden prosperity in a child from a poverty home, unexpected academic failures, etc. For clinical purposes a check list would include over forty terms such as: restlessness; excitability; "nervousness"; boastfulness; sensitiveness; worrisomeness; dull, slow manner; selfishness; changes in personality; depressed or discouraged attitude; bed-wetting (beyond early age); absent-mindedness; daydreaming; shyness; seclusiveness; failure to adjust with other children; preference for younger children; disobedience; temper display; incorrigibility; fighting; quarrelsomeness; swearing; stealing; lying; truancy from home; truancy from school; begging; association with bad companions; sex misbehavior; acts of violence; physical complaints, nail-biting; convulsive attacks; sleeping sickness; speech defects; retardation in reading; retardation in school; advancement in school; exclusion from school; exceptional brightness; slowness in learning to do things. (3, p. 264)

The main thing the teacher as a diagnostician should guard against is the pedagogical attitude which E. K. Wickman described as early as 1928, but which nonetheless is as valid today as it ever was. That is, in attempting to identify cases of maladjustment, too many teachers are prone to look for disruptive classroom behavior, which, in terms of mental hygiene, can be of little significance, while they disregard the inconspicuous and often significant symptoms, as, for instance, absent-mindedness, shyness, seclusiveness, and the like. (**37**, p. 73) In other words, the teacher is thinking more in terms of her own favorable adjustment than of the child's. Furthermore, some teachers, Fenton points out, tend to disbelieve what the psychologists and mental health authorities have told them; for instance, they will discredit the high IQ of "the slow, awkward type of child," alleging that they "know more about him than the psychologist" because they have the child in class every day and have "observed what a source of irritation his clumsiness is." (**12**, p. 128)

The introduction of objective measures of individual difference, he goes on to say, has overcome a good deal of this kind of emotional assessment by teachers. On the other hand, like the wonder drugs, these objective measurements have given rise to a new strain of virus in the teacher. As a result—

Some teachers now tend to accept too unquestioningly the finality of test scores. They may need to be warned about the limitations of the tests, because sometimes they put more faith in them than the authors of these measurements would advise. (**12**, p. 128)

Origins of Maladjustment

As was mentioned earlier in this chapter, virtually all social maladjustment seems to spring from environmental causes. That environment can be, first of all, the larger environment—the town, the state, the nation, even the world. The current almost schizoid state of society has produced tremendous, often conflicting forces that assail every one of us from all directions, so that it becomes almost a feat to retain some degree of balance underneath such pressures. In this connection, Clinard has observed that—

The mobility and impersonality of an urban world and the restrictions on personality present in the traditional family methods of rearing children in such a world appear to produce individuals who are prone to mental disorder. . . . (5, p. 330)

Another even more basic factor held by many investigators to be a prime source of the prevalence of emotional maladjustment in our society is the fact that our culture, and, hence, our social institutions, have lagged far behind our technology. This holds true in the concrete as well as the abstract interpretation, as Carr has stated, "for the average man there is no appreciable carryover of adjustment techniques from physical to social situations." (3, p. 17)

Although these larger issues are no doubt ultimately responsible for many if not most of the psychological disturbances we find among school children, it is rare that these issues are directly responsible, but affect the individual only as they are channeled down to affect his immediate environment. To most people, the world—sometimes even the nation—is an abstract concept, having real existence only in the newspapers and on radio and television broadcasts; what is real to them are the community, the home, and the school. Moreover, even if it were agreed that the state of the world is what is causing the state of social maladjustment that we are attempting to combat, what individual or local group of individuals can even attempt to reorganize our whole social structure in one blow? Hence, any preventive or ameliatory program would, of necessity, have to start with a discussion of the immediate environmental factors.

Goldberg has written concerning the adjustment—or, rather, maladjustment—of the exceptional that—

. . . if a child lives in an environment in which he is opposed, thwarted, or rejected, as happens often with the exceptional, he will begin at an early age to develop the kind of behavior which we find in a person who perceives himself as one being abused. He will feel hostile and probably will project his hostility into others. (**18**, p. 120)

This, of course, is applicable to the average or retarded individual just as well.

Specifically adverse environmental factors include racial and religious discrimination, which have always been strong forces in promoting the kind of resentment that can lead directly to social deviation. Poverty and substandard housing, with its concomitant of overcrowding, are other responsible factors. Then, of course, there is always the question of the broken or disorganized home, which is supposed to be so characteristic of American society today. Referring to the maladjusted gifted, Cutts and Moseley have reported that "research into the background of disturbed children has shown that from 35 per cent to 50 per cent of them come from homes where strong emotional tension is evident." (**9**, p. 157) And the same investigators point out further that "frequently homes are broken or cracked because the parents are themselves maladjusted" (**9**, p. 158), thus giving a frightening picture of what may happen to current generations unless the present rise in personality disorders is curbed.

Sad to say, even the school can play a part as an adverse environmental force. Heck—who uses the term "social handicap" in its narrowest sense—ascribes one of its causes to "lack of curricular adjustment in the regular school." (**20**, p. 33) Conversely, Cutts and Moseley state, "studies of well-adjusted children from bad environments show that the saving factor has often been a teacher who took time to be interested and to help." (**9**, p. 157) On the whole, though, the school situation as it exists in many, if not most, communities today is generally conceded to be provocative of a considerable proportion of the total maladjustment in our population. Clinard has given a picture of the school in its capacity as a psychologically destructive force:

> Unfortunately, some school situations add to personality difficulties and to intergroup tensions, and may even contribute to truancy and to more serious delinquency. Many professional educators agree that schools are often places where juveniles, during the school day, are bored, subjected to monotonous routine, crushed when they try to express any individuality, or thrown into needless competition with others instead of learning how to cooperate with them. In many urban areas the relation of teacher and pupil is impersonal. Nevertheless, the school situation is one of personal interaction, and too frequently those selected to educate others are themselves uninspiring and may even be seriously maladjusted. (5, p. 528)

Extremely personal factors can, of course, play a major role in emotional maladjustment, with their effect on the environment, and the environment's effect on them the causative force of disturbance. As has been stated, the child who is defective, either from the point of view of organic or mental handicap—or even, as a matter of fact, the cosmetic viewpoint—can readily become maladjusted. Furthermore, sibling rivalry, competition, and other aspects of a normal, well-ordered existence can become sources of serious disturbance. According to Karen Horney, the disturbed or neurotic individual is the one who cannot succeed in resolving the inherent dichotomies of our own culture *in the ways provided by that culture for their resolution.* (21, pp. 286–88)

Insecurity is, of course, a major factor in emotional maladjustment, and that insecurity can be produced, Horney says, from "a wide range of adverse factors in the environment":

> . . . direct or indirect domination, indifference, erratic behavior, lack of respect for the child's individual needs, lack of real guidance, disparaging attitudes, too much admiration or the absence of it, lack of reliable warmth, having to take sides in parental disagreements, too much or too little responsibility, over-protection, isolation from other children, injustice, discrimination, unkept promises, hostile atmosphere, and so on. . . . (22, p. 41)

Everyone experiences some degree of frustration, and often it is the degree of individual tolerance rather than the amount of outside pressure that determines how well each person will be able to preserve his own stability. Nonetheless, the neurotic child is behaving normally by becoming disturbed under pressure. Carr has adjured us to—

Remember that the characteristic of frustration (wish blockage) is *suffering*. Remember that the tendency to escape suffering is a fundamental biological drive in every organism. The child denied physical care, emotional satisfaction, and the skills normal for his age-group, sex, and social class is suffering. Hence he is driven by uncontrollable biological forces to try first one thing and then another to reduce his suffering. It is purely a trial-and-error process. . . . (**3**, p. 137)

So far, it is the child who is at conflict with his environment that has been discussed here. However, Clinard points out that sometimes it is not the child who is at conflict with his environment, but the immediate environment that conflicts with the over-all social structure:

. . . Much juvenile delinquency . . . arises from the growth of subgroups which, although in physical contact with the rest of the society, may have different norms. . . . (**5**, p. 15)

He explains this further by stating that different worlds, in effect, exist side by side in the same city, even on the same street: "Many local communities have norms so different from those of middle-class neighbors that they might be part of a separate culture." (**5**, p. 120)

New York City, specifically Manhattan Island, is perhaps the most conspicuous example of this kind of culturally diversified environment in the United States, for here the different worlds are clearly visible from one block to another—and the resulting differences in cultural values, although they do not necessarily produce delinquency, are bound to produce a considerable degree of social maladjustment. Carr has summed up the results of various studies of all the large cities in the United States when he declares that—

. . . there are areas in our great cities where (antisocial) patterns are omnipresent, where they affect all areas of life, and where the pressure for conformity to them is very powerful. . . . The antisocial pressures in such areas are *numerous, varied, powerful, widely deviant,* and *continuous.* In contrast, the antisocial pressures in a residential (presumably middle-class residential as opposed to tenement) district are *few, simple, weak, little divergent,* and *intermittent.* (3, p. 127)

And, finally, still another source of mental conflict related to this is what Clinard has described as "the inconsistent value patterns of the adult world," which very understandably "constitute one of the chief moral hazards to the juvenile in the modern world" (5, p. 110), and which may be a prime causative factor in juvenile delinquency.

TWO SPECIAL PROBLEMS

Certain types of social handicap have received so much attention that, even though they are properly part of the total situation, they will be given special treatment here as well. These are delinquency and maladjusted feeblemindedness.

Delinquents

Obviously one reason why delinquents have received so much more attention than the other emotionally disturbed is that their maladjustment affects not only themselves but the whole community, which is forced to attempt to cope with the problem not so much out of regard for the general welfare as out of sheer self-preservation. The current rise in the incidence of juvenile delinquency can be described by no other word short of appalling. According to Strang's statistics:

During the last twenty years the number of murders committed by boys under the age of sixteen increased 47 per cent, sex crimes 69 per cent, attacks on people 71 per cent . . . young people in the United States commit a million and a half major crimes every year. This is nearly sixty per cent of all major crimes. . . . (**34**, p. 4)

Furthermore, her statistics, and the others available, do not, according to Schwartz, give a complete picture of the total situation—which, he says, is even more serious:

Operating statistics . . . cannot supply all the important kinds of data on juvenile delinquency which are needed. The statistics presented . . . for example, do not give information on children whose behavior is contrary to the law but who are not apprehended or brought to the attention of an official agency. . . . (**32**, p. 9)

It might be well at this point to attempt some clarification of the terms "juvenile delinquent" and "juvenile delinquency"—which are not as susceptible to definition as they might appear at first glance, since there are both legal and social aspects to be considered. "Antisocial acts of juveniles," Clinard says, "include not only those which would be crimes if committed by adults but many other offenses which are peculiarly juvenile, such as truancy, incorrigibility, and vandalism." (**5**, p. 16) Strang has observed that "a young person is legally considered delinquent only if his behavior has brought him into contact with the law," but she adds that "social delinquency ranges all the way from minor offenses to serious crimes." (**34**, p. 7)

She goes on to list a series of characteristics by which the juvenile delinquent may be identified, although she takes pains to stress the fact that not all juvenile delinquents manifest these characteristics, nor are all who manifest these characteristics juvenile delinquents:

Juvenile delinquents usually have several or more of the following characteristics: They have been neglected by their homes, schools, or communities. They have somehow got off the track and have been

thrown into association with groups that exert a bad influence. They
are dissatisfied with school either because they fail in their work or
because the subjects they are taking have no meaning for them. They
are not liked and accepted by the young people they would like to
have for friends. They have not been given the love and affection they
need from their parents. They lack self-confidence, a feeling of being
likable, worth-while individuals. They are always in search of excite-
ment, of wild, daring things to do. They have a reckless, I-don't-care
attitude toward life. . . . (34, p. 15)

While not minimizing the importance of juvenile delinquency
as a manifestation of individual adjustment, Shulman gives the
concept a broader sociological significance by terming it "more
than a formal breach of the conventions; it is indicative of an
acute breakdown in the normal functions of family life." (33,
p. 21) And Carr, bringing us back to the lamentable state of the
world today, has described it as one symptom of a vast social
disorder:

. . . delinquency is only one small part of the problems which "social
engineers" face in trying to organize the good life in American communities. . . . research in social work has shown that juvenile delinquency as such tends to appear in association with clusters of other
troubles in a community. The whole complex of troubles that bring
individuals into contact with the police, the relief administration, or
with other agencies, has been called *social breakdown*. . . . (3, p.
212)

Traditionally, delinquency has always been the type of maladjustment that is said to derive from a substandard background,
and Clinard has commented in this regard that—

. . . delinquency is primarily a lower-class phenomenon. According
to one explanation . . . it represents largely a protest by lower-class
boys against the virtues of honesty, cleanliness, and hard work represented by the middle class and particularly by the middle-class teachers
of lower-class boys. (5, p. 22)

The Gluecks found in their 1934 study of one thousand juvenile
delinquents that 76.3 per cent came from families in poor eco-

nomic circumstances, and only 23.7 per cent from families who might be described as "comfortably-off." (**16**, p. 69) However, these findings could be interpreted in a number of ways—first of all, that the social maladjustment of the child of better financial status might manifest itself in other ways, since he does not have the *need* for this kind of misbehavior. According to Shulman:

. . . The delinquencies of the lower-class child arise from the conditions of his rearing—greater deprivation of material means to pleasure and greater clash of temperaments in family life owing to the inconsistencies and lack of discipline in rearing. His offenses (among boys) consist largely of various types of stealing, and (in girls) of waywardness and ungovernability. . . . In contrast, and in the absence of scientific data, we may speculate from scanty evidence that the characteristic offenses of middle-class children consist of malicious mischief occurring under group stimulus, and sex offenses that are privately dealt with. (**33**, p. 30)

Second, the child of the better cultural background might be cleverer about concealing his misdeeds. Shulman has further pointed out that the middle-class delinquent generally does not come into full bloom until adulthood:

. . . The characteristic offenses of the middle class do not show up in criminal statistics until adult life, and are then occupationally differentiated from the offenses of the poor, tending toward fraud, in contrast to assault and theft among the poor. Aside from occupational opportunities, it may be pointed out that the personality structure involved in successful fraud is wholly consistent with middle-class education and training, depending not on a single successful attack or raid . . . but on a more carefully controlled aggression involving knowledge and application of a wide range of technical skills and patience and fortitude in planning and carrying out extense frauds as nearly within the letter of the law as technical skill will permit. This suggests that the middle-class child who in later life resorts to crime does so in the light of earlier experience which has taught him that the social order has few loopholes and many restrictions; whereas the poor child resorts to types of crime which suggest that earlier experience has taught him that the social order has many loopholes and few restrictions. (33, p. 31)

However, social conditions are in a notable state of flux, and today it certainly does appear as if—so Dorothy Barclay writes in the *New York Times*—juvenile crimes were increasing among middle-class youth . . . which, if true, is a very sinister symptom of the deterioration of our social order. Barclay qualifies this assumption by the statement that the facts are not yet proven:

> Statistics on this point are unclear, but whether or not delinquency has increased among middle-class youngsters, it is our opinion that concern about it among parents definitely has. (1, p. 56)

Much has been said about organizing programs to prevent the rise of delinquency, but, as Russell pointed out, "existing facilities and institutions for observing and preventing early traits which may lead to delinquency are inadequate," and "the emphasis still remains on rehabilitation rather than on prevention." (31, p. 73) Moreover, there is a good deal of doubt as to how effective the rehabilitation techniques that do exist actually are.

Children's courts have been established for youthful offenders and, in connection with or as a result of these, child guidance clinics have been set up in cooperation with both courts and schools. Special "disciplinary" classes have been organized in many public school systems for those children consistently truant or delinquent, and their worth, of course, depends upon the individual program utilized. Some are mere catchalls for hard-to-teach children; others do make valuable adjustive contributions.

The accepted solution for so-called incorrigibles is still all too frequently indiscriminate institutionalization. Institutionalization per se is not necessarily an evil; the trouble is that the role of the institution is not clear. It can do much, or little, to help the delinquent, depending upon its purpose, its organization, and its facilities. The prevailing system, however, is inadequate, and

John Costello has described its outstanding inadequacies as follows:

> The institutions for juvenile delinquents are still in precarious position as child caring agencies. This is especially true of state institutions, which are commonly considered the dumping grounds for communities which do not have adequate facilities for the youngster in trouble. With a few exceptions, state training schools must receive the feeble-minded, the potentially psychotic, sex deviates, the physically handicapped, and aggressive delinquents. . . . (8, p. 166)

Frank Cohen has declared that any method of institutionalization which is not based on a sound program of rehabilitation not only does not solve the delinquency problem but may, in fact, increase it, by "hardening" the juvenile delinquent in the criminal mold:

> It serves no purpose to attempt to establish order and discipline if there is no understanding of the forces that make for disorder and revolt and no effort to deal with those forces both in the children and in their environment. To hold youngsters in custody with no other purpose than to keep them as quiet as possible is to fall into an inhumane pattern. Moreover, it is a pattern which is at odds with society's best interests. For these children will almost all graduate to the community sooner or later. Either they will be prepared to take a useful place in society or they will be so firmly set in patterns of defiance or withdrawal that they can only express their hostility in repeated antisocial behavior. . . . (6, p. 6)

On the other hand, even where there is a rehabilitative program—or an attempt at one—it may, if it is not adequately based on sound adjustive techniques, fail as a corrective measure. Without a thorough knowledge of the delinquents and their problems, educators are likely to plan a program that will appear to the children concerned as primarily a retribution rather than education. Feeling the "revenge" thus exacted to be unjust, the children may refuse to cooperate. Cohen has suggested that—

. . . a boy who has been arrested for an act of delinquency and placed in detention is seldom conscious of the cause-and-effect sequence of his crime and its punishment. Society may be firmly convinced of its right to take steps to protect itself against those who attack it; yet we cannot overlook the fact that the child concerned sees the same events in a different light. To him his arrest and incarceration are just further evidence of the injustices which have always pursued him. (**6**, p. 7)

Even in terms of the community's welfare rather than the child's, a blanket policy of institutionalization can merely heighten the problem of delinquency by sometimes effectively training the children in their delinquency, in that it gives them the opportunity to associate with more experienced delinquents and perhaps learn the professional techniques of crime. Certainly it seems to have little or no effect as a deterrent to further delinquency.

Traditionally the delinquent child was placed in an institution in order to remove a menace from the community. It was also hoped that if he lived in a regimented, controlled situation, he might be sufficiently discommoded by the loss of freedom and community privileges and the necessity of conforming to a strict regime, so that he would think twice before committing another act which would return him to such an existence. Yet these methods have not deterred delinquents from a repetition of their unlawful acts. . . . At best they have done no more than delay a repetition of crime for the period of incarceration. (**6**, p. 9)

To show how little those traditional methods of institutionalization have helped, the Gluecks discovered in a follow-up study of a thousand delinquents fifteen years after they had been originally identified as such and given such adjustive techniques as were available at the time that 85 per cent of them had nonetheless become adult criminals. (**15**, p. 215) McKay is also of the opinion that our method of dealing with juvenile delinquents often is a causative instead of being a deterrent factor in their later criminal careers:

. . . when children are arrested for relatively minor offenses, the treatment accorded them in the police station, the detention home, or the court may provide the basis for their coming to conceive of themselves as offenders or delinquents. . . . Thus efforts to prevent misbehavior may be the efforts through which it is created. (28, p. 39)

In attempting to organize an adequate rehabilitative program within the institution, the administrator will run into many difficulties. Not least among them is the problem of academic education for the delinquent, which, to a lesser degree, will also exist in the public school's "disciplinary classes," and that is that, in addition to representing a combination of handicaps, the delinquent generally is most unwilling to submit himself to the learning process, for he has already found school a highly traumatic experience. Costello has described the situation in which both teacher and pupil will find themselves:

Education in a school for delinquents presents a special problem. The students have a deep-seated hatred for school. For the most part they are badly retarded scholastically, and they are literally afraid of school. They associate most of their previous failures with their school experiences. This means that the institution's school must be different if it is going to catch hold. . . .

Teachers in schools for delinquents must be persons who can be comfortable working with the public school failures. They must be able to accept the fact that their students are retarded [that is, culturally and educationally] and their job is to try to rebuild in the pupil confidence in his ability to learn. . . . (8, p. 171)

To describe all the other problems which face the staff of an institution for juvenile delinquents would require an entire volume. Therefore, to sum up the problem of institutional organization and policy, it seems appropriate to offer Cohen's description of, not what the present-day institution *is*, but what the future institution *should* be:

The institution of tomorrow will be a permissive environment in which the child will feel free to express himself, and through this expression to work toward a satisfactory resolution of his difficulties. He will be given an opportunity to evaluate for himself any unacceptable means he has taken to deal with his problems while at the same time he is redirected toward more constructive solutions. . . .

The juvenile institution of tomorrow will be a place of service for children without label. . . . [The inmate] will be identified simply as a youngster in need of help, for whom the institution is the best resource available at the time. . . . (6, p. 171)

The Maladjusted Feebleminded [1]

There still is a tendency today for many among the lay public—and sometimes among those who are, or should be, better informed—to think that there is a direct correlation between feeblemindedness and delinquency, i.e., that those of low intelligence are especially susceptible to criminally deviant behavior. Most researches into the subject appear to have refuted this myth quite conclusively. Clinard, for one, has declared that "most of the studies of the intellect of deviants have been based on institutional populations or detected deviants, and the fact that the studies sometimes indicate that deviants may have a low intelligence may simply mean that the samples are biased." He adds that "there may be . . . a relation between intellect and certain types of offenses," but that is the only connection there could possibly be. (5, p. 118)

Carr believes that the original misconception regarding the retardate's delinquency came into being and may still appear on the surface to have some weight because "mental deficiency and delinquency tend to some extent to go together in the court statistics." However, he adds:

. . . These statistics are, of course, notoriously skewed in favor of the more comfortable neighborhoods. In other words, the same factors which boost the delinquency rates in certain areas probably also oper-

---

[1] The terms "mentally defective," "feebleminded," and the like, are used interchangeably in this section, since the authorities quoted have adhered to no single standard of definitions.

ate to draw the duller and less successful types into those areas and to make adjustment more difficult once they are there. . . . (**3,** p. 134)

Louttit has observed, to explain the fact that juvenile delinquents tend to rate lower on IQ tests than the general population, that, since "delinquents appear more frequently from homes of low socioeconomic status and with unacceptable moral standards; [and] further intrafamily relationships are psychologically poor," it appears that the background, and not the criminal traits, is what seems to correlate with the tested intelligence. (**25,** p. 370) However, logically speaking, there is, as Clinard points out, "nothing in the nature of subnormal intellect that implies a relationship with either attitudes or personality traits." (**5,** p. 119) And Karl Birnbaum, writing in the *Annals of the American Academy of Political and Social Science,* agrees that—

. . . mental deficiency is not inseparably connected with criminal propensities, nor is there any unequivocal correspondence between the grade of the mental defect and the seriousness of the delinquency. There are low-grade feeble-minded persons without any antisocial inclinations, and conversely there are persons who show a very moderate intellectual deficiency but an outspoken readiness for criminal actions. (**2,** p. 58)

There is no doubt that there are mentally handicapped individuals who are maladjusted to the point of delinquency. The basic reason for this, and for all behavior problems of the mentally handicapped, according to Martens, is that these children did not receive proper training at the start. "There is a tendency," she says, "for disciplinary problems to be concentrated among retarded children who are not given the special educational help that they need." (**27,** p. 7) She goes on to describe some of the factors that can cause maladjustment, but not necessarily delinquency, in the mentally handicapped:

One of the dangers often encountered in the life of the high-grade mental defective is that too much is expected of him. . . . The majority of people who meet him may think of him as normal. As a result, he is frequently directed to tasks that he is unable to perform. He fails, with disastrous results to himself and to others. One who understands his weaknesses would never have assigned such tasks to him. (**27**, p. 30)

Conversely, it often happens that the higher-grade defective becomes delinquent, not because his intelligence is low, but because it is too high for the dependent role the community has implicitly assigned to him. As Strickland has commented, "in some cases a more accurate description than socially incompetent (for the defective delinquent) might be anti-socially competent, in the sense that the defective is competent to maintain himself in society at the expense of society." (**36**, p. 509)

It is unfortunate that the institutions established for disturbed children generally refuse to accept the mentally handicapped unless the powers that be in those institutions have reason to believe that these children are suffering from pseudo feeblemindedness. On the other hand, the institutions for the mentally handicapped often do not. Martens maintains, segregate the psychotic and delinquent mental deficient from the "normal" one. (**26**, pp. 91–92) Such a policy—or, rather, lack of one—not only will hinder the potential adjustment of the severely disturbed retardate, but may affect the favorable adjustment of his associates, for, as T. E. Harms has pointed out—

. . . there is no doubt that we must have different educational setups to train and adjust mongoloids, schizophrenics, and spastic children, and behavior-disorder types, to mention only some major groups. Those working with a mixed group of mentally impaired children know that one case of behavior disorder often makes any average tie work with the others almost impossible because the one child needs constant watching and holding back. . . . (**19**, p. 229)

Even where the mentally handicapped child is unquestionably delinquent, there is no reason to institutionalize him for the rest of his life, as so many believe to be the only solution in his case. Hungerford, to name one investigator among the many who subscribe to the same view, feels that a remedial training program, within or without the institution, can help the delinquent retardates as much as the delinquents of normal intelligence, and that "they can still be rehabilitated after succumbing to environmental pressure." (23, p. 760)

REMEDIAL PROGRAMS

What Has Been Done

On the whole, very little effective work has been done to cope with social maladjustment in the child—even when the programs for the delinquent and the mentally handicapped are taken into consideration. One major reason for this virtually medieval state of affairs is that, although the component parts of the program have been given spasmodic attention, it was not recognized as a *whole* problem until quite recently, and, even then, the recognition was more one of theory than of practice. The public schools of the United States, Carr says, have "hardly even recognized" the problem of "emotional education . . . except in conferences and periodical publications!" Yet they are ignoring an area that is at least as important as any subject or combination of subjects being taught in the schools.

. . . In its social consequences, emotional illiteracy is probably more serious than any other kind. We have a tradition of more than two thousand years for eliminating intellectual illiteracy but of less than a generation for dealing with emotional illiteracy. . . . (3, p. 489)

The public schools have made a few feeble efforts to keep up with the times by establishing some special classes; however, Mackie and Dunn point out, relatively few of the children, even those suffering from serious maladjustment, are in such classes:

. . . some are in residential schools for delinquent boys and girls; some are in psychiatric hospital wards. The majority of these children, however, are regarded by state and local school systems as a responsibility of the general education program, and, for the most part, are in regular classes. . . . (**26**, p. 32)

Yet special classes cannot conscientiously be offered as the ideal solution here, because the disturbed children cannot, by and large, be considered as a homogeneous group. Each is *sui generis*, and their presence might have a deleterious rather than a beneficial effect upon each other. On the other hand, the presence of the socially maladjusted is not particularly desirable for the well-adjusted child, since maladjustment is one handicap that can be acquired by association; hence, in some of its manifestations, it could almost be considered contagious.

Many schools offer facilities outside the classroom proper, which are useful according to their nature and extent. Mackie and Dunn report that "emotionally disturbed children in school systems are frequently aided by visiting counselors, visiting teachers, guidance personnel, clinical specialists, and other school personnel." (**26**, p. 32) Maladjusted bright children have received some specific attention, though far less than the maladjusted retarded. "A very small number of seriously disturbed bright children," Strang mentions, "have been treated in special schools." (**35**, p. 158) The Connecticut State Board of Education has described its work with a school of this kind:

. . . One [school] district is experimenting with a clinic school: children who are discovered by test and teacher observation to be performing far below their ability are assigned to this clinic school for a period of time. . . . (**11**, p. 15)

Strang has also recommended for treatment of the seriously disturbed gifted children a number of methods that, in the main, would apply to all the socially handicapped: "milieu therapy, play therapy, counseling and psychotherapy, group therapy, psychiatry, and psychoanalysis." (**35**, p. 161)

The Chicago school system apparently has given more consideration than most public school systems to the fact that social handicap includes more than active delinquency. Its methods of dealing with both types of maladjustment are noted by Mullen:

> Truancy and other symptoms of maladjustment in the regular grades are problems every school must face. Frequently in certain schools, occasionally in any school, children will be found whose problems seem insoluble with the resources available to the regular school. Such pupils are given another chance in our day schools for the socially maladjusted. . . . (**29**, p. 197)

There are also in existence residential schools for disturbed children which are conducted outside the regular school system; most are institution and school combined, although there are instances like Hawthorn-Cedar Knolls, which, as Leonard Kornberg describes it, is "an institution for children who are emotionally disturbed who live there and who attend a public school specially maintained for them." (**24**, p. 4) According to him, "there are hundreds of schools all over the country where disturbed children, taken out of their homes and communities, are forced to live in a special institutional environment." (**24**, p. 113)

Some of these institutions are engaged in valuable work and research; some are catchalls—and the same is true for the public school classes. Carr has summarized the outstanding examples of the good work that is being done for disturbed children in this country, but he takes great care to emphasize that, however beneficial the individual school or program may be, the total mounts up to an aggregate that is not nearly enough in terms of our needs:

> . . . Here and there throughout the United States, enterprising school officials have tried a variety of methods, ranging from the provision of specialized services for exceptional children as in the Montefiore special school for Problem Children in Chicago, the Binet Schools of Newark, the Testing and Clinical Program for Maladjusted Children

in the Detroit Public Schools, to the visiting teachers of Rochester, Cincinnati, and many other cities. Such demonstrations include also the integration of schools, police, and other agencies in Jersey City, and the far-reaching community integration activities centered in the schools as in the late Dr. Nathan Peyser's program in Brooklyn and in the Columbus (Indiana) Foundation for Youth. (**3**, p. 494)

What Should Be Done

Whether or not institutionalization is the best solution to the problem of social handicap, even where that institutionalization is not intended to be of a punitive nature, is a moot question. Certainly, whatever the intentions of those who put him there, the child will tend to regard the institute as punitive. On the other hand, in cases where the child is so seriously disturbed as to come perilously close to the psychotic, he cannot be treated in the ordinary public school system. The public welfare comes before the individual good. He must be institutionalized or, at least, dealt with in some way outside the classroom. Similarly, many disturbed children who come from substandard or broken homes might be better off under some kind of institutional care.

Of course, teachers will be needed within the institution as well as without, and they will face one of the most difficult tasks a pedagogue might have, for they will find themselves confronted with the kind of group that Kornberg had to deal with, and which he has described in the following terms:

. . . Not only were there extreme personality and ability differences among these children . . . there were also the diverse impact of therapy, the constant turnover in group membership, and the classroom as affected by the situational dynamics in Hawthorne. . . . As a teacher of disturbed children, I knew that I faced a group teetering on the edge of violence, where each child was either too blocked or too uncontrolled to face others calmly. I would have to be and provide the relational bridge, linking the isolates until the group was a calm, satisfying fact. . . . (**24**, p. 19)

A good deal of the program of social handicap is outside the province of the teacher, belonging more properly to the clinician or psychiatrist. As far as the public school teacher goes, her greatest value, when it comes to the seriously maladjusted child, is diagnosis and referral; she should never attempt to tamper with a badly disturbed child or she may cause permanent injury to him (and, sometimes, to herself).

Where the child is not severely disturbed, however, the regular public school teacher can do a good deal to help him—and the following applies to the delinquent as well as the nondelinquent, the one of inferior intelligence, as well as the one of normal and superior intelligence. First of all, she can develop in him the feeling that he is accepted, that he belongs to the group; and, by so doing, she can gradually build in him the self-respect that most maladjusted children so sadly lack. She can give him the opportunity to express himself and his own identity, to learn that he is of some moment in this world and that what he says and does really matters. She can, in short, give him the recognition and status of which he stands in need.

After teaching a class for the socially handicapped, Kornberg came to the following conclusions:

. . . among several aims that directed me and that would do so again, here are a few. I tried to create a purposiveness in the life of my classroom, by encouraging tasks that drew on the needs and motives of my boys. I tried to insure success, status, and feelings of adequacy—of which they all had been so deprived. I wanted to avoid the "bad adult" personifications these children had formed, and build a trust and consensus between us. I strove to support expressive behavior and to clarify necessary limits, to check competitiveness and conformity's frustration. I sought to nourish the rudiments of a group and build cooperative, problem-solving action. And, in the end, my goal was the slow drainage of anxieties . . . preparing a base for more effective conduct. (**24**, p. 99)

Where there is a physical handicap in addition to the social one, the teacher will need to help the individual to adjust to his own limitations. As Frampton and Gall observe, "the body image held by the individual is important to his life adjustment." On the one hand, "he may set totally unrealistic standards for himself or be unable to allow for the necessary adjustments in his environment," going so far as to believe "he has no disability." On the other hand, "school efforts toward social integration may be defeated if the child believes that he is a malformed monster." (13, p. 113) But what the teacher should certainly try to do, and what may be the most important task of her whole program, is, in Fenton's words, "to separate in her own mind (and perhaps in the child's) the unfortunate behavior and the potentially adequate development of the pupil's personality." (12, p. 122)

Since it is impossible to secure a homogeneous group of emotionally disturbed pupils, Kornberg's method of dealing with his special class might well be considered as a possible, though difficult, technique. What he essentially did was to make himself as diversified as the group, by following—

. . . a pattern of multiple roles enacted simultaneously for individuals and for subgroups. To some of my boys I was a guide, to some a disciplinarian, to others a supporter, to still others a nag. . . .

I built . . . a role proliferation in which I was many things for everyone, and for the group the important (because satisfying) central (because responsive) person. Sometimes, if this role variance was in conflict with itself, there would be misunderstanding and resentment. But it did not occur frequently, for the boys grew to accept my consistent differences; and, also, they often saw the justice in handling different individuals differently.

One of the very important ways of securing the right personification of myself lay in anticipating and averting my boys' hostility and aggression. One of the ways I did this involved the function of humor in easing role acceptance; affectionate kidding was often the medium in trying to dissolve some tension, for instance. . . . (24, pp. 107–109)

Although she may find it difficult to emulate Kornberg's multiple personality, the public school teacher should give careful attention to each individual's particular difficulties and project herself, as well as she can, into the role necessary for dealing with each. At the same time, she and the school should not overlook the fact that every constructive step they take in dealing with a maladjusted pupil should become part of an over-all methodology, with the aim of developing effective techniques in this area. According to the bulletin put out by the New York State Board of Education:

. . . There is a tendency sometimes to deal with the cases of difficulty which arise today simply in terms of the individual children concerned. These immediate situations should help point the way to the improvement of school services. From our work with the failing child, the maladjusted child, or the unhappy child of today, we should constantly be trying to learn better ways to help their brothers and sisters of tomorrow. . . . Through such efforts we will come closer to the goal of an educational system which will fulfill, to far greater degree than may be the case today, the responsibilities and opportunities for child adjustment which lie within our grasp. (**30**, p. 17)

Of course, there are some investigators who feel that all the programs that have been organized to combat maladjustment, even more, all the programs that have been *proposed*, are, although well meaning, futile, because they do not strike at the heart of the matter. Harms is one of these. According to him:

. . . we know that all recent progressive programs designed to help in the serious problems of youth—its neuroticism, insecurity, delinquency, etc., make innumerable suggestions as to better housing, food, day care, schools, and even psychological and child guidance procedures. Occasionally education of parents is suggested or improvement of their social or financial status, but seldom as a major remedy the actual reconstruction of the family as the fundamental task of really sane and sound human economics. Unfortunately we believe that we can improve our present social and communal status by external measures such as better food and housing, easier communications, shorter working hours, better leisure-time facilities and more highly developed educational methods. (**19**, p. 21)

But the fault, we believe, lies in our basic social organization, and all the programs that have been organized, whether on paper or in actuality, are designed to attack *effects*, not *causes*, and so, in our opinion, are doomed to failure, because "we do not realize that" all our sociological and economic and psychological remedies will not succeed in restoring "the most elementary relationship need," which is "that of properly bringing up human offspring and of returning our life, in all that results from it as civilization or culture, to its healthy basis." In short, Harms feels, "the real task is simply to bring parents back to their human job in regard to the physically and mentally healthy growth of their offspring." (**19**, p. 21)

However, the "simply" is far from being as simple as Harms would have us believe. However much we may be in accord with Harms' basic thesis—and, fundamentally, it has one great drawback, that it necessitates a turning "back" rather than a seeking for a *new* solution to problems which have arisen in consequence of our contemporary civilization—it is far easier to change environmental conditions one by one than to attempt a drastic alteration of our cultural structure at one fell swoop.

In a democratic society, progress in any direction must be slow and subject to the will of all the people, as it should be. Only a dictator can deliberately reorganize a civilization from the top, and history has shown us that such reorganizations are retrogressive rather than progressive in nature. All that the schools, the community, and the parents can do to combat the growing question of social maladjustment among our children is to attack each maladjustive factor individually and hope that, as they are solved, bit by bit they will help to solve the larger problems of which they are perhaps only a part, but a very important part.

References

1. BARCLAY, DOROTHY. "Helping the Youngster in Trouble," *New York Times Magazine,* September 27, 1957. P. 56.
2. BIRNBAUM, KARL. "A Court Psychiatrist's View of Juvenile Delinquents," *Annals of the American Academy of Political and Social Science,* CCLXI (January, 1949), pp. 55–63.
3. CARR, LOWELL J. *Delinquency Control.* New York: Harper and Brothers, 1950.
4. CHAMBERLAIN, NAOMI B., and DOROTHY H. Moss. *The Three R's for the Retarded.* New York: National Association for Retarded Children, n. d.
5. CLINARD, MARSHALL B. *Sociology of Deviant Behavior.* New York: Rinehart and Co., 1957.
6. COHEN, FRANK J. *Children in Trouble.* New York: W. W. Norton and Co., 1952.
7. CORRIGAN, MARIE A. "Tests and Measurements," in (12). I, 152–61.
8. COSTELLO, JOHN B. "Institutions for Juvenile Delinquents," *Annals of the American Academy of Political and Social Science,* CCLXI (January, 1949), 166–218.
9. CUTTS, NORMA, and NICHOLAS MOSELEY. *Teaching the Bright and Gifted Child.* Englewood Cliffs, N. J.: Prentice-Hall, 1957.
10. *Education of the Gifted.* Washington, D. C.: National Education Association, Educational Policies Commission, 1950.
11. *Education for Gifted Children and Youth.* (Connecticut State Department of Education. Bulletin No. 77) Hartford, Conn.: 1955–56.
12. FENTON, NORMAN. *Mental Hygiene in School Practice.* Stanford, Calif.: Stanford University Press, 1943.
13. FRAMPTON, MERLE E., and ELENA D. GALL (eds.). *Special Education for the Exceptional.* Boston: Porter Sargent, 1955. Vol. I.
14. FRAMPTON, MERLE E., and HUGH GRANT ROWELL. *Education of the Handicapped.* Yonkers, N. Y.: World Book Co., 1940. Vol. 2.
15. GLUECK, SHELDON, and ELEANOR T. *Juvenile Delinquents Grow Up.* New York: Commonwealth Fund, 1940.

16. —— — ——. *One Thousand Juvenile Delinquents.* Cambridge: Harvard University Press, 1934.
17. —— — ——. *Unravelling Juvenile Delinquency.* New York: Commonwealth Fund, 1950.
18. GOLDBERG, I. IGNACY. "Mental Health for the Exceptional," in (**13**). Pp. 116–22.
19. HARMS, T. ERNEST. *Essentials of Abnormal Child Psychology.* New York: Julian Press, 1953.
20. HECK, ARCH O. *The Education of Exceptional Children.* (2nd ed.) New York: McGraw-Hill Publishing Co., 1953.
21. HORNEY, KAREN. *The Neurotic Personality of Our Time.* New York: W. W. Norton and Co., 1937.
22. ——. *Our Inner Conflicts.* New York: W. W. Norton and Co., 1945.
23. HUNGERFORD, RICHARD H. "The Young Retardate Outside His Home Community," *Journal of Mental Deficiency,* LI (April, 1947), 758–65.
24. KORNBERG, LEONARD. *A Class for Disturbed Children.* New York: Bureau of Publications, Teacher's College, Columbia University, 1955.
25. LOUTTIT, C. M. *Clinical Psychology of Exceptional Children.* New York: Harper and Brothers, 1957.
26. MACKIE, ROMAINE P., and LLOYD M. DUNN. *College and University Programs for the Preparation of Teachers of Exceptional Children.* (U. S. Department of Health, Education, and Welfare. Bulletin 1954, No. 13.) Washington, D. C.: Government Printing Office, 1954.
27. MARTENS, ELISE H. *Curriculum Adjustments for the Mentally Retarded.* (U. S. Department of Health, Education, and Welfare. Bulletin 1954, No. 2. 1950.) Washington, D. C.: Government Printing Office, 1950.
28. MCKAY, HENRY D. "The Neighborhood and Child Conduct," *Annals of the American Academy of Political and Social Science,* CCLXI (January, 1949), 32–41.
29. MULLEN, FRANCES A. "A Metropolitan Area Plans for Special Education," in (**13**). Pp. 194–205.
30. *Reducing Juvenile Delinquency.* Albany: New York State Department of Education, 1952.
31. RUSSELL, J. C. "The Place of Home and School in Delinquency," *The Commonwealth,* XXVIII (March 31, 1952), 73–81.

32. SCHWARTZ, EDWARD E. "Statistics of Juvenile Delinquency in the United States," *Annals of the American Academy of Political and Social Science,* CCLXI (January, 1949), 9–20.

33. SHULMAN, HARRY M. "The Family and Juvenile Delinquency," *Annals of the American Academy of Political and Social Science,* CCLXI (January, 1949), 21–31.

34. STRANG, RUTH. *Facts about Juvenile Delinquency.* Chicago: Science Research Associates, 1952.

35. ———. "Mental Health of Gifted Children," in Paul Witty (ed.). *The Gifted Child.* Boston: D. C. Heath and Co., 1951. Pp. 131–62.

36. STRICKLAND, C. A. "The Social Competence of the Feeble-Minded," *Journal of Mental Deficiency,* LII (January, 1944), 504–515.

37. WICKMAN, E. K. *Children's Behavior and Teacher's Attitudes.* New York: Commonwealth Fund, 1928.

CHAPTER NINE

The Psychology of Teaching the Physically Handicapped

THE ancient Greeks used to exterminate the handicapped among them on the principle that only the fit have the right to survive, for only the fit are of value to society. Our American democracy considers that any individual born into this world, no matter how defective he may be in mind or body, has the same right to live as the normal person, whether or not he can contribute anything of value to society. However, by allowing these handicapped individuals to survive, our democracy, at the same time, automatically assumes a threefold obligation toward them: (1) that of educating them to the limit of their abilities; (2) that of training them, if possible, to be self-supporting; and (3), if that is not possible, that of taking care of not only their physical but their mental well-being.

Our entire program of educating the handicapped has begun to assume particular significance today in view of the fact that the number of handicapped children in our total population is increasing steadily as a result of the increase in the birthrate combined with the decrease in infant mortality. As a result of this growth in the numbers of the handicapped, the field of special education is going to include more and more of our total school population within its scope—a prospect that is both genetically and socially alarming, for the aim of our society's humanitarian attitude is, of course, to help the physically unfit, not to propagate them. However, where the handicaps, or a predisposition to them, are of a hereditary nature, our society is not only preserving the unfit but directly contributing to the rise in their numbers. Therefore, in order to protect ourselves against gradually becoming a nation of the handicapped, we must implement, along with a program of care and education for these unfortunates, a preventive program directed against those factors that have caused their various disabilities, for, fortunately, a good many of these handicaps can be prevented or ameliorated if their basic causes are attacked vigorously.

WHY EDUCATE THE PHYSICALLY HANDICAPPED?

Society's regard for those who are not physically complete or totally functioning is not purely an altruistic one, even though humanitarianism is its basis. It has been rewarded many times over by the contributions which have been made by those who, in another age or another culture, at best might have been permitted to exist and degenerate, at worst might have been exterminated.

History has shown us that a physical handicap per se is no barrier to achievement. Many of the world's greatest leaders in various fields of endeavor suffered from physical handicaps. Franklin D. Roosevelt was crippled by poliomyelitis; Charles Steinmetz, the electrical genius, was born a cripple. The pianist, Alec Templeton, was born blind. Thomas Alva Edison and the detective story writer, Edgar Wallace, were born deaf, while Beethoven lost his hearing at the age of twenty-eight. Winston Churchill was born with a defective palate, which gave him a lisp, to which was added the further handicap of stuttering. Arnold Bennett and Somerset Maugham both were stutterers.

Yet, in spite of their handicaps, and, in spite of the fact that the preceding centuries were even less sympathetic to handicaps than ours, all of them succeeded. It is to be hoped that, given training commensurate with their needs and abilities, many more of the handicapped will make equally valuable contributions to our society. Of course, the likelihood that any individual will become one of the world's "greats" is a remote one whether he be normal or handicapped. However, it is expected that, suitably educated, most of the handicapped will be able to make as useful a contribution to society as if they were normal in every respect.

THE PSYCHOLOGICAL FACTOR IN PHYSICAL HANDICAP

It must be remembered that the actual physical defect does not necessarily account for all that is deviant in the child, although it is certainly a temptation to ascribe every out-of-the-ordinary factor appearing in his total personality to his handicap, particularly if it is an adverse factor. A deaf child, for example, may seem dull because of his affliction. He may also seem dull because he *is* mentally retarded, and no amount of learning how to lip-read will upgrade his intellectual inadequacy, although it very likely will enable what intellect he has to function at closer-to-maximum efficiency. Mental retardation is not uncommon among the handicapped, largely because the factors that gave rise to the physical effect often prove to have affected the brain as well.

Mullen has commented, in speaking of the work done in special education by the Chicago public school system, that a greater number of the children who attend the special schools for the handicapped test below average in intelligence rather than above.

However, she accounts for this manifestation by explaining that it "is due in part to the presence of associated and inherent mental defects in some of the physically handicapped group and also to the many restrictions which limit the opportunity of others to experience the social stimulation received by normal children." (47, p. 21)

On the other hand, it is true that a physical defect, particularly when it is not a readily observable one for which allowances will be made more or less automatically, may cause the child's intelligence to appear substantially less than it is, especially in a test situation, because the handicapped, having been deprived of the environmental stimuli and contacts normal for children of their age, can hardly be expected to respond in the manner standardized as normal for that age. Thus, the idea that those with orthopedic or sensory handicaps are, as a rule, less intelligent than those who are physically normal is entirely fallacious.

Furthermore, although it is true that the physical deviant tends to be maladjusted, since it is more difficult to make an adequate adjustment with insufficient or flawed equipment—whether we are speaking of people or of machinery—it by no means follows that there is a direct correlation between a specific set of behavior patterns and a specific deviation, as is so commonly supposed. There are no obligatory peculiarities of the blind or the deaf, in the sense that such peculiarities are a necessary accompaniment of that condition. Sometimes deviants, whether consciously or unconsciously, *do* tend to "trade upon their misfortunes." As Lavos has pointed out:

. . . Unusual, annoying, immature, or emotionally disturbed behavior in exceptional children may be accepted by parents as invariable concomitants of the condition in somewhat the same fashion that certain theories link physical defects and personality traits. . . . More than one parent has taken a deaf child for his first day of school, thinking that a temper tantrum was a normal way of behaving on his part.

Such permissive attitudes on the part of the family may encourage behavior which will be unfavorable at a later time. (34, pp. 137–38)

Directly related to this problem in the physically handicapped child's behavior is the tendency of some, as noted by Mullen and others, to refuse to exert themselves by attempting to acquire the degree of independence for which they have the physical capacity. (47, p. 29) Because these children have been overprotected in the home and in the community, they have acquired ingrained dependency patterns from which they are reluctant to break away. In any educational program, therefore, the attitude must always be that the handicapped individual is there to be developed rather than protected, and that the "coddling" approach is fully as injurious to him as the "sink-or-swim" one.

Although there is, then, no one psychological syndrome appertaining to each particular handicap, all physically handicapped children are, as has already been pointed out, psychologically disturbed to some extent, since it is almost impossible to make a ready adjustment to a world based on norms that the individual is constitutionally incapable of meeting. It is generally agreed that often the behavior problem becomes more serious than the actual handicap. Morton states that "a severe handicap of physique often imposes very definite restrictions upon the range of choices open to an individual," with the result that "a very definite problem" of personal adjustment is apt to arise. (45, p. 132) "The hardest thing for the physically handicapped child to overcome," Mullen has commented, in this connection, is "not his physical disability but the mental set which it often induces." (47, p. 26)

Such behavior problems can, of course, approach the point of actual delinquency. It is surprising how many delinquents are handicapped to some degree, although usually not to any significant extent, because practical delinquency is, as a rule, infeasible for the severely handicapped child, no matter how ill-willed he may be. Cohen has observed that most children who are put into detention homes for the socially maladjusted—and, in this instance, he is referring primarily to the delinquent—prove to have physical handicaps ranging from the slight to the fairly serious:

. . . Preponderantly these children require dental care; many reveal a need for eyeglasses. A high percentage show evidence of nutritional disorders, varying from mild to severe deficiencies. Skin and scalp conditions are much in evidence, and respiratory infections are not uncommon. A fair number suffer from some form of genito-urinary problem. Some show real or suspected heart conditions. These are situations which show up with fair regularity; many others occur with sufficient frequency to demand provision in the medical program of the institution. (8, p. 104)

A further disadvantage for the crippled and afflicted is that they tend to be "mainly the children of the poor," because, as Carr has pointed out, the poorer the child's family and the neighborhood, the greater the likelihood of such infections as infantile paralysis, and "the greater the likelihood that treatment will be slighted and that after-care will be inadequate." (6, p. 134) Therefore, such children have their physical handicap as an *addition* to the handicap of poverty and possibly that of discrimination. When the inevitable social handicap is added to these, the child is laboring under a very heavy burden, indeed.

ORGANIZING A PROGRAM

The main principle to be applied in the education of the physically handicapped, as in the education of all the exceptional, is that of working out a program which will be based on the child's strengths rather than his weaknesses. A positive approach is always preferable to a negative, and Darrel Mase has strongly emphasized that workers in the field should—

. . . Never speak of a blind child, deaf child, cerebrally palsied child. If we think and speak of disability first, we may fail to see ability. The clinical approach demands that first we see abilities, capacities, strengths, and then turn to disabilities and weaknesses. . . . (**42**, p. 23)

It would, of course, be unreasonable to expect that, where the handicapped child is included in the regular school system, he will be able to participate in every activity on an equal basis with the normal child. However, a well-regulated program should see to it that, as Fenton suggests, "the child who is different, whether he is crippled, slow to learn, foreign-born, or deviates in some other fashion, should be accepted by the group as different without being made to feel inferior." (**15**, p. 193)

In theory, this might well be the best solution to the whole problem. In practice, such a result is difficult, often impossible, to achieve, for there are too many uncontrollable factors involved—the parents, the other children, and the community at large. According to the government bulletin, *Emotional Problems Associated with Handicapping Conditions in Children:*

. . . The child with a crippled leg soon becomes aware of his inability to run and play with his age-mates. The disappointment of the parents in the child heightens his sense of inferiority. If he is disfigured, as by a cleft palate and lip and "talks funny," he is apt not to be ignored by other children but to be taunted by them and to be the recipient of cruel pranks. When these handicaps are obvious there is little protection from episodes which give great mental pain. . . . (**22**, p. 13)

Most of the ordinary school subjects can be mastered to some degree by the handicapped child, once he has mastered the techniques of his disability. One subject that is likely to prove the greatest stumbling block for both the handicapped child and the teacher or administrator is physical education, even specially adjusted physical education. As Frampton and Gall have noted:

. . . The physical education program for sight-saving classes has been greatly limited by the belief that actual damage to the vision of the child might result from bending and from certain other activities. Other areas have similar problems. Obviously, to the child who has chronic osteomyelitis there is very real danger of fracture and even occasionally the possibility of amputation, as a result of an unwisely planned physical education program. The cerebral palsied child, or the child with multiple sclerosis or polio presents very real and practical problems. . . . (**17,** p. 169)

SPECIAL CLASSES, SCHOOLS, AND INSTITUTIONS

One question that is bound to occur over and over again in connection with the handicapped is: What are the advantages of the special classes versus the special schools, versus the institutions; and what are the advantages of any or all of these over the regular class in the regular school? There are many who maintain that it is best for the handicapped children to be retained in the regular school system, even at considerable sacrifice of educational advantage, because, if there is a choice to be made, community contacts are more important than superior educational adjustment.

"Wherever possible," Gisela Konopka has said, "when the handicap is not too severe, when the home situation is healthy, when special teaching facilities are available, this seems the best solution, since it minimizes segregation for the child." (**32,** p. 28) Ray has suggested that even blind children be educated within the regular school system, though not in the regular classes (**53,** p. 16), and Postlewait, declaring that "wherever possible a handicapped child should be integrated into a regular classroom," recommends that sight-saving students not only be kept in the regular schools but eventually be transferred back into the regular classes. (**52,** p. 78)

Numerous others are in agreement with the policy of keeping the handicapped in the regular classes, or, at least, returning them to the regular classes whenever it is at all possible. There are many, however, who feel, like Mullen, that a warning note must be sounded here, that "this trend toward regular class placement for a child with a degree of handicap formerly thought to demand special placement can be carried too far. Physicians and others not close to the educational needs of a child sometimes become over enthusiastic advocates of regular grade placement." (**46**, p. 198)

The greatest drawback of the special class is that it must, of necessity, be multigrade, for no one school, no matter how large, is likely to have sufficient students in the same grade with the same disability. The special school, of course, has far more chance of surmounting this difficulty because there are more handicapped students from which to attempt homogeneity of classification. And Mullen has pointed out that when children are placed in the special schools of the public school systems they have made such striking improvement in social adjustment as to place the worth of such schools beyond doubt.

In a regular school these children would be helped and pitied by others but they would be isolated because of their inability to be a member of the groups at play or work. In a special school their handicap, their deformity, their slowness or inability to walk or write are no excuse for failure. . . . (**46**, p. 26)

Thus the child receives the education he needs, without sacrifice of community contacts.

Where institutionalization is recommended, as in the case of certain handicaps which cannot be effectively treated otherwise, it is not considered advisable for the small child, as it may induce severe emotional retardation:

Separation from the parents may be very traumatic for the preschool child and may seriously interfere with his ability to form satisfactory emotional relationships with people. . . . If a child under six . . . needs hospital care, the care should be given in small units so that a mother figure can be provided. Institutional care, except for necessary brief periods of acute illness, is definitely undesirable for young children. When young children are kept too long in institutions or have a succession of mothers, they often revert to infantile habits . . . and their mental and emotional growth is seriously delayed. (**35,** pp. 4–5)

As for the older child, "separation is usually less traumatic . . . from six years to adolescence, but may be serious for some children of this age." (**35,** p. 5)

If children must be institutionalized, there is no reason why they should be deprived of all those community contacts that have been felt to be so desirable. Under such circumstances, Jack Hartong has stated, the institution should arrange a program which would enable the children to become a part of the community in which the institution is situated, by, for example, participating—

. . . in a variety of social and group activities in the local community, such as attendance at churches and Sunday schools, integration in "Y," Scout, and other group activities. Such an integrated program affords the handicapped child an opportunity to be with and to share in the experiences of other children of the district. (**23,** p. 32)

The principal purpose of specialized education is, it is agreed, to enable the child to become a functioning member of the community. Therefore, it is undeniably the goal of all such education to return him to the regular schools and classes whenever it is possible; i.e., whenever he has been trained to the degree *where he is able to compete on an equal basis with the unhandicapped child.* On the other hand, indiscriminate return of the handicapped child to the regular classes or retention of him in them is almost as harmful as indiscriminate institutionalization.

LIMITATIONS OF SPECIAL EDUCATION

As in the area of mental retardation, the opportunities for charlatanry are lamentably rife in the area of physical handicap. Too many anxious parents are ready to grasp at straws, even though they know them to be straws. There is a school of "quack-ery" (sometimes honestly misguided), based on the premise that all emotional maladjustment can be traced to some sort of physical handicap, and, once that handicap is found and corrected, the child will automatically become a normal, functioning individual. Even where the handicap is real, even where it *is* the cause of the maladjustment, removing it will not automatically remove the maladjustment, which almost always will need therapeutic treatment. The charlatan also finds a fertile field in promoting hearing aids that are alleged to produce phenomenal (and, of course, virtually impossible) results, and so on. One of the school's tasks is to attempt to educate the parent against such victimization and, incidentally, to avoid falling into that pitfall itself.

Following are brief summaries of what is being done and needs to be done in each of the principal fields of special handicap. Of course, in a work of limited size, such treatment is necessarily far from comprehensive and merely gives an inkling of what only an entire volume for each of the areas described would be able to give in even adequate detail.

VISUAL DEFECTS

The American Medical Association has officially accepted the following definitions of the various types of visual defects:

1. *Absolute blindness:* inability to perceive light.
2. *Economic blindness:* inability to do any kind of work for which sight is essential.
3. *Vocational blindness:* impairment of vision which makes it impossible for a person to do work which he had formerly done to earn a living.
4. *Educational blindness:* such loss of sight as makes it difficult, dangerous, or impossible to learn by the methods that are commonly used in schools. For sight-conservation classes the re-

quirement is vision in the better eye of less than 20/70 and better than 20/200. For admission into a school for the blind the vision in the better eye must be 20/200 or less (with correction). (**18**, p. 116)

The Blind

It is generally agreed that those who are totally blind are those whose visual handicap is so great as to prevent them from doing anything that involves the use of sight. Even though they may still retain some degree of light perception, nonetheless, since this perception is of no functional value, they are still classified as blind. The total number of blind persons in the United States was estimated by Hurlin in 1953 as about 308,500, on the basis that blindness occurs "at the rate of 1.98 per 1,000 population." (**25**, p. 190) However, since it is a generally accepted fact that over half of all blind persons are more than fifty years old, since it comes as the result of many diseases of later life as well as of occupational accident, unquestionably the incidence is much smaller among the school-age population. According to Rice and Hill, there were 839 blind children enrolled in the public schools and classes of the United States in 1952–53. (**54**, p. 19) Without a doubt, this meager number does not include all or even a majority of the blind of school age, since most of those who are being educated at all are probably being trained in the residential schools. Blind children tend to be found very often in the underprivileged areas, since, among the social causes of blindness, are malnutrition and unhygienic conditions of living.

Stringent efforts should be made to discover all blind children well *before* they are of school age, so that their education and adjustments can be started to some degree at home, in the normal environment, before they are sent either to the public or the residential schools. Residential schools offer better facilities to treat the very special problems of the blind, but it is not impossible to educate them in special classes within the regular school system. In Ohio, for example, McIntire states that "early counseling services make it possible for blind children to come into nursery school at the age of three years." When the child reaches the age of six, he may then be assigned to a special Braille class located in a regular school. Throughout elementary school, he will have "the services of this special class . . . with emphasis on the development of the special techniques that he will need to carry out his academic program, and upon growing participation in activities with regular class children." (43, p. 187)

New York City also has Braille classes, which, since they include 15 per cent of all the children in the United States enrolled in such classes, as of 1951–52, probably represent the most extensive system of that kind. (59, p. 227) And, in line with the New York and Ohio policies, there is an increasing tendency in some states toward, as Marie Beynon Ray has observed, "putting the blind in separate classes in the regular schools. Thus they never lose contact with the sighted world, never cease trying to adjust to it, to act like the sighted." (53, p. 165)

It is true that these public school programs for the blind have, in Mary Bauman's words, "the advantages of special materials, relatively individual attention, and some areas of competition only with children of like physical handicap, while they also provide opportunity for contact with seeing children in social and some athletic activities and permit the child to reside in his own home and community." (4, p. 9) At the same time, their limitations in scope aside, they are by no means in extensive use throughout the country, as most public school systems simply cannot afford to give the blind even a modicum of the training and techniques they need.

Therefore, although it is not to be questioned that contacts with the sighted are eminently desirable for the blind, as normal contacts are desirable for all the handicapped, the question that does arise is whether these contacts are sufficiently important to outweigh the advantage for the blind child of attending a school designed specifically to fill his needs. Bauman has outlined in considerable detail just what it is that the special school has to offer that the special class cannot—and the school's advantages are considerable:

> The two channels chiefly used to replace the lost channel of vision are hearing and touch. Both are, of course, also much used in the education of seeing children but there are many who feel that so much more material must be presented orally and tactually to blind children and that so much more individual attention is needed by blind children that special schools for the blind are necessary. . . . These schools can tune their whole program to the blind child teaching what he needs and only what he needs. These schools can provide competition not only in academic areas but also in social and athletic areas with other blind children and protect the blind child from what might be unfair competition with seeing children. . . . (4, p. 8)

If the blind child's education is efficiently adjusted to his visual loss from the start, or as close to the start as is feasible, he not only enters school earlier, but "remains in school longer, reaches a significantly higher educational level with more academic success and a greater feeling of satisfaction on his part." (4, p. 132) Only the special school, whether day or residential, can afford to devote sufficient time to developing the particular aptitudes the blind child needs. There is, of course, no evidence whatsoever to support the popular legend that the blind have superior auditory and tactile abilities. It is merely that they have *needed* to develop what capacities they have in these areas to their fullest extent, and it is in the development of these skills that the special schools can be of outstanding service.

An adequate curriculum for the blind child would, of course, include Braille reading and writing, as well as the usual academic subjects necessary to complete his education—English, mathematics, and the sciences. Special emphasis should be placed on those subjects in which he can compete on an equal basis with the sighted, notably music and foreign languages; and, since the blind often suffer from speech defects, considerable attention should be devoted to speech and speech correction.

But a program cannot be organized without due consideration of the blind child's physical and emotional make-up. Logically, the blind child should show no signal difference from the sighted child physically, unless his blindness was caused by some disease with accompanying handicap or debility. Perhaps because of the sedentary life they are often forced to lead, perhaps because of "impairment of the nervous system and general neglect" (18, p. 139), the blind do not usually seem to be in good physical condition, but tend to be weak and listless.

Emotionally also they deviate from the norm, experiencing considerable difficulty in making satisfactory personal adjustments for, no matter how well disposed their sighted contacts are, they cannot help but suffer a feeling of being alien and alone, especially when out of touch with other sightless individuals.

Further maladjustments often arise when the blind person, in an effort to make his cruel fate seem less unjust, blames himself for his handicap. Farfetched as it may seem, this often happens. Bauman reports:

> It is often said that one of the reasons for intense emotional reaction to loss of vision is a sense of guilt, a feeling that blindness is a punishment for some misdeed. In our total study, 97 persons [out of 443] said that they did feel, or at times had felt, that blindness was a punishment. . . . (4, p. 125)

Obviously, the degree of adjustment or maladjustment will depend to a great extent upon the blind person's own personality, rather than upon the nature of his handicap. However, some of the psychologically disturbing factors come from outside him and cannot help but shake the most stable to some degree. The chief source of this disturbance is the unhappy fact that blindness appears to arouse a more emotional reaction in others than do most other handicaps.

The Partially Sighted

A distinction is sometimes made between the partially blind and the partially sighted. By legal definition, pupils who have 20/200 vision or less or who have better than 20/200, but whose peripheral vision is limited to twenty degrees or less in the widest diameter are considered partially blind, even though they can see to some extent. The partially sighted are those with 20/200 to 20/70 vision—sometimes those whose vision is better than that but who have specific defects or who are suffering a gradual loss in vision.

There were 8,104 public school children listed as enrolled in the special schools and classes in 1952–53 (**54**, p. 15); however, this by no means implies that very much more than a few of the total extant in the population are included. Unlike the blind, who are immediately identifiable once they actually appear in the schools, the partially sighted child, if his defect is not too great, may not be apparent as such to the teacher untrained in diagnostic procedures. Therefore, Garrison advises:

The teacher should possess the ability to recognize certain gross symptoms which suggest the possibility of visual defects. . . . A few of these common symptoms of eyestrain . . . are undue stooping to read and write, too frequent headaches, inflammation of the eyelids . . . granular eyelids . . . watery eyes, discharge from the corners of the eyelids, swollen appendages. Variation of the pupil of the eye . . . is another symptom of eye trouble. . . . Other external symptoms . . . are tense facial expressions, knitted eyebrows, blinking, screwing the eyes when looking at books or blackboard, squinting, styes. . . . (**20**, p. 229)

It is essential that those with visual defects be identified as soon as possible, and this includes those children with simple problems—such as myopia that can, if discovered, be readily corrected by glasses—as well as those with more serious problems that require special medical or therapeutic treatment. Otherwise, there is always the danger of these children's frustration and resentment boiling up into antisocial behavior, as Frampton and Rowell have intimated:

> In the public schools visually handicapped children sometimes become behavior problems. Cases are cited of juvenile delinquents whose maladjustments were finally traced to some visual handicap as the primary cause. The visual handicap may intensify undesirable behavior problems. Pupils may have fought their way through several years of schooling before the eye difficulty was discovered. Eyestrain and fatigue may lead to exhaustion and neurasthenic conditions. (18, pp. 143–44)

The partially sighted may be, and, in fact, should be taught in sight-saving classes conducted within the regular school, because their educational needs are not as highly specialized as the blind's, so that the facilities they require are well within the scope of most well-equipped schools. In the sight-saving classes which many communities have established, the pupils have the opportunity both to enjoy the best program possible for their education along with maximum community contacts. "Essentially, such classes emphasize the use of material in large type, optimum lighting conditions, and considerable individual help." (4, p. 9) The Ohio program is typical of an effective class arrangement for the partially sighted:

> . . . Most of the larger cities in Ohio operate "sight saving" classes with a special teacher in a special room. As with other special classes, the child remains here while he is acquiring those skills needed to help him adjust to his handicap in a school situation but participates in the regular classroom for much of his school work. . . . (43, p. 188)

The sight-saving classes at the Humboldt School in Alton, Illinois, are, as described by Postlewait, another well set up system, being, first of all, "blessed with . . . teachers . . . who are

well trained, who use sound judgment, and possess an understanding knowledge of children." Considerable attention is given
to the physical arrangements of the rooms used for these classes.
Each "is well equipped with the proper tilt-top desks, fluorescent
lights, typewriters and stands, Venetian blinds, special blackboards and chalk, specially designed paper, and . . . the special
textbooks . . . necessary for Sight Saving pupils." (**52,** p. 78)
New York City has probably the most outstanding system of
sight-saving classes in that, in 1951–52, 17 per cent of all children
enrolled in such classes throughout the country were in the
classes of that city. Totalling over 1,300, they probably represented only a fraction of those in the city, requiring such classes.
(**59,** pp. 215–16)

In Alton, according to Postlewait, experiments have been
made in returning sight-saving children to the regular classes
with, she feels, favorable results. At first the children were sent
only to such classes as "music, art, and physical education." Then
the school placed several sight-saving pupils in the regular classes
for "practically their complete program." They returned to the
sight-saving room only "for personal help from the teachers and
to do their close study work under the proper illumination." (**52,**
p. 79) Although Postlewait seems enthusiastic about this procedure, it has not been used sufficiently—or, at least, reported on
sufficiently—to warrant recommendation at this juncture. In fact,
a word of caution might be introduced here against too facile
return of the visually handicapped child to the regular classes.
A poorly sighted student *can* compete with one of normal sight,
but he will do so at the cost of a considerable degree of strain,
both to his vision and his emotions.

Vocational Opportunities

If it is presumed that current conditions will remain static,
then less than 1 per cent of the blind has much chance of ever

being employed in jobs outside the sheltered workshops, because of prejudice rather than their inherent disabilities.

. . . Some of the limitations arise from the fact that certain kinds of work are difficult or impossible without vision, but equal difficulty arises from the fact that employers are unwilling to accept the blind worker. Suffice it to say that a few kinds of work have been regarded traditionally as work for the blind: caning chairs, basketry, weaving, broom and mop making, making mats from rubber links, leather work. Such work is still offered in many communities on a sheltered shop basis, which usually means that the shop is not supposed to pay its way nor is the blind person expected to produce enough to "earn" the money he receives. . . . (**4, p. 11**)

When it comes to jobs outside the workshop, piano tuning or running a newsstand are among the few occupations considered suitable for them.

However, far more of the blind than is commonly believed possible are capable of filling many different kinds of positions, if employer resistance could only be broken down. In studying the problems of the blind, Bauman discovered that, among the well-adjusted and fully employed individuals in the group she was investigating, those who were within the legal definition of total blindness included eight teachers and ten social workers, as well as five in other professions. There were fourteen office workers, three masseurs or physiotherapists, fourteen vending-stand operators and one individual in another type of sales work, thirty-two employed in factory or trade jobs, four in service and labor, and seven farm workers. (**4, p. 178**)

It is by no means necessary for the blind person to be above-average in intelligence for him to be able to secure employment, for, as Bauman states, "there is no evidence that employment is open only to the mentally superior blind person," adding that "it is encouraging to find how many blind persons of very limited mental ability can and do find employment." (**4, p. 84**) She comments that there does seem to be a definite tendency for persons who attended schools for the blind to hold "white collar" jobs, but ascribes this to the fact that those who had the opportunity for adjusted schooling generally also had the opportunity of receiving a higher education, so that this factor "may be the result of more adequate preparation rather than of prejudice against work with the hands." (4, p. 93)

As for the partially sighted, their vocational opportunities depend upon the degree of handicap. Those with minimal handicap will find little or no difficulty in securing employment. Those considerably handicapped may find themselves put in the same category as the blind.

AURAL DEFECTS

The Deaf

In Chapter Two, it was noted that there are approximately two hundred thousand deaf persons in the United States between the ages of five and seventy. Approximately thirty-five thousand children of school age are considered totally deaf. Since, however, the definitions in this field have not been absolutely standardized, there are varying opinions as to what precisely constitutes total deafness.

One definition describes a totally deaf individual as either one who was born deaf or one who lost his hearing before learning how to talk; hence, in both cases, one who never acquired speech habits. The reason that the speech factor is given so much importance in this connection is that the inability of children in these categories to hear spoken language culminates in their lack of awareness that there are such symbols as words which can be utilized orally as instruments of communicating or receiving ideas, information, and thoughts. The child who not only cannot speak but has no idea that there is such a method of communication as speech is as effectively cut off from his own species as if he were an alien life form born and bred on another planet; in a sense, he *is* an alien life form, for he lacks the shared experiences that bind us together far more cohesively than any identity of shape.

Nonetheless, other investigators do not weigh the factor of speech quite so heavily from the standpoint of evolving adequate definitions, although it is, of course, of paramount importance in originating and carrying out any program of work in the field, be it educational, therapeutic, or even custodial. The fact remains, however, that those individuals who have completely lost their hearing after learning how to speak still must be classified as totally deaf, which would vitiate the definition.

Another definition of those who are deaf is that adopted by the membership at the 1937 Conference of Executives of American Schools for the Deaf:

. . . Those in whom the sense of hearing is nonfunctional for the ordinary purposes of life. This general group is made up of two distinct classes, based entirely on the time of the loss of hearing: (a) the congenitally deaf—those who were born deaf; (b) the adventitiously deaf —those who were born with normal hearing but in whom the sense of hearing has become nonfunctional through illness or accident. (18, p. 196)

Mackie has approached the matter most practically when she states that "obviously, from the physiological standpoint, a child is deaf when his hearing is so impaired that he cannot understand connected speech through the ears even with amplification." (38, p. 21)

Just as in the case of the blind, deaf children must be discovered as long as possible before the compulsory school admission age, if they are to be given the fullest possible chance to achieve normal educational status, since their disability in itself cannot help but be a cumulatively retarding factor. The longer their deafness remains neglected, the longer they are cut off from any real communication, and, furthermore, the harder it becomes to establish communication patterns. As a matter of fact, a concept with which most, if not all, workers in the field of special education would agree is that deafness, which is severe and profound at the onset, is probably the most serious of all the types of disabilities from an educational point of view.

Another imperative reason why deafness should be discovered as early as possible is that even total deafness is not always irremediable, particularly when it is treated during the individual's formative years. Certain kinds can be eliminated or substantially reduced through surgery or medical treatment. Removal of adenoids or tonsils sometimes helps, and there are operations for the relief of Ménière's disease, and for mobilization of the stapes, as well as the fenestration operation. Plastic surgery can correct malformation of the outer ear. Radiation and chemotherapy have been found useful in treating some aural conditions. The earlier the stage at which the potentially corrigible aural defect can be treated, the greater the chance that the techniques applied may be successful.

It is imperative that hearing tests should be given at a very early age to children who manifest the slightest of difficulties in speech. Also teachers and parents, especially, should be alert to delayed speech and difficulties on the part of children to identify the directions of sound. Whenever children seem to use their hands excessively to make themselves understood or to make their wishes known, parents and teachers should direct their attentions to test the hearing of such children. Poor intonation and resonance along with poor articulation and difficulties in using and pronouncing common words may indicate signs of deafness, which should encourage immediate examination and testing. Then, too, obviously organic disorders of the ear, such as a discharge of some sort, should be given prompt attention. Sometimes the constant turning of the head to catch sound may be another indication of hearing defect. Other symptoms of hearing disorders in children may be an abnormal manifestation of loss of balance and equilibrium and a feeling of unsteadiness. Finally could be added nystagmus, which is a kind of involuntary movement of the eyeball, and which may be a warning sign that the child has a serious hearing loss. All or any one of these difficulties, as soon as they are discovered, call for immediate diagnosis.

In some larger cities, provision is made for organizing classes for the deaf, as for the blind, at the preschool age level, so that the early period of isolation is shortened as much as possible. Many schools, as, for instance, those in the state of Ohio, have lowered the admission age for deaf children to three. It is entirely possible to train the deaf within the regular public school system, although the special curriculum required will make it difficult for them to keep up to normal grading. However, specialized teaching methods plus an earlier starting age at school for deaf and hard of hearing children can conceivably curtail the educational differential. It would be expedient, moreover, that deaf and hard of hearing children should receive an early and systematic training in language which would continue after the school hours with parents cooperating in the program, and, if parents are not proficient enough to assist, then other adult substitutes must be secured. Precisely, if well organized supplementary opportunities for training deaf and hard of hearing children outside of school are not provided, then it is unlikely that classes in the public day school, even at a preschool age level, would be very effective. In any case, children who will be able to succeed in public school day programs will not be numerous, since few deaf children of elementary school age have sufficient language development and the minimum skills in speech and in reading. Every child, once he has had some special class training, should be given the opportunity to study in the public day school, if it is thought that there is a reasonable prospect of success.

As for extant programs, in Ohio, according to McIntire, deaf children are educated in the public schools by teachers who are trained "not only in methods used for hearing children but also in special techniques of teaching language and speech to the deaf."

. . . In the public school classes the oral method is used exclusively. The work is begun at as early an age as possible to at least partially overcome the child's speech and language retardation before he reaches regular school age. (**43**, pp. 186–87)

And Watson has noted, concerning the system in use in his own state, that "in California deaf children may receive the special education they need in special day schools or special classes operated by the public schools or in one of the two residential schools for the deaf maintained by the state." (**61**, p. 35) Some cities, notably New York, Chicago, Los Angeles, Cincinnati, and Minneapolis, have elaborate systems of special classes for the deaf within the public school system; these may be situated either in the regular schools or in special schools. In New York, according to O'Brien, the deaf are educated in special schools, contrary to the city school system's usual nonsegregation policy, because—

. . . the very special and intensive problems these children present, particularly during the early part of their education, require that the programs be conducted in highly specialized settings. However, as soon as these children have been benefited sufficiently from these programs so that they can maintain themselves with no or very little special help, they are returned to regular classes or to special classes in a regular school. (**50**, p. 210)

On the whole, since the number of totally deaf children is small and scattered widely throughout the country, it has proved most feasible in all but the largest communities, such as those cited, to educate the totally deaf in special day or residential schools.

Noteworthy among the day schools is New York City's Junior High School 47, which Harriet McLaughlin has described as the largest school devoted entirely to acoustical handicaps in the United States. (**44,** pp. 200–208)

At the present time, about fifteen thousand of the approximately twenty thousand totally deaf children estimated to exist in our population are being trained in residential schools. Most of these schools are public institutions, although there are also some twenty-five private residential schools for the deaf in the United States. All of the states, except four, have residential school facilities for the deaf, either public or private.

Watson has given rather a complete picture of the attributes that are considered to be indispensable to the well-equipped classroom for the deaf. First of all, it should be "large enough to accommodate the special equipment and teaching materials used in their instruction." Then it should have electrical outlets sufficient in number and so located as to permit "the convenient use of group hearing aids." Adequate lighting is most important in this area; "the light should be of steady intensity," with all glare and undesirable light reflection eliminated.

These classrooms for the deaf should be situated far from sources of noise, "for it is essential that the teacher be able to hear readily all aspects of each deaf pupil's effort at speech," and also so that "deaf pupils having any residual hearing"—which, of course, would apply to the hard of hearing also—"may better sense the various components of the teacher's speech." The rooms should be soundproofed, with the ceilings and upper walls constructed of some type of sound conditioning material, while the floor should be covered with cork or rubber tile, or, if these are impracticable, rugs. Finally, each classroom for the deaf should contain "a large mirror on a flexible mounting for showing deaf pupils speech positions and articulation movements." (**61,** p. 42)

Educating the deaf requires that the teacher be skilled in a good many competencies, for there are a number of techniques used in this area, and, although certain favored methods might be the ones actually in use at her school, she should have some knowledge of all of them. Basically, the language techniques may be subdivided into the oral, the manual, and a combination of the two. The oral, of course, emphasizes lip reading; the manual, sign language.

Formerly, although the oral method was certainly not unknown, it had been the practice in the United States to teach virtually all the deaf children how "to talk on their hands," which, of course, restricted their communication to other persons with similar training and virtually cut off all normal community contacts for them. Then, about the middle of the nineteenth century, more emphasis was placed upon the oral method of teaching deaf children. The oral method actually is a type of oral education which stresses training in speaking and in reading lips, and it includes specialized instruction in phonics and articulation while employing visual, tactual, and kinesthetic aids.

Today, the manual alphabet is little used by itself, the emphasis in most educational programs being laid on communication which utilizes the maximum development of skill in lip reading (or speech reading . . .), hearing aids, auditory training, and the teaching of speech. One of the reasons that the manual alphabet held sway in this country for so long is the existence of a popular legend to the effect that sign language is the "natural" language of the deaf, because the deaf child will, of course, use signs in his attempts to communicate. However, that is simply because he does not know that there is such a thing as speech. The fact that he uses the only means available to him does not mean that they are necessarily the best.

The idea that sign-language . . . is the "natural" language of the child with profound hearing impairment can be maintained only in spite of—not because of—known facts of infant and childhood behavior, the neurophysiology of the association centers in the brain, and the use of compensatory adjuncts to the impaired hearing mechanism in early linguistic and behavioral training. . . . (**35**, p. 15)

The combined method is still in use because the oral method alone is really successful only in day schools where the children are under the teacher's supervision all the time. Furthermore, the employment of the manual alphabet and sign language does not necessarily deter a child's ability to utilize the speech and speech reading that he acquires in his classes. Actually, sign language may afford a deaf child the opportunity to give vent to many of his ideas in a more effective and spontaneous manner. It also happens that certain deaf children do not seem able to master lip reading and speech; therefore, the manual method must be taught them if they are to achieve any degree of communication at all. In such cases, it has sometimes been found possible to teach the child the oral techniques *after* he has mastered the manual method.

Within the framework of the oral method, deaf children can be taught to speak by either "the oral method" or "the synthetic [natural] method," both of which Frampton and Rowell have described as follows: In the oral method, the children "are taught isolated sounds, including the vowels, consonants, and diphthongs." Once these speech sounds have been mastered by the child they are combined into words.

The synthetic method represents the newer approach to the problem. The child here "is encouraged to try to pronounce whole words and use them for self-expression purposes before the phonetic elements of which words are composed have been taught." (**18**, p. 206) Other methods of learning language development and voice improvement are "the kinesthetic and auditory." (**38**, p. 7)

On the whole, as soon as the communication techniques have been learned, the deaf child's curriculum should follow the one used in the regular classes, insofar as is possible, considering his handicap. And, in giving attention to the deaf child's inherent deviation from the norm, program planners must pay attention to the particular difficulties that seem to accompany this deviation. Although deaf children should not be extremely different in physical development from the hearing children, there is, Helmer Myklebust maintains, more physical difference than might be supposed, for deafness "causes the individual to see differently, to smell differently, to use tactual and kinesthetic sensation differently" . . . and every single one of these factors must be taken into account when organizing a program for them. (**49**, p. 177)

Emotional consideration must be given their due weight, too, because socially the deaf person is possibly the most maladjusted of all the handicapped. This, Wright ascribes to the fact that—

. . . So much of social intercourse depends upon hearing. It has been said that hearing is our social sense and the one most closely allied with our emotions. We are inspired and uplifted by great music; we are gay when there is laughter around us; we weep at certain inflections in the voice when touching words are spoken. We are depressed if we do not hear the sound of the human voice for any length of time. These emotions caused by sound are denied to the deaf. (**64**, p. 8)

Although deafness may seem superficially to be less of a handicap than blindness, the deaf may manifest a much greater degree of antisocial behavior than the blind. Of course, maladjustive responses to the loss of hearing will assume different forms and proportions in different individuals, since it may cause all forms of poor adjustmental behavior, such as frustration, hostility, fear, inadequacy, guilt, excessive embarrassment, and depression.

The Hard of Hearing

It is generally conceded that, when a child has a hearing loss of 20 decibels or more in both ears, he is considered definitely handicapped as far as normal educational environment in our public day schools is concerned.

The Conference of Executives of American Schools for the Deaf has defined the hard of hearing as "those in whom the sense of hearing, although defective, is functional with or without a hearing aid." (18, p. 196) Therefore, the hard of hearing generally have acquired some development of the faculty of speech before their hearing loss, whatever its extent, and their psychological maladjustment will, as a rule, be less severe than the deaf's. However, they are subject to a considerable degree of psychological disturbance. One description says they—

. . . often shun society because of [the] strain of trying to keep up— often with the result of continuing withdrawal from social gatherings. The hard of hearing are often ashamed—they are afraid they will be thought stupid or queer. They get panicky sometimes when people speak to them, and often walk along the street with fear showing in their eyes. (64, p. 10)

How disturbed they are depends partly upon individual personality traits, partly upon the extent of their handicap. Some degrees of hearing impairment are so slight as to be an inconvenience rather than an actual disability; others verge on actual deafness.

It has been estimated that between 4 and 5 per cent of school-age children have some degree of hearing impairment, which would mean that there are more than 1,200,000 school children who could fall into the hard of hearing classification, although only about twelve thousand hard of hearing children were listed as being enrolled in the United States public schools. (54, p. 15) There are no certain figures as to the number of children under five with impaired hearing, but an estimate of six hundred thousand would be a conservative one. According to Eleanor Ronnei, hearing loss is on the increase in the United States, because a good many infants whose lives have been saved by modern medical science, particularly the premature, R H factor, and tubercular meningitis cases, seem to have defective hearing. (**55,** p. 261)

Charles Watson has outlined four general types of hearing impairments: the *conductive,* where "the deafness is caused by some condition in the outer ear or middle ear partially or totally obstructing the passage of sound vibrations to the inner ear"; the *perceptive,* which results "from an impairment or degeneration of the sensory structures located in the inner ear"; the *central,* where "the difficulty is located in the central nervous system"; and the *psychogenic,* where the difficulty is, of course, psychological. (**61,** pp. 6–7)

Whatever the type of impairment, the more severely handicapped of these children will need to be taught to lip-read, as well as to develop their own voice qualities, while, at the same time, making optimal use of hearing aids. The amount of help that can be obtained from a hearing aid does vary with the individual, depending upon—

. . . both the amount of hearing loss and the type of loss. Hearing aids usually give more help to individuals who have a conductive type of deafness. Those who have suffered involvement of the inner ear or the auditory features of the central nervous system resulting in perceptive deafness are less likely to derive help from a hearing aid. . . . (**61,** p. 29)

The hearing aid is not simply an amplifier; it may also have "important secondary values," helping "deaf children to develop greater skill in articulation and acquire a more natural quality of voice." (**61,** p. 30)

However, simply equipping the hard of hearing child with a hearing aid is not going to provide a complete solution to all of his difficulties, but only a tool with which he can help himself to solve them. Watson says:

Obviously he will not be able to hear and understand speech solely through the use of a hearing aid. He is going to need the special skills of speech reading and language to do this. Nor is he going to learn speech through the use of the hearing aid. He will require skilled, intensive, special instruction in speech development. (61, pp. 29–30)

Furthermore, the hearing aid of itself, while serving to solve one problem will create another, namely that of adjusting the child to the concept that the aid is to be an extension of his own sensory equipment, in other words, a new part of himself.

Since most hard of hearing children will have achieved some degree of communication, they should, if possible, attend classes in the public schools lest they lose whatever favorable adjustments they have managed to make on their own behalf. Putting such children in a school for the deaf, as was often the procedure before the widespread use of the oral method in this country, was a cruel and senseless procedure, making a severe handicap out of what might have been a comparatively slight one.

Probably children who show the effects of defective hearing in their schoolwork will need to be put in special classes; however, there are few, if any, hard of hearing children whose work does not suffer to some degree from their handicap. If no special classes are available for them, they should have additional work beside the regular school curriculum. Special classes with a suitably modified curriculum would be preferable, not only because of the disability itself, but because the children will probably be physically and perhaps emotionally in advance of the grade they have succeeded in reaching and may need adjustments on that score. Ohio may be cited as an illustration where hard of hearing children are taught effectively in the regular classes under the supervision of specialized teachers who have access to the necessary physical resources and devices. The crux of the matter is that the teacher must be especially trained to teach hard of hearing children in the regular classroom and she must have the necessary instrumentalities to do effective work. Without the special teacher, hard of hearing children would be practically wasting their time in public school day classes; and many of them do waste their time, because of administrative short-sightedness and parsimony on the part of too many school boards.

Special Problems

There are two specialized problems in the area of aural disability which, including only a few of the handicapped in their scope, can be touched on only briefly in this volume. One is an error of diagnosis, in that sometimes aphasic children are inadvertently enrolled in special classes and schools for the deaf. "This situation," Watson says, "exists because aphasic and deaf children often have common developmental or functional deficiencies:"

. . . The aphasic child, for instance, often appears not to hear and he frequently fails to learn to talk. His understanding of spoken or printed language is often limited or lacking. These are conditions that also characterize the deaf child. . . . (**61**, pp. 14–15)

However, aphasia is a disorder not related to deafness, for it is not located in any of the hearing organs, but in the central nervous system. The educational needs of the aphasic child, therefore, differ considerably from those of the deaf child, and those who work with the deaf must be on the watch for cases of aphasia enrolled in their classes by mistake. The symptoms of this disorder are mixed laterality; delayed response; inconsistency; distractibility; hyperactivity; perseveration; difficulty in shifting from one activity to another; disinhibition; catastrophic reaction, persistent repetition of questions; meticulosity; aimless movements, abnormal clumsiness; aggressive, antisocial, or uncontrolled behavior; phlegmatic behavior; and short attention span.

The deaf-blind child also presents a special problem, which, though pertinent, can be given only passing mention in a text of limited scope. His needs combine those of both the visually and the aurally handicapped, but they combine algebraically, rather than arithmetically, presenting a teaching problem that is many times more difficult than either handicap alone:

> The deaf child relies heavily on vision in his learning activities while the blind child depends primarily on hearing and touch in his learning activities. Vision and sight are denied the deaf-blind child. Touch is his chief avenue for learning activity. Since the learning task confronting the deaf-blind child is extremely difficult, it naturally follows that teaching him requires a high order of general ability, extensive training in the fields of the deaf and blind, and demonstrated skill. (**61**, p. 16)

Vocational Opportunities

Employment opportunities for the deaf vary greatly. The totally deaf will experience some difficulty in finding jobs—though they are better off than the blind in this respect—but the partially deaf are eligible, in theory, at least for 90 per cent of all factory jobs, 71 per cent of mechanical jobs, and 61 per cent of office jobs. On the whole, job opportunities for both the deaf and hard of hearing are becoming far more numerous, even though some employers still continue to—

> . . . place too much emphasis on the communication problems of the deaf and not enough emphasis on the deaf worker's production potential. The same attitude often extends toward the hard-of-hearing even when their communication difficulties, as far as the jobs are concerned, are overcome by lip-reading and the use of a hearing aid. (**64**, p. 11)

However, Elstad says, "in normal times most deaf people are employed. Those who wish to work can find work." (**14**, p. 163)

Concerning the hard of hearing, it must be remembered, Wright has emphasized, that "a hearing impairment is not usually static"; hence the hard of hearing individual should not be guided toward an occupation for which the amount of hearing he currently possesses may be sufficient, but with which he could not cope should his hearing loss become more severe. (**64**, p. 29)

Furthermore, he must not be guided toward an occupation for which he might be qualified, but which might represent a risk for the degree of hearing he still does possess.

SPEECH DEFECTS

In 1952, there were over three hundred thousand speech defectives enrolled in the public schools of this country. (**54,** p. 15) Although defects in speech, therefore, make up the largest quantitative handicap, they also make up the handicap about which the least is known, except in cases where the defect stems from an obvious physical abnormality, such as a cleft palate or malformation of the jaw.

The line between merely faulty and actually defective speech has never been clearly delineated, for it may be possible that there is no such thing as a minor speech disorder. Overtly, an individual with even the slightest sound deviation may be deeply disturbed because of his inner reactions to his defect. On the whole, then, speech might be defined as defective when—

(1) it interferes with the individual's ability to communicate.
(2) it is conspicuously different from the speech of his peer group.
(3) it causes psychological disturbance in him.

Classifications

Speech handicaps are the most difficult of all to standardize, even for purely organizational purposes, because, even where their cause is known or suspected, few of them can be traced back to one basic origin, most arising from a combination of several causes. From the etiological point of view, speech abnormalities may be classified into four general groups: the physiological, the anatomical, the psychogenic, and the imitative.

Those defects that are classified as physiological would occur as part of a general physiological condition, such as a marked retardation in the area of one's perceptual development. These defects may also be evident in the poor functioning of an individual's sensory receptive areas for speech or in a definite retardation of his conveying of speech impulses to the motor areas of the cortex. They may also be the result of a child's inability to understand the multifarious kinds of association imperative to the understanding of meanings and the reception, retention, and the reproduction of speech.

The anatomical category would include all oral deformities that generate or influence speech, such as harelip, cleft palate, and orthodontic defects. Speech disorders may also be caused by nasal obstructions or by abnormalities in the larynx or pharynx. Many disturbances of the central nervous system can also result in speech pathology, and the side effects of numerous diseases and infectious conditions can also produce disorders of speech. For example, the effects of poliomyelitis may result in speech disturbances, and cerebral palsy almost invariably does have that result. However, this entire category would include relatively few of the defective because most speech-defective children will be found to be physically normal.

Speech defects associated with psychogenic disorders constitute the largest group of all. Here usually no organic defect is present, but speech disorder is manifested outwardly because of a psychophysical situation.

The fourth, and last, the imitative speech defect, is self-explanatory. If caught early, speech defects arising from imitative causes rarely develop into a serious problem. The existence of such a defect, however, serves to point up the fact that all teachers, not merely those employed as speech correctionists, should use optimal speech themselves, for children have a very natural tendency to use their teachers as linguistic models.

Van Riper classifies speech disorders into four groups, which he categorizes according to symptoms rather than causes. Under *disorders of rhythm,* he includes "stuttering and cluttering." Stuttering he describes as consisting "of moments of speech interruption of such frequency and abnormality as to attract attention, interfere with communication, and produce maladjustment," whereas cluttering "is characterized by slurred and omitted syllables, by improper phrasing and pauses due to excessive speed."

Disorders of articulation comprehend "substitution, omission, addition, and distortion of the speech sounds," while *voice or phonation disorders* encompass disorders of pitch, of timbre, and of intensity. *Symbolization disorders* or dysphasia are rarely met with in the public school system, but are manifested by a difficulty in use or comprehension of linguistic symbols, "whether they be written or spoken." (They are discussed briefly in this text under the heading of aural disorders.) And finally there are the *mixed disorders,* among which are the cleft-palate speech and foreign accent, both of which involve an articulatory plus a voice defect. (**58,** pp. 17–35)

An additional complication here is the fact that many speech abnormalities arise in conjunction with physical abnormalities. That is, they do not occur merely as the result of abnormalities of the vocal apparatus, but as accompaniments of virtually any type of physical (or mental) handicap:

Few persons realize that impairments of speech may exist simultaneously with, or arise secondarily in practically all types among the exceptional. One reason for this is the presence of fatigue and neuromuscular tension in individuals who are trying to meet normal competition with certain senses that function at anywhere from zero to perhaps near normal expectancy. . . . There are also, in certain types of the exceptional, speech defects arising from intrinsic causes. (**17,** p. 167)

On the whole, then, it can be stated that all speech defects are psychological, physical, or functional in cause, and usually contain elements of all three.

Incidence and Types

The average estimate of the number of speech defectives in the United States school population ranges from 8 to 10 per cent. Wendell Johnson believes that 2 to 3 per cent of the total number of school children are seriously defective and another 2 to 3 per cent less seriously defective. (**29**, p. 177) Backus is far more generous with her figures, maintaining that 16 to 25 per cent of all elementary school children have defective speech (**1**, p. 21–22), and Garrison would go as high as 30 per cent. (**20**, p. 339)

However, the discrepancy here seems to be one of definition rather than of statistical inexactitude. Apparently Backus and Garrison feel that other investigators are inclined to give insufficient weight to defects which they consider serious. The White House Conference made the very conservative estimate that only 5 per cent of the total school population have defective speech (**22**, pp. 353–56) and, since most of the figures given for the individual defects in the following paragraphs are based on the White House reports, it must be borne in mind that they probably represent an absolute minimum.

The most common speech problem is faulty articulation, which is responsible for about 3 per cent of all the speech difficulties found in the elementary schools, and comes to a total of more than all the other speech difficulties put together (**22**, pp. 353–56) since 75 to 80 per cent of the children enrolled in speech therapy classes suffer from this defect. According to Ogilvie, the causes of faulty articulation are varied, including "organic difficulty of the articulatory organs, dull hearing, psychological difficulty, persistence of childish habits, and faulty learning." (**51**, p. 236)

The most common speech defect, lisping, falls in this category. Others are lallation—in which the *r*, *l*, *t*, *d*, and/or *s* sounds are defective—and oral inaccuracy, which Van Riper describes as a wastebasket term for any mild articulatory defect. (**58**, p. 26)

About .2 per cent of all school children and 4 per cent of all speech-handicapped persons have voice difficulties, which are classifiable as disorders of quality, of pitch, of volume, and of rate. Defective voice qualities include huskiness, hoarseness, stridency, hypernasality, hyponasality, and so on. Pitch disorders would be represented by the too high and too low voice, as well as the monotone and the singsong. Disorders of volume occur when the voice is too soft or too loud for the purpose for which it is needed, and sometimes when it is lost entirely. Again, these disorders can be combined to make an infinite variety of other disorders, such as the falsetto voice—which is definitely a handicap to the male and certainly no asset to the female. Disorders of rate occur when the speech is too fast, too slow, or too jerky.

A total of .17 per cent of all school children stutter. Curiously enough, the number of boys who stutter far exceed the number of girls who do (this inequity seems to exist in all areas of speech defect, but reaches its greatest variance here). However, although many hypotheses have been advanced to account for this egregious disproportion between the sexes, the basic causes are not known any more than the basic causes of stuttering itself are. Each investigator seems to have a different theory concerning the origins of stuttering. According to Van Riper, for example, stuttering springs from a complex of causes:

> Stuttering then has a multiple origin. It can emerge out of backgrounds of emotional conflict, low frustration tolerance, a speech environment filled with fluency disruptors, a poorly timed dysphemia, parental labeling of the normal non-fluencies as abnormal, and from the stress felt by most children if, driven by their parents, they try too swiftly to master the art of talking in phrases and sentences. Of all these factors, the last is probably the most common source of stuttering. (**58**, p. 349)

In contrast, Johnson seems to feel that the cause of stuttering can be traced back to one rather broad origin, and that it initiates from a situation existing outside rather than inside the stutterer. "The problem of stuttering," he says, "would seem to start, not in the speaker's mouth, but in the listener's ear," for what "the speaker"—i.e., the child—does is respond to what "the listener"— i.e., the adult—does. "And what the listener does seems to be more or less unnerving to the speaker." (**28**, p. 11) On the whole, then—

Stuttering appears to be anxiety-motivated avoidant response that becomes "conditioned" to the cues or stimuli associated with its occurrences. Like other anxiety-motivated avoidant responses, stuttering is anticipatory. . . . The expectation of stuttering is apprehensive, characterized by anxiety in some degree, ranging from near panic to [a] very mild sort of affective reaction. . . . (**28**, p. 23)

In collaboration with John Knott, Johnson has made a series of attempts to isolate the basic factor underlying the stuttering syndrome. Terming that factor "the moment of stuttering," he and Knott have identified that moment as starting before "the actual spasm" and continuing until that spasm is terminated, which will happen—

. . . whenever the psychological field becomes charged either with a totally positive valence, in which case nonstuttering speech is immediately resumed, or with a totally negative valence, in which case the communicative act ceases. In either case, the conflict has ended. . . . (**30**, p. 31)

As a result of all these investigations, Johnson has finally come to the conclusion that—

. . . much of what we call stuttering behavior involves reactions on the basis of statements (or assumptions which become known to us when they are stated), the inferential terms in which are either implicitly false or else meaningless. . . . (The stutterer's habitual use of inferential terms, without examination of their factual implications, prevents his taking the first step toward better adjustment, namely recognition of the facts in terms of which he must make an adjustment. . . . (**28**, p. 435)

The explanation that Dean E. Williams gives of the origins of stuttering bears many points of resemblance to Johnson's. It is Williams' opinion that—

The person who stutters is motivated to govern the things he does as a speaker by the way he feels. . . . He evaluates his emotional reactions to speaking situations as "feelings-of-stuttering." . . . Following the occurrence of a set of stimuli which he evaluates as "trouble," or even "doubt," he responds by "getting set." . . . He tenses stomach, throat, or jaw muscles . . . increases or decreases speaking rate . . . restricts the breath flow . . . and imagines that "it" is now beginning. When he reaches this point, these are the *results* of his doings, and not the beginning of anything new. . . . (**63**, p. 396–97)

Stutterers themselves do recognize the emotional origins of their handicap, for Jeannette Fraisier reports, when asked to give their own explanations for the existence of the handicap in them, they will usually ascribe it to psychological factors, though not always the correct ones. (**16**, pp. 325–34) Curiously enough, Jean Maraist has pointed out, a person who has less than normal hearing acuity is not likely to stutter, for "when the stutterer is unable to hear himself, he stutters less." The theory that she has evolved to account for this phenomenon is that—

. . . the stutterer misevaluates his own speech output at some point in the control system and finds error where, in reality, no error exists. The result of his attempt to correct this non-existent error is stuttering behavior. . . . (**41**, p. 385)

Finally, there are the speech defects which arise as the direct result of physical abnormalities. According to the White House Conference, .1 per cent of all children have cleft-palate speech and .2 per cent of children from five to twenty-one are afflicted by cerebral-palsied speech. (22, pp. 353–56) Under the general classification of physical handicap, we might also include those whose speech defect accompanies another handicap. Half of 1 per cent of all children, the White House Conference reported, have impaired hearing accompanied by speech defects. Ogilvie has said, in describing the speech problems of the aurally impaired that—

. . . the hard-of-hearing youngster often has an articulatory difficulty. The difficulty is sometimes accompanied by one in voice. In some instances, a hearing loss may not be significant enough to cause any speech difficulty. Nevertheless, even in these cases . . . although the child can speak properly, he may not be hearing all that goes on around him. . . . (**51**, p. 236)

And, finally, .3 per cent of all children suffer from impaired hearing accompanied by defective speech. Mental deficiency is also accompanied by defective speech; usually over 50 per cent of all retardates have difficulties with their speech.

Correcting the Defects

The early discovery of the speech defective is of vital importance, as it is comparatively easy to correct a speech defect in a young child, harder in an adolescent, and extremely difficult, if not impossible, in an adult. Before mechanical and therapeutic adjustments are undertaken, the speech correctionist must make sure that the full resources of medicine and surgery have been utilized to correct or ameliorate the defective condition wherever possible. Surgery or prosthetic devices can do much to help cleft palate and harelip. Orthodontia, too, may prove useful in the case of such speech disorders as arise from mouth deformities. The speech teacher, therefore, should have the ability to make at least elementary diagnoses in this area.

And, not only the *speech* teacher, for, although specialists are needed to cope with all really serious speech defects, *every* classroom teacher should be able to "pinch hit" for them. Accordingly, she should have a good deal of training in speech, for "knowledge of some of the minor defects and of the methods used for their correction can often prevent more serious development of the defect." (**18**, p. 239) This is important also in that the speech defectives are not put in special classes, except for the therapy itself; otherwise they do their work in the regular classes.

The main principle to be applied in the area of speech correction is for the teacher to stimulate the child toward initiating motivation that will lead him to correct his defects, for, until the child realizes the urgency of correcting his defects, he will not put forth the necessary effort. Ear training is also of great importance in the education of the speech defective, because, in general, except for the stutterer, once the defective is able to *hear* his own mistakes it is far easier to correct them. Voice defects are far less usual in those individuals possessing what is known as "a good ear," and, in fact, some of them, notably the monotone, are often symptomatic of a hearing impairment. The various mechanical methods are still of great value in correcting speech defects, despite the asseverations of therapists, such as Backus and Beasley, who believe that effectively changing speech behavior depends "less upon devices for breathing, blowing, tongue exercises, 'ear training,' and the like, and more upon forces operating in the interpersonal relationships between child and therapist and among children as a group." (**2**, p. 4) Important as the therapy undeniably is, the mechanical devices should not be discounted, as they serve very useful purposes.

However, it is true that, since so much of speech deviation is of psychological origin, the teacher should make an attempt to get at the emotional roots of these disorders. Stuttering is, of course, the most obviously psychogenic of all the speech defects, and, although Ray may have exaggerated a trifle in her description, it is true that it is a far more serious handicap to the stutterer himself than it might appear to the observer:

We may not consider the stutterer handicapped to the same degree as a blind or a deaf person. To himself he seems just as effectively cut off from society. For while he possesses all his faculties, no one has the patience to communicate with him. (**53**, p. 198)

Van Riper calls for two different kinds of therapy in the treatment of stuttering, one for "the young stutterer in the primary state of the disorder," the other for the "advanced or secondary stage stutterer." (**58**, p. 350) The primary stutterer, Van Riper says, "reacts unconsciously and automatically to his blocks"; hence "his symptoms are the short, effortless, rapid repetitions or the equally short, easy prolongations." As training increases the child's stability, his speech blocks often vanish. However, Van Riper maintains, they will disappear "only if, during this period of instability, the child has not become aware of them as a definite handicap." The method of treating "the secondary stutterer" is more complex. As befits the advanced nature of the ailment, it—

. . . points its therapy at the following goals: (1) Decrease the practices that reinforce the strength of the stuttering reaction. (2) Help the stutterer solve as many of his emotional conflicts as possible and change, if we can, the environmental conditions which tend to keep him a fundamentally hesitant person. (3) Decrease the fears and mal-attitudes by teaching the stutterer to admit and accept his stuttering as a temporary problem which must be faced and conquered. (4) Modify and lessen the severity of the stuttering blocks by eliminating the secondary symptoms of stuttering. (5) Teach the stutterer not to avoid fears or blocks, but to use them in learning how to stutter in an easy, effortless fashion, with a minimum of interruption or abnormality. . . . (**58**, p. 414)

Johnson offers a rather less elaborate system, which he calls "descriptional therapy" for dealing with stuttering:

. . . The basic principle is that of translating inferences into their descriptive equivalents, of keeping discussion and instruction on a descriptive level consistent with the specific adjustments required and of planning any adjustments (exercises, drills, analyses, counseling, etc.) on the basis of the descriptions achieved. (**28**, p. 435)

Here the stutterer must continue his own training by himself for, outside clinical periods, he should, in addition to the assignments he may have been given by his teacher—

. . . speak and react to the greatest possible extent on the basis of the new inferences which he will be gradually developing. For example, it should become reasonably clear to him within a few weeks that his hypothesis concerning the necessity of unusual tension or strain is unfounded. The modification and finally the elimination of this hypothesis or inference should be reflected in a decrease, and finally the elimination, of tension and strain in the stutterer's speech. Essentially the same statement is to be made with regard to any other particular aspect of his stuttering behavior. . . . (**28**, p. 442)

It must not be thought that stuttering is the only speech disorder of psychogenic origin. Many others can spring from emotional difficulties. In fact, most of them, even if not originally psychological, are compounded by the emotional disturbance arising from the consciousness of defect. Van Riper has commented that "a good share of the total handicap . . . is emotional in nature . . . and the speech correctionist who thinks that he deals with lisping rather than lispers, and with stuttering rather than stutterers, will find discouragement at every turn." (**58**, pp. 40–41)

Most voice disorders are said to be of psychogenic origin. The reason for the poor speech of many of those with visual defects has been ascribed to emotional rather than physical factors. (**18**, p. 55) The continued possession of a foreign accent may also be the result of emotional maladjustment arising from the original reactions of the individual's associates to that accent. And, as far as the cleft-palate speaker is concerned, his emotional adjustment is much more important than his actual speech defect. There is often a strong relationship between speech and personality disorders and, while the personality disorder may be the result of the defective speech, the defective speech can also be the result of the personality disorder.

Special attention should be given to those whose speech problems are the by-products of other handicaps. Some authorities recommend that the blind and the part-blind should have their speech carefully checked, for they have a tendency toward defective speech, and it is possible that sometimes a weak poor quality of the organs of speech may accompany a weak quality of the organs of sight. Furthermore, even though a cleft palate is surgically treated, special training is still needed afterward. Coordinated exercises of the muscles employed in articulation are necessary before specialized treatment can be given the spastic and athetoid types of cerebral palsy.

Some speech correctionists believe that, if possible, those with defective speech should be segregated and taught according to the nature of their particular disorder. Backus and Beasley disagree, holding that this practice—

. . . stems from the assumption that there is a different type of therapy for each different type of disorder. This in turn stems from an implicit assumption relating to classification: namely, that all persons who have one set of symptoms in common are alike in all other ways. . . . In point of fact . . . no two persons within a given classification present identical patterning in speech symptoms, nor in functional organization. . . . (2, p. 43)

Vocational Opportunities

It may not be realized that the speech defective, even where he is not suffering from an accompanying physical disability, will find his handicap a vocational drawback. And it is probable that in unskilled and nonprofessional work, a speech defect like faulty articulation or stuttering will not handicap him too greatly. But such a speech defect will certainly prove to be a hindrance in the white-collar or professional areas, and its greatest vocational drawback is that persons who are qualified for a superior type of work are likely to undertake a less congenial occupation simply because it would not require good speech. Some authorities have estimated that the speech defective's earning power is 25 per cent deficient by reason of his handicap.

THE ORTHOPEDICALLY HANDICAPPED

Types and Incidence

The term "orthopedic handicap" includes a wide range of defects which contribute to crippling conditions—those resulting from infection, such as poliomyelitis, bone and joint tuberculosis, rheumatoid arthritis, rickets; cerebral palsy; birth injuries (club foot, cleft lip and palate, and so on); injuries received through accident, and a variety of other causes. Birth injuries are not as rare as might be supposed and are increasing in proportion as superior obstetric techniques are increasingly saving more and more children who would probably have died at birth in the not so distant past.

Sometimes children with cardiac conditions are classified as crippled, sometimes as special health problems. The reason that some communities do enroll these children, as well as others "with certain other handicaps of marginal classification" in classes for the crippled, is, Mackie has explained, out of expediency, because no other suitable provisions are available to them; not that they are officially considered to rank among the orthopedically handicapped. (36, p. 2)

A sound working definition of the juvenile cripple has been put out by the Committee for the Study of Crippled Children, which describes him as—

. . . An individual under twenty-one years of age who is so handicapped through congenital or acquired defects in the use of his limbs and body musculature, as to be unable to compete on terms of equality with a normal individual of the same age. (36, p. 2)

In the following table, Mackie has listed the percentage frequency of particular disabilities among handicapped children who were enrolled in special day schools and classes, in hospitals, convalescent homes, and sanitoria, or receiving home instruction in forty states and Hawaii:

Handicap	Percentage of cases
Infection due to poliomyelitis, tuberculosis of the bones, osteomyelitis, and other diseases	37.3
Cerebral palsy	17.7
Cardiac conditions	13.4
Congenital anomalies	8.5
Traumatic conditions resulting from burns or accidents	3.9
Birth injuries	1.3
Conditions of unknown or uncertain cause, and miscellaneous	17.9

(36, p. 7)

Since the etiology of many of these crippling factors is not known, they are especially difficult to treat from either the physiological or the psychological standpoint. At the same time, however, since we refuse to accept the premise that the weak and disabled among us should be exterminated, it is imperative that we establish a sound program of education for the orthopedically handicapped or crippled children. Many of these children, of course, in spite of this training can never become self-sufficient, but a wholesome education can help them to adjust to their deficiencies and enjoy, to the greatest degree possible, whatever life span has been allotted to them.

However, the more research that has been done, the more we realize how many of those cases that formerly were thought hopeless can be rehabilitated into contributing social units, and the more we realize how much we have lost and wasted by not appreciating their potentialities sooner. And, even though we are aware of those potentialities now, the potentialities of these individuals are still going to be valueless to us, unless we make a positive effort to exploit them. In Mackie's words:

> Much can be done for crippled children today. Under an adequate program of care, many of them can be cured, and large numbers of them will improve to the point where they will be able, for all practical purposes, to lead normal lives. Only a small percentage must remain totally dependent. The happy results, however, do not come about if the care of the crippled child is left to chance. . . . (**36**, p. 1)

There is a total of approximately six hundred thousand crippled individuals under twenty-five in the United States. Studies indicate that 50 per cent of those cases of crippling can be cured entirely or in large part if they are discovered before the age of six. Since so many of the children afflicted in this way come from the lower socioeconomic groups, the percentage of those not cured is tragically higher than it need be, as such children often are not located until either after they are attending school or the school social service worker starts to investigate the reasons for their nonattendance. Therefore, one of the most imperative needs in this area is, again, an early identification program, so that the handicapped children can get the training and treatment they require as soon as possible.

There will be a tremendous variety of differences among the cripples. They cannot ever be considered as a homogeneous group, not only because of the diversity of the handicaps that will be found among them, but also because in some the crippling factor does not affect their health and in others it does. "Some of the crippled children in schools are physically well even though they are limited by handicaps," Mackie says, "but others are below par and will need rest periods in varying amount." (**36**, p. 22)

Some will be multiple-handicapped. For instance, children with cerebral palsy generally have more than one disability. According to the American Public Health Association, over 50 per cent of the cerebral palsied suffer from mental retardation, have speech defects, and/or visual problems. Over 25 per cent have hearing problems and over 25 per cent suffer from convulsions. (**56,** p. 14) Many other disabilities can have associated handicaps, either by chance or because there is some etiological relationship. The multiple-handicapped were for a long time considered as uneducable, particularly when at least one of the disabilities was severe. However, the tendency nowadays is to attempt to educate them, classifying them according to their major handicap.

School Facilities

Ideally, crippled children should be educated in specially designed classrooms within the regular schools. Such specially designed classrooms would be located on the ground floor, so that children can alight from the school bus and reach their classrooms with a minimum of difficulty. If that is not feasible, the school should have ample elevator service and/or inclined ramps.

Inside the classroom, there should be ample space for wheelchairs and other orthopedic equipment, and desks and chairs should be constructed so as to make each child as physically comfortable as possible, in order that he should be able to work and play with maximum efficiency. Handrails should be placed in areas which the child will be using in order to move from one place to another, and floors should be of some composition designed to minimize the effects of a possible fall. Toilet facilities should be located either immediately adjacent to the classroom or very close by, and provision should be made for easy access to the lunchrooms. Not only should a special teacher be provided, but also one or more attendants to help those most severely handicapped and those who may need additional assistance in carrying out their toilet needs. Then, too, assistants are needed to administer to children in wheelchairs and those who walk unsteadily.

In addition to specially designed classrooms, specially designed instructional equipment will also facilitate the child's training. For example, Mackie has suggested that large crayons or pencils may be easier to manipulate for those crippled children who find difficulty with the standard sizes. And the crippled child who cannot manage to write with a pencil or pen may be able to learn the use of the electric typewriter. Some few cerebral-palsied children have scored a great success with the latter. (**36**, p. 30)

Koenig has proposed the use of green blackboards with yellow chalk, "because these colors are more restful to the eye and tend to eliminate glare." She has also suggested that the ideal arrangement would be for each classroom to be accompanied by a second room equipped with cots, where the crippled child can get the rest he generally needs. (**31**, p. 394)

Many of the larger cities have such specially designed classrooms where—

. . . medical treatment (including therapy) goes on simultaneously with the educational program, and thus the efforts of the medical and educational staff are coordinated. Children in need of intensive medical supervision, adjustment in school materials and instruction, the help of trained personnel, special housing and equipment, speech training, and children in need of nutrition and rest should be able to find all of these things in the special classes. (**36**, p. 12)

Chicago is one such city, where extensive arrangements are made for the safety and comfort of the physically handicapped child:

. . . Loading platforms, ramps, and elevators eliminate stair climbing. Spacious classrooms and corridors permit the use of wheelchairs, crutches, walkers, canes, and specially built tables and chairs. Rest rooms are as necessary as libraries and laboratories. . . . (**47**, p. 9)

No matter how well equipped the regular school, it will not, as a rule, be able to cope with the needs of those whose handicaps are of a particularly serious nature, so that special classes alone will not suffice. As O'Brien observed:

. . . children who are extremely handicapped physically and require such costly facilities as therapeutic pools, cannot be admitted to special class programs that are organized in the average regular school building. They should receive their clinic-educational help either in special school buildings or hospitals that are equipped for this purpose. (50, p. 211)

And Heck has described, as particularly outstanding, the Sunshine Orthopedic School, which is part of the regular San Francisco school system:

. . . The upper floor has special glass in the roof which permits indoor sun-bathing. The rooms on the lower floor open through French doors into a central court; thus children in wheel chairs can be moved quickly and easily into the court. There is a modern pool for exercises and treatments. (24, p. 140)

Home and Hospital Facilities

In rural and sparsely populated areas, the schools may not be large enough to justify even special classes, to say nothing of special schools. Under such circumstances there may be a program of home instruction for the handicapped. Actually thirteen of the forty-eight states have no other system of education for crippled children. In too many cases this method has not proved very effective, because the teachers generally have been trained to cope with the children's problems, not the mothers', and the rural housewives, living in relative isolation, often seem to believe that the teacher has come to chat with them rather than to instruct their children.

Where children are so weak that they must be confined to a hospital or at home, provision should be made for specialized teachers to instruct them. In 1949, according to a study put out by the Commonwealth Fund, about 1,850,000 children were admitted to general hospitals every year. (**7**, p. 73) However, many of these general hospitals do not have children's units, with appropriate facilities for taking care of the children's educational and mental well-being, as well as their physical well-being.

In addition to the children admitted to general hospitals, a smaller group, about ninety-one thousand, is admitted every year to the eighty-two children's orthopedic hospitals and ninety-one convalescent homes which, Shands has noted, make up the total of United States institutions of that kind. (**57**, p. 408) The children admitted to these special hospitals, Mackie and Fitzgerald explain, "are usually long-term patients who have tuberculosis, contagious diseases, rheumatic fever, orthopedic disabilities, and various types of illness." Yet, even in these institutions, educational facilities are not always adequate:

Thousands of children would make a more speedy physical recovery; they would be happier; and they would make better adjustments if they had a full and constructive school program in the hospital. When this is provided, there is no time in the child's day for worry about himself and the things he is missing at home and at school. (**40**, p. 1–3)

Aside from providing educational facilities, the hospital should also provide transitional facilities, i.e., an adjustive process for the time when the child will be able to leave the hospital and go to a regular or special school. This change can be highly traumatic for the child who has grown accustomed to "living" in the hospital.

Although all these hospital facilities exist to some degree throughout the United States, they are grossly inadequate in terms of the actual need. Not enough progress has been made in establishing programs for those who are unable to attend classes in any of the schools.

Planning a Program

As far as the curriculum goes, for the most part, the physically handicapped are capable of studying most of the same subjects as the normal children—all the academic subjects, and very likely the greater part of the nonacademic ones, when sufficiently adapted to their needs. They will, even though not retarded in intelligence, probably be behind in grade for their age, because of having been held back by periods of confinement, either at home or in the hospital. The grade lag may be widened even more appreciably in the case of those who need considerable rest, because they will not be able to follow as full a program as the unhandicapped children. Furthermore, certain aspects of their education may need to be rather different from those of the average children. Most of them will need some sort of physiotherapy. Also, because so many of them do not experience everyday activities of the more vigorous boys and girls, rather than have intensive drill in the academic subjects, they will need special curriculum enrichment in the shape of as many field trips away from the school as can be arranged, considering the practical difficulties involved.

Psychological Problems

The orthopedically handicapped child often suffers from extreme maladjustment. Even when his particular handicap is not disfiguring, the child may feel himself to be repulsive to others. As a matter of fact, it has been said that some individuals without obvious handicaps suffer more than those for whom a visibly handicapping condition offers a measure of protection to the ego.

As the crippled child grows older, his psychological problems become more acute. Finding himself "deterred in making social adjustments because of the handicap," he tends, Garrison declares "to become more and more introverted"—especially the girls, to whom personal appearance and social acceptability are particularly important. (**20**, p. 363)

The general attitude of the community often is not conducive toward the child's adjustment:

> Many people are uneasy when they are with handicapped people. This may be because they have fears about things which are different . . . or it may be because they are self-conscious and uncertain how to behave without being patronizing or unnatural. Disfigurements . . . seem to create feelings of revulsion in some people. . . . (**35**, p. 17)

And often the layman does not understand the sometimes erratic behavior of the handicapped. Cruickshank has suggested in this connection that both professionals and lay persons try to conceive of "the adjustive attempts of crippled children", not as "an inherent part of being crippled", but as "part of normative development . . . as efforts on the part of the child during normative development processes to integrate the crippling condition and his understanding of it into his life space." (**11**, p. 285)

Vocational Opportunities

A large number of crippled individuals may never be able to hold jobs except possibly under sheltered workshop conditions. In 1955, Koenig estimated that 93 per cent of all the orthopedically handicapped (excluding the cardiopathic and the cerebrally palsied, who did not come within the scope of her study) were unemployed. (**31**, p. 387) However, the largest obstacle in the way of a crippled individual's making a contribution to society is not his handicap but society itself. Many employers are too prejudiced to hire the orthopedically handicapped, even though the individual's particular handicaps may not stand in the way of his doing the particular type of work involved. Those employers who have been broadminded enough to hire the crippled have, in the main, been very well satisfied with them as employees.

The amount of vocational opportunity open to the crippled depends, of course, upon the nature and degree of his handicap, as well as the kind of work he is seeking.

SPECIAL HEALTH PROBLEMS

Incidence

About 11,500 children are listed by Rice and Hill as being in the public school classes for special health problems (**54**, p. 15), although Mackie and Dunn estimated that actually 510,000 stood in need of such services. (**39**, p. 3) As a matter of fact, Heck has added together the numbers of all the children who fall into the various classifications considered under this category, using the White House Conference figures, and came up with the incredible total of 8,607,000—"a number that is slightly less than one third of all school children of the United States." (**24**, p. 313) Of course he could not allow for duplication of effects, but his figure is still startling.

Identification of these children is extremely difficult, as there are no rules of any kind to go by. Teachers should look out for pupils who seem unusually thin, pale, and listless, lacking in resistance to disease and often seeming to show signs of mental retardation. Actually, this is the group which, more than any of the others, could benefit from an adequate preventive program, for most of the defects are neither congenital nor adventitious, and, if these children had had adequate nourishment and favorable home conditions and a sound program of medical care from the start, they might never have entered into a debilitated state.

Types

Various states use different terms to describe the category of special health problems. Michigan and New Jersey's phrase is "children with lowered vitality," New York's "cardiopathic" classes, and Pennsylvania's "convalescent, tubercular, and physically delicate" children.

The category is rather an ambiguous one, which often overlaps the category of orthopedic defects; in many cases the defects here are modified or less severe versions of those generally listed under the other heading. Cardiac involvements are occasionally included in both classifications. Those handicaps almost always considered under special health problems are epilepsy, diabetes, hemophilia, tuberculosis, anemia, chronic illness, and other debilitating conditions. Often diseases of psychosomatic origin, such as asthma and the other allergic reactions, are considered in this category. Sometimes lowered vitality is categorized as a special health problem, since this is a defect which may isolate a child from his peers. The lack of vitality can be the result of another health problem, such as malnutrition, lack of proper rest, emotional disturbances, or physical illnesses.

Planning Programs

Many of the children considered in this category can be taken care of to some extent in the regular public school classes, or in a combination program of regular plus special classes. Epileptics—petit mal especially—are generally able to follow a regular program, as are the inactive tubercular. Sometimes, however, there are special schools and classes for these children, notably the open-air and open-window variety. It would be a sound idea that such children be supervised in school throughout the summer; otherwise, the progress made during the rest of the year might be negated. Frankly, in an urban quasi-automated society that prevails in the United States, the idea of the twelve months' school is wholesome for all children, healthy as well as handicapped.

The curriculum is usually the same as in the regular classes, except that it may have to be reduced because of the children's inability to sustain a normal work load. The exercise activities of the cardiac and diabetic will have to be carefully supervised and regulated, since children in these special health groups can hardly surmount the factor of fatigue, even though they conceivably may possess the intellectual potential of the nonhandicapped. A series of rest periods in addition to a special program of instruction in health crammed into the standard school day makes it virtually impossible for the child with special health conditions to compete with healthy children and to complete the normally prescribed curriculum.

Adjustments

Social adjustment problems may loom large here, for the child may be baffled as to the reasons for his having been set apart from the others. Furthermore, if his condition is the result of acute or prolonged illness, he may need to be guided away from the habits of overdependency that he has formed, since some handicaps have a stigma attached to them, which are often repulsive when observed in a person who appears normal. Since the psychosomatic disorders generally fall under this category, naturally there would be a great incidence of psychological distress among the children concerned. Allergies are said to produce irritation and behavior abnormalities. Hence, an epileptic, for example, is likely to suffer considerable psychological disturbance, which, in its turn, can be responsible for bringing on one of his seizures, as they are said to have some emotional basis. While it is true that the theory that idiopathic epilepsy is basically a psychogenic disease, making emotions causal and not merely precipitant, has been advanced, it is not necessarily generally accepted.

In a brief summation on problems of social adjustment, special teachers must consider objectively a child's reaction to a physical handicap and/or a special health condition rather than simply the intellectual and physical potential of such a child. It would be folly, and even risky, for special teachers of these children to work apart from the medical men and the psychologists especially trained for dealing with such children in relation to their attitudes and reactions to their disabilities. Too often teachers are prone to consider the mechanical or intellectual IQ apart from the handicapped child's emotional feelings and inner quests.

Vocational Opportunities

Vocational opportunities open to these children depend on the degree to which they have surmounted their handicaps. Except in the case of the epileptic, against whom there continues to exist considerable social prejudice, the question of what kind of jobs they can fill depends upon their own capacities. Since their defects are not obvious, there is no popular feeling against them.

GOALS

All the programs that have been outlined are excellent in theory but not good enough in practice, since they help only a part, and that the smaller part, of the handicapped. If our society's policy is to preserve the handicapped, it must establish programs to include every one of them. If vegetation is to be the lot of any, then we are inadvertently exterminating from our society by way of dereliction many potentially useful citizens and denying the right to a satisfying life for those who never will be able, because of severe handicaps, to become self-sufficient. In an ethical democratic society all individuals are considered dignified and worthy.

DiMichael has pointed out how well the handicapped can do occupationally when given a chance. They are, he says, to be "found in all fields of employment":

. . . The yearly statistics of the Office of Vocational Rehabilitation have shown repeatedly that the disabled who were rehabilitated were employed in occupational groupings almost similar to those of the United States Labor Force. Moreover, studies of comparable groups of disabled and selectively placed non-disabled workers have shown almost similar records in such factors as production, job stability, absences, number of accidents, duration of illness due to accidents, earnings, and efficiency ratings. . . .

Each handicapped group has a wide scope of jobs in which individuals have been, or may be placed. . . . For the physically handicapped and the emotionally disturbed, one will find individuals in job categories ranging from the professional to the unskilled. . . . It is obvious, then, that the problem of suitable placement is dependent upon a skillful exploration of the field of work, and the strengths and limitations of the individual, with a matching between the two that also recognizes human adaptability to several kinds of jobs. (12, p. 343)

Undoubtedly it is expensive to educate the physically handicapped child. Not counting transportation, in 1951–52 it cost New York City, for example—to take the metropolis with the most elaborate system of special education—up to twice as much to educate the orthopedically handicapped, the partially sighted, and those with special health problems, as the normal child, and between three and three and a half times as much to educate the blind and the deaf. This is all very well, the taxpayer says, when the money is used to rehabilitate those who can contribute to society, but why are we educating those who can never be rehabilitated?

In the first place, it is surprising how many seemingly hopeless cases can, given the proper training, become useful and self-supporting citizens. That proper training will give due weight to psychological as well as physical factors, not only attempting to adjust the handicapped individual to occupational and educational techniques, but adjusting him to himself—breaking him of any habits of dependency and self-pity he might have formed.

In the second place, it may be trite to say "where there is life there is hope," but it still holds true. As long as the child is alive, we must treat him as if he would some day be able to take his place in society. After all, the handicapped child, having been born, has a right to live; it is society that does not have the right to ask him to justify his existence.

References

1. BACKUS, OLLIE L. *Speech in Education.* New York: Longmans Green and Co., 1945.
2. BACKUS, OLLIE L., and JANE BEASLEY. *Speech Therapy with Children.* Boston: Houghton, Mifflin Co., 1951.
3. BARRY, HORTENSE. "Classes for Aphasiacs," in (**17**). II, 362–67.
4. BAUMAN, MARY K. *Adjustment to Blindness.* State Council for the Blind, Department of Welfare, Commonwealth of Pennsylvania, 1954 Pennsylvania Division of Documents, Department of Property and Supplies, Harrisburg, Pa.
5. BROIDA, DANIEL G. "Psychological Aspects of Education," in (**10**). Pp. 345–90.
6. CARR, LOWELL J. *Delinquency Control.* New York: Harper and Brothers, 1950.
7. *Child Health Series in Pediatric Education.* I. The Commonwealth Fund, 1949. Vol. I.
8. COHEN, FRANK J. *Children in Trouble.* New York: W. W. Norton and Co., 1952.
9. CORRIGAN, MARIE A. "Tests and Measurements," in (**17**). I, 152–60.
10. CRUICKSHANK, WILLIAM M. (ed.). *Psychology of Exceptional Children and Youth.* Englewood Cliffs, N. J.: Prentice-Hall, 1955.
11. ———. "Psychological Considerations with Crippled Children," in (**10**). 284–344.
12. DiMICHAEL, SALVATORE G. "Vocational Rehabilitations," in (**17**). I, 343–44.
13. EISENSON, JON. "The Nature of Defective Speech," in (**10**). Pp. 184–213.
14. ELSTAD, LEONARD M. "The Deaf," in (**17**). II, 163.

15. FENTON, NORMAN. *Mental Hygiene in School Practice*. Stanford, Calif.: Stanford University Press, 1943.

16. FRAISIER, JEANNETTE. "An Exploration of Stutterers' Theories of Their Own Stuttering," in (**28**). Pp. 325–34.

17. FRAMPTON, MERLE E., and ELENA B. GALL (eds.). *Special Education for the Exceptional*. Boston: Porter Sargent, 1955.

18. FRAMPTON, MERLE E., and HUGH GRANT ROWELL. *Education of the Handicapped*, Yonkers, N. Y.: World Book Co., 1940. Vol. II.

19. GALL, ELENA. "The Child with Multiple Handicaps," in (**17**). II, 534–49.

20. GARRISON, KARL C. *The Psychology of Exceptional Children*. (Rev. ed.) New York: Ronald Press Co., 1950.

21. ————. "The Role of Psychology in Special Education," in (**17**). Vol. I.

22. *Handicapped and the Crippled, The*. White House Conference on Special Education. New York: Appleton-Century-Crofts, 1931.

23. HARTONG, JACK. "The Community and the Institution Cooperate," in *The Handicapped Child in the Mainstream*. Chicago: State of Illinois Committee for Handicapped Children, September 25, 1953. Pp. 32–33.

24. HECK, ARCH O. *The Education of Exceptional Children*. New York: McGraw-Hill Book Co., 1953.

25. HURLIN, RALPH G. "Estimated Prevalence of Blindness in the United States," *Outlook for the Blind*, XLVII (1953), 189–96.

26. INGRAM, CHRISTINE P. "The Prevention of Handicaps," in (**17**). I, 320–35.

27. IRWIN, RUTH B. "Speech Disorder," in (**17**). II, 324–45.

28. JOHNSON, WENDELL. *Stuttering in Children and Adults*. Minneapolis: University of Minnesota Press, 1955.

29. ————. "Teaching Children with Speech Defects," *Forty-Ninth Yearbook*, National Society for the Study of Education. Chicago: University of Chicago Press, 1950.

30. JOHNSON, WENDELL, and JOHN R. KNOTT. "A Systematic Approach to the Psychology of Stuttering," in (**28**). Pp. 25–36.

31. KOENIG, FRANCIS G. "The Orthopedically Handicapped," in (**17**). II, 384–97.

32. KONOPKA, GISELA. "Sharing the Community with the Child," *The Handicapped Child in the Mainstream*. Chicago: State of Illinois Commission for Handicapped Children, September 25, 1953. Pp. 27–31.

33. LAVOS, GEORGE. "Economic Security," in (17). I, 354–76.

34. ———. "Guidance for Exceptional Children and Youth," in (17). I, 137–38.

35. LESSER, ARTHUR (ed.). *Emotional Problems Associated with Handicapping Conditions in Children.* (Federal Security Agency. Children's Bureau Publication No. 336.) Washington, D. C.: Government Printing Office, 1952.

36. MACKIE, ROMAINE P. *Crippled Children in School.* (Department of Health, Education, and Welfare. Bulletin 1948, No. 5. Reprint.) Washington, D. C.: Government Printing Office, 1953.

37. ———. *Education of Crippled Children in the United States.* (Federal Security Agency. Leaflet No. 80.) Washington, D. C.: Government Printing Office, 1952.

38. ———. *Teachers of Children Who Are Deaf.* (Department of Health, Education, and Welfare. Bulletin 1955, No. 6.) Washington, D. C.: Government Printing Office, 1956.

39. MACKIE, ROMAINE P., and LLOYD M. DUNN. *College and University Programs in the Preparation of Teachers of Exceptional Children.* (Department of Health, Education, and Welfare. Bulletin 1954, No. 13.) Washington, D. C.: Government Printing Office, 1954.

40. MACKIE, ROMAINE P., and MARGARET FITZGERALD. *School in the Hospital.* (Federal Security Agency. Bulletin 1949, No. 3.) Washington, D. C.: Government Printing Office, 1954.

41. MARAIST, JEAN ANN. "Efforts of Auditory Masking upon the Speech of Stutterers," *Journal of Speech and Hearing Disorders,* XXII (September, 1957), 385–87.

42. MASE, DARREL J. "The Clinical Approach in Special Education," in (17). I, 21–31.

43. McINTIRE, HAZEL C. "A State Program of Special Education," in (17). I, 182–93.

44. McLAUGHLIN, HARRIET S. "A Modern Day School Program for Teachers of the Deaf," in (17). II, 200–208.

45. MORTON, VELMA Y. "Basic Problems in Guidance in the Field of the Exceptional," in (17). I, 131–74.

46. MULLEN, FRANCES A. "A Metropolitan Area Plans for Special Education," in (17). I, 194–95.

47. MULLEN, FRANCES A. *The Needs of Physically Handicapped Children*. Chicago: Chicago Public Schools, 1954.

48. MYKLEBUST, HELMER R. "Aphasia in Children," *Exceptional Children*, XXIX (October, 1952), 9–14.

49. ———. "Toward a New Understanding of the Deaf Child," in (17). II, 176–84.

50. O'BRIEN, FRANK J. "Special Education in New York City," in (17). I, 206–213.

51. OGILVIE, MARDEL. *Speech in the Elementary School*. New York: McGraw-Hill Book Co., 1954.

52. POSTLEWAIT, GRACE. "Role of the Regular Teacher," *The Handicapped Child in the Mainstream*. Chicago: State of Illinois Commission for Handicapped Children, September 25, 1953. Pp. 78–81.

53. RAY, MARIE BEYNON. *How to Conquer Your Handicaps*. Indianapolis: Bobbs-Merrill Co., 1948.

54. RICE, MABEL C., and ARTHUR S. HILL. *Statistics of Special Education for Exceptional Children*. (U. S. Department of Health, Education, and Welfare) Washington, D. C.: Government Printing Office, 1954.

55. RONNEI, ELEANOR C. "The Hard of Hearing," in (17). II, 260–84.

56. *Services for Children with Cerebral Palsy*. New York: American Public Health Asociation, 1955.

57. SHANDS, A. R., Jr. "The Care and Treatment of Crippled Children in the United States," in (17). II, 405–17.

58. VAN RIPER, C. *Speech Correction, Principles and Methods*. Englewood Cliffs, N. J.: Prentice-Hall, 1954.

59. WALLACE, H. M., J. W. WHITESTONE, and ELENA GALL. "Special Classes for Handicapped Children," in (17). I, 224–27.

60. WARREN, MARJORY C. "Meeting the Special Needs of Handicapped Children through Group Work," *The Handicapped Child in the Mainstream*. Chicago: State of Illinois Commission for Handicapped Children, September 25, 1953. Pp. 91–100.

61. WATSON, CHARLES W. *A Guide to the Education of the Deaf in the Public Schools of California*. California State Department of Education (August, 1955), XXIV, 5.

62. WESTLAKE, HAROLD. "Understanding the Child with a Cleft Palate," in (17). II, 346–54.

63. WILLIAMS, DEAN A. "A Point of View on Stuttering," *Journal of Speech and Hearing Disorders*, XXII (September, 1957), 390–97.

64. WRIGHT, BETTY C. *Orientation Training for Vocational Rehabilitation Counselors*. Washington, D. C.: American Hearing Society, 1956.

CHAPTER TEN

The Public School Administrator
and Special Education

ADMINISTRATIVE ATTITUDES

When it comes to establishing and operating a program of special education, it is the administrator who is in the key position. He is close enough to the children themselves to know from first-hand experience what their needs are and how those needs can best be met. He is also close enough to the members of the school's governing board and to local officials to know what *their* needs are and how these can best be met. Therefore, it is his attitude that counts most of all in this field, for he is the individual who will secure the official permission and the funds to support any extensive educational program, and he is also the one who will be called upon to organize that program and to carry it out in the school.

Precisely who is the administrator in relation to the educational hierarchy? He can be any one of a number of functionaries. He can be the school superintendent (or assistant); he can be the school principal (or assistant); he can even be the grade supervisor or guidance counselor. Generally, in this chapter, it is the school principal who is referred to, unless another person is otherwise specified.

What attitudes, then, do contemporary public school administrators take toward the concept of special education? Certain of them do recognize its necessity and attempt—insofar as it is feasible, considering both the facilities and limitations of their particular schools—to implement programs adjusted to the concept that there are and always will be individual differences inherent among any given group of children. On the other hand, there are other administrators—far too many of them—who refuse to recognize that such specialized programs are vitally important for the health and progress of our educational system.

All children who are physically and mentally capable of attending school, this second group of administrators maintains, are then equally capable of being educated together in the same classes and of following the same programs. To segregate the gifted from the retarded, the physically well from the handicapped, is "an undemocratic practice"—so runs one of their favorite slogans. All children should be grouped together in the regular public school classes, and those who cannot keep up with what these administrators feel to be a "democratic" education should not be in a public school at all. Perhaps these children should be in a private, even a custodial, institution, perhaps they should be kept at home, but they do not, these administrators seem to believe—for this is the only logical inference that can be drawn from their arguments—belong in the public school system. That is designed for the average, the normal child . . . or those who come close enough to the norm so that their deviations do not preclude their following with some degree of success a curriculum adjusted to its standards.

Those sociologists who have suggested that one of the basic weaknesses of our society is the failure of its culture to keep pace with its technology could easily prove their case by this one point alone, for what these administrators are actually attempting to do is foist eighteenth- and nineteenth-century standards of education upon a twentieth-century culture, just as if, in effect, they were to insist that schools should give preference to the old communal dipper and water bucket over the sanitary drinking fountain.

Of course the idea of the communal water bucket would horrify them, for they have learned to accept the principles of physical hygiene. Insofar as mental and social hygiene are concerned, however, they are not in as relatively modern an era as the eighteenth and nineteenth centuries. They are much farther back than in the Dark Ages, for, during the eighteenth and nineteenth centuries, the principle of equal education for all was a practical one, because it fitted the school population of that particular time. The mentally deficient and seriously disturbed children generally stayed at home—with their presence kept a dark secret, if possible, for, in those unenlightened days, their very existence was considered shameful. Children who had serious physical handicaps were also kept at home, because, under the relatively primitive living conditions of the day, it was usually not feasible to send them to school—the question of transportation alone made it hard for them to get an education.

Those who could not keep up because of mental inadequacy or other reasons simply dropped out to become part of the nation's labor force—on the farm, in the home, in the burgeoning industries of our young nation. And they were needed and welcomed in all of these because of the acute manpower shortage, and, of course, the fact that their services could be obtained much more cheaply than those of adults. Even the gifted were often better off in those days. Since, except in the largest communities, classes and schools were small, sometimes the teacher would have the opportunity to take a real interest in a child who seemed to manifest exceptional abilities.

Thus, the public school classes in the colonial period and the following century were essentially homogeneous, and, this being so, one educational program could serve adequately for all. It might not have been the best possible education, but, in relation to the actualities of the culture at that period, it served the needs of its society far better than today's education serves the needs of ours.

THE ROLE OF THE SCHOOL

Today there are no profitable outlets on the farms or in industry for our youth. Although there is no excess of manpower at the present moment, except in individual localities, neither is there a dearth. Furthermore, the growing mechanization of our society added to a decline in the death rate that extends the working life of adults, means that we may aggravate an excess of unskilled and semiskilled labor. Hence, to protect our labor force from juvenile competition, the law says that all children must go to school until they reach a certain age. There is no room for the young and unlearned in our complex society, where the increase in automation has put a premium upon brains rather than brawn and energy.

Therefore, it is necessary that the school consume a substantial number of years of a youth's time until he reaches the age where he is considered ready to compete on an adult level with adults. The school functions as a guardian agency appointed by the government to fill as wholesomely and usefully as possible those unproductive years of a young person's life during which he is not legally permitted to work. Since those early years are the formative ones, during which the youth's major skills will be learned and his major adjustments made, they are probably the most important years of his life, for his whole life will be based upon what he learns, consciously or unconsciously, during that period.

This places a tremendous responsibility upon the school. What is it going to do in all those years of guardianship to ready the youth for the adult world? Is it going to try to prepare him to become an efficiently functioning social unit by developing his capabilities to their utmost and by equipping him with those skills which will make him of maximum value to his society? Or is it going to assume that its principal function is the sloughing off of the excess energies of youth—in short, a quasi-custodial function—with the result that its curriculum must be watered down to meet the limited capacities of the lower-level majority, and thus keep as many children as possible "quiet and occupied" until it comes time to release them into the community?

Is it going to smooth the transition from a role of dependence to one of independence by making the young person as potentially self-sufficient as possible; and, by showing him how the contributions he can make are of value to the community, giving him a sense of personal worth? Or is it, through a system of "social promotion," going to pass along as dead weights from class to class those whose mental capacities are inadequate to cope with that curriculum's meager requirements so that, if they do not experience any educational advantage, neither will they experience "the emotional maladjustment" of being left back?

Is it going to take cognizance of the fact that, though all can and should contribute, the leadership of our nation will rest primarily in the hands of the gifted, and to take steps to ensure that those of superior intelligence will be trained to become leaders worthy of their heritage? Or is it going, under the rationalization of still another slogan, "if they're so smart, they should be able to take care of themselves," to leave the gifted to the mercies of the regular teacher—who, no matter how conscientious she may be, cannot, in today's crowded classrooms, afford to give individual attention to any few children?

In short, is the school going to assume the role of an agency designed to assist each child in reaching his ultimate development in personality and in educational attainment, which would include assisting the handicapped to become self-sufficient rather than a burden to their communities and families? Or is the school going to assume the role of nothing more than a gigantic baby-sitter in its efforts to keep as many children as possible within its walls, going from grade to grade until they are legally eligible to take on the adult responsibilities for which they have not been trained; will it, then, doom the handicapped to a continuation of the same vegetable existence they have been leading in the regular classes of the public school system?

SOCIAL—OR ANTISOCIAL—PROMOTION?

What does the term "social promotion," as used in many of our schools today, mean? Simply that, in this method, children are kept together in school on the basis of chronological age. That is, the children all enter school at the same age and are passed on from class to class in a group, with little, if any, regard for the educational attainments they have succeeded in achieving; they are classified and educated according to the number of years they have spent on this planet, not according to their mental or physical development.

Certainly the term "social promotion" is a misnomer to describe this procedure, for there is nothing social about it. Age does not make up a social grouping, and it should not be allowed to make up a societal grouping. Moreover, an outstanding anomaly in a procedure that is allegedly based on "democratic" methods is that ranking the child according to age is just as much a form of segregation as if he were classified according to his IQ, except that segregation by age has far less validity. Whatever the IQ's limitations, at least it is a factor that relates directly to the child's educability, whereas his chronological age has as little to do with his scholastic aptitude as the length of his nose!

However, grouping children according to their age does have

this one advantage; it requires no tests or diagnoses on the part of the teacher or administrator to make sure that the children are grouped correctly. All that is needed is a birth certificate for each one. So it is, of course, the simplest method, and the cheapest one . . . which probably accounts in some measure for its wide popularity in our schools.

THE CASE AGAINST SPECIAL EDUCATION

Special Education as Inexpedient

Some administrators are opposed to inaugurating a system of special education in their schools, largely because they feel it will complicate their tasks and their budgets. They are against special education because they know that starting so extensive a program would mean a good deal of additional work and additional responsibility for them. Furthermore, feeling that it might be difficult to convince a conservative school board of the necessity of establishing an educational program based on the principle of individual difference; perhaps disliking the awkwardness of appealing to the local and state governments for the necessary funds; and undoubtedly unwilling to take any chances on risking their jobs—or, at least, their popularity—for a principle, they yield to outside pressures which may not, in fact, exist. If such administrators had the courage to present the case for special education forcefully and authoritatively to their superiors—be they school superintendents or boards of education— they might find their arguments receiving more sympathetic attention than they had anticipated.

The job turnover among school executives happens to be exceedingly high. However, it does not seem to be any higher among the sincere administrators who will stand up for their principles than among the conscienceless ones who are willing to sacrifice so much for their own peace of mind and security

that it may turn out that they lose that peace of mind and security as well, for, though a school board may be conservative,
that does not render it incapable of telling an efficient administrator from an inadequate one.

Special Education as Unrealistic

There are also many honest administrators who believe in all
sincerity that special education is undemocratic, that the classroom should reproduce the cosmos in miniature—in other words,
that it should be as heterogeneous in character as chance makes
it. Their contention is that, when the child becomes an adult,
he will not be confined to a homogeneous group of individuals all like himself, but will be called upon to mix with all the
different types of individuals that inhabit this heterogeneous
world of ours. Therefore, he should begin learning how to adjust
himself to actual life conditions while he is still in the classroom.

There are two basic fallacies inherent in this argument. In
the first place, special education does not promote exclusiveness;
an engineer does not, as a rule, mix only with other engineers—
save, perhaps—in the course of his work—a doctor, with other
doctors, a musician, with other musicians. Yet, it would have
been impossible for each of them to have achieved their professional status if they had not had the advantage of highly specialized education. A class could not be organized which would
teach music, medicine, and engineering as part of one program
and expect that program to produce qualified musicians, doctors,
and engineers. And, despite the fact that educationally they were
segregated from one another during the latter portion of their
school years, still all three types of professional men are considered equally worthy in the world's eyes, and all three are
likely to mingle and interact both socially and professionally.
Moreover, the reason for that segregation was specifically so that

they could be trained in the particular functions they are expected to perform as part of that interactive process.

This same principle could be extended on a broadened basis to apply to the general education of children as well as the professional training of adults. It is only in the special class that children of one kind, whatever that kind may be, can be specifically trained to get on with children of another.

The second fallacy in the concept of the heterogeneous class as a miniature of life is that in real-life situations people do tend to segregate themselves into groups that share a community of interests, financial status, education, or what have you. They may be on perfectly amiable terms with individuals whose interests and status are different from theirs, but, on the whole, like tends to be attracted by like. The college professer will not invite the refuse collector to dinner, nor will the refuse collector under ordinary circumstances suggest that the professor come sit at his table, yet both may have the highest respect for each other and his indispensable function in the world's work.

Furthermore, even within the heterogeneous school environment, the gifted child who will one day become an atomic physicist is not likely to fraternize, either during school days or afterward, with the dull one who will become a factory hand—not, at first, out of snobbery, but simply because their interests and outlook are so diametrically opposite. However, if the gifted child is placed in the same classroom as the dull one and is forced to follow the same curriculum, if he observes that his own educational progress is being retarded as a result of the other's inadequacies, *then* he may develop an antagonism that will ultimately manifest itself in the snobbishness of intellectual superiority. And the dull child, equally antagonistic at being forced to compete with someone so much better equipped than he by nature for the intellectual battle, may emerge not only with a specific hostility toward the one gifted individual, but a general hostility toward all those whom he will learn to call "eggheads."

THE CASE FOR SPECIAL EDUCATION

Under a system where children are grouped chronologically and, as a result, promoted "socially," not only do many of them fail to get an education at all—and most fail to get an education commensurate with their needs and abilities—but resentment and hostility are often encountered in all those outside the dull normal. And even this group does not always escape scot free, since its individual talents, as opposed to its collective ones, may not have received recognition, either. The more retarded children will find themselves in a situation where they sit day after day in a classroom while matters utterly outside the scope of their comprehension are discussed over their heads. The fact that each term they are promoted to classes which continue to deal with more and more bewildering subjects is hardly conducive toward a happy adjustment for them. The above average are resentful because the program as planned is so far beneath their capabilities that they conceive themselves to be—and, in fact, are—insulted by having it offered to them as in any way suitable for their needs.

In addition, often this educational system of rewarding the dull child for what he cannot do and does not appreciate inculcates a talent for deceit in the other children, particularly the more intelligent ones. They discover that it is not necessary to do one's lessons in order to pass, for even the pupils who cannot understand what is going on are passed. Why, then, should they, "the smart ones," waste their time on unnecessary studying, when it seems as if any efforts they do put out are unappreciated?

Those who advise the promotion of the dull child from one grade to the next regardless of his scholastic deficiencies contend that "it is unreasonable to punish him, since he cannot do the work." Does it not occur to them that setting him a task he cannot possibly hope to do is a far greater punishment than anything else? In real-life situations we do not suffer because we receive poor grades. No such things as grades exist outside of the classroom. In the adult world, we suffer because we are frustrated, because we find ourselves personally and socially inadequate to cope with the situations that confront us.

Are these educators going to argue that, since the backward child is bound in the nature of things never to derive any sense of accomplishment from life once he is out in the adult world, it is the classroom's task to harden him in advance to frustration? Even the most cynical, politically minded educator would not put forth such a premise, though he might unconsciously act upon it.

It is true that education does not aim simply at the acquisition of subject matter, that it must build character as well. However, emotional maladjustment does not build character, and the system of education that has spawned "social promotion" does not, as has already been indicated, tend to produce good adjustment. Obviously, the retarded child can develop a sense of adequacy only if the classroom teacher shows him the few things that he can do instead of the many things he cannot do. And, in his turn, the gifted child can develop a sense of adequacy only if *he* is taught that educational accomplishment is worth while, and that his classroom lessons are not merely a means of marking time for him, but are valuable training for the future.

THE CHALLENGE TO THE ADMINISTRATOR

What He Is Faced With

Our educational system is, as recent global events have demonstrated to our chagrin, something less than adequate. Some other countries may have outstripped us, both qualitatively and quantitatively, not only in the sciences, but in some other aspects of the educational program. If our schools want to regain the educational lead they once held, or even to keep up with modern education in this world, they must—all of them—stop and realize the importance of an educational system based on individual differences. To develop as a nation, we need to develop the talents that lie within each child who is, or will be, a functioning part of the nation.

Past research has proved conclusively that no one—educator or layman—can take a group of individuals of varied cortical make-up and physical construction and ability, and expect each of them to master the same tasks with equal facility. And yet, ignoring this proved fact, school personnel exert veritably Procrustean efforts to teach a child a skill long after diagnostic tests have assured them that he is incapable of acquiring it. Since it is a part of the curriculum, every child is supposed to learn it, and so they pursue their dogged and futile way. Paradoxically enough, these educators will accept the existence of the tests themselves as being a necessary part of modern education. They will swear by the tests as such, but they may not pay attention to the findings derived therefrom.

Nor do they always pay appropriate regard to the true function of the guidance counselors in their schools. Too many schools today tend to relegate these workers to the category of psychometrists, registrars' assistants, and vocational reference librarians, instead of acknowledging them as trained social educators. Such an over-all attitude in a school is largely the administrator's fault, for most intramural attitudes tend to take their coloring from his. It might be argued that the guidance counselor should "stick up for his rights," and probably there is some justice to that contention; nonetheless, there is nothing inherent in his position that calls for strength of character, while it is certainly a vital part of the administrator's job to ensure an adequate program of guidance and to keep trained psychologists from being used to serve as little more than clerks—or merely as human tranquilizers.

Too often this emasculation of the guidance department's function stems from the administrator's own feeling that there is no real necessity for such a department, that he himself "knows as much as any counselor," and, hence, is fully equipped to handle any guidance program. However, the truly mature and efficient administrator will realize that, just as his training and education qualify him for his particular job, so the training and education of the guidance counselor qualify him for the kind of work he does, and neither can replace the other. Again, special education has fitted each one for the role he is to play in life.

The Administrator's Functions

Just what does the administrator's job consist of? It is true that it involves many of the routine aspects of school management, such as school budgeting and bookkeeping, filing reports, and so on. However, these are not the basic problems that concern him; his primary task is to deal with the problem of the children themselves. If the school is to be considered as comparable to a large industrial plant, then dealing with children is its business. And, since the administrator is the head of that plant, dealing with children is his responsibility.

Some administrators do not know how to handle that responsibility from the very beginning. For example, let us take a school principal who heads an elementary school with an enrollment of nine hundred children. He might reason that, since classes in his school number thirty pupils each, all he has to do is arbitrarily divide the nine hundred by thirty—which will give him thirty teaching units. Then he will get thirty teachers to teach these units, instruct each one to teach every child as an individual and, at the same time, fulfill the course requirements—and his job, he thinks, is done! Every child will be receiving the education to which he is entitled.

There is only one thing wrong here: The administrator's job is not done; it has not even started. He has failed as an executive. He would not last a minute in the executive offices of any of our large industries, where personnel policies are conducted according to far more complicated procedures than in many of our schools. Before a worker is hired by one of these industrial plants, he is given a battery of tests to determine whether he is fitted physically, intellectually, and emotionally for the job, or—in the case of a labor shortage—to determine what jobs within the company are best fitted physically, intellectually, and emotionally to him.

There is no reason why our school system should be less exacting than our industry. What the principal should do in this case is try, within the limitations of thirty set teaching units, to group those nine hundred children according to previous educational attainment and demonstrated abilities, so that they can most efficiently be educated, that is, to group them as much as possible with their peers. He should also try, within the undeniably scant limits of what candidates are available, to secure thirty teachers, each of whom is especially well qualified to teach a particular one of those thirty classes. Only then will he have made a first step toward giving each child the education to which he is entitled.

Again, that same principal very probably would reply to a teacher who complains—with considerable justification—that it is virtually impossible for her to give adequate instruction to each child in such a diversified group as she has been assigned, that a really good teacher should be able to teach any individual child in any group. However, he might, if he is kindly, add that she should do the best she can and, if she needs help, call on the supervisor. He might also suggest that, since the teacher will need to take certain courses for alertness credit in any case, it might be a good idea for her to take those courses in differential psychology, choosing the various fields of exceptionality that seem to present themselves most often in her classroom. It will not occur to the principal that, no matter how many courses the teacher takes, she will not be able to give individual attention to the children in her classes, when, in addition to a heavy teaching load, she has bus duty, study hall duty, and playground duty; she has to keep voluminous records and file intricate reports; she has to collect book fees; she has to sell refreshments at the school football games; and, to top all this, she may also be serving as faculty advisor for one or another of the school's extracurricular activities.

He is far more likely to suggest that the child who seems to present an insoluble problem be sent to the testing bureau (of course, when the results of the tests come in, they will probably be, in many cases, disregarded) or to the reading clinic, which—since certain educators made the discovery that poor reading ability in a child can be a sign of poor emotional adjustment—is rapidly becoming a catchall for any problem that does not fit in elsewhere. Our eighteenth- and nineteenth-century ancestors were not too sophisticated to overlook the obvious; they could have told him that poor reading ability in a child can also be the result of poor teaching ability in the instructor or poor cortical make-up of the child and/or a combination of both, or, in the case of today's educational methods, it could be the result of a poor school program.

A good administrator must be carefully fitted to his job. Not only must he have all the necessary degrees and skills, but he should have the quality of being able to encourage and inspire the teachers on his staff. A truly gifted administrator, with a reputation for being dedicated to his profession, will often have much less trouble than other principals in recruiting teachers for his school, in spite of current shortages, even though he may not be able to offer anything more substantial than they in the way of emolument or even physical working conditions.

The good administrator must constantly be in contact with his staff so that he has a personal awareness of any difficulties under which they may be laboring, and he must try to minimize such difficulties wherever it is even remotely possible to do so. Further, he must keep pace with the latest trends and research in his field as conscientiously as a manufacturer keeps up with the latest developments in his. He must be familiar with the educational problems of the handicapped, as well as with the educational problems of the normal, with special education as well as the standard curriculum.

He must be able to understand, and to make his superiors understand, that perhaps heterogeneous education may be costing the school less money than an equivalent system of special classes—though even that need not be true in all situations—but it is costing the nation a good deal more in conspicuous waste of human resources. Under normal conditions, no factory executive would consider using the machinery in his plant at less than full power. Why, then, should any school fail to make use of a program that will use the children who are the machines in that plant to the fullest extent of their potentialities? Why should any principal continue to plod along utilizing an outmoded program that has been clearly shown to breed intellectual attrition, social maladjustment, and even delinquency, when applied to the conditions of twentieth-century life?

The Outlook for the Administrator

Watering down the curriculum by depriving it of a good deal of its intellectual content means reducing the goal of our children's abilities to the lowest common denominator. But children cannot be lumped like arithmetical symbols; every one of them is an individual, with individual needs which must be considered by the educational program before they can perform their individual functions competently. There is no reason why the dull, the average, or the gifted child should be forced to submit to a curriculum that fits him no better than a pair of shoes lasted for someone else. All three have contributions to make, and all three should be allowed to make them in their own way, rather than to be battered into a low-level mediocrity (or a vegetable existence) by the school's effort to achieve "sameness" in every one of the children in its charge.

The administrator's task is to see that the facilities of his school are expanded to the utmost in order to make it possible for each child's potentialities to be developed. It is up to him to try to get the funds for such special programs as he feels are not only needful but feasible for a school of the size of his, and it is up to him to try to convince his board or superintendent, when they are reluctant, that such programs are vitally important.

Where the school is small and its budget limited, so that, no matter how liberal his and his board's outlook, special classes must be few, if any, then it is up to him to try to discover what enriching opportunities or experiences the community can offer the children to supplement the education that the school *can* afford to give them. He must, moreover, also see to it that his school is serving as *many* of the children in the district as it possibly can, as *well* as it possibly can. Even when his school does have a program of special education, he must make sure that it is the kind that is most appropriate to the needs and demands of his particular type of community. He should see to it that children are sent forward in grade according to a truly social type of promotion—and that it is the kind of promotion that advances the child on the basis of his successful completion of a given amount of the work that has been determined to be well within the scope of his capabilities.

The problem of educating all of our children to full capacity is a pressing one today, for, in the ideological kind of wars we are fighting, education has become one of our most powerful weapons. As the president of this country, Dwight D. Eisenhower, has stated:

> Our schools are strong points in our national defense. Our schools are more important than our Nike batteries, more necessary than our radar warnings nets, and more powerful even than the energy of the atom. . . . To maintain the common defense and to guarantee the progress of our nation, each of us must discharge his own rightful and proper role in developing the intellectual capacities of all children . . . in every corner of our land. . . .[1]

The challenge to the administrator, therefore, is that he re-examine his school program through the light of current research in the psychology of teaching children who are different, because the very weighty problems in our schools today arise from our failure to consider seriously the individual child, although we do pay lip service to individual differences. The schools must cease tranquilizing a sizable number of our very valuable human resources until they are "promoted" out of the school into frustration, hostility, delinquency, sorrow, unhappiness or bitterness. This is the challenge: Political expediency under the guise of a questionable social psychology must give way to a reality that embraces strong moral, spiritual, social, and intellectual values.

[1] Eisenhower, Dwight D., "Education, the Most Important Subject," NEA *Journal,* XLVI (May, 1957), 300–302.

Subject Index

Name Index